Introduction to Artificial Neural Networks

INTRODUCTION TO ARTIFICIAL NEURAL NETWORKS

Dr. S.N. Sivanandam
Professor and Head
Department of Computer Science and Engineering
PSG College of Technology, Coimbatore
Tamil Nadu, India

Dr. M. Paulraj
Computer Science Program
School of Engineering and Information Technology
Universiti Malaysia Sabah, Kota Kinabalu
East Malaysia

VIKAS PUBLISHING HOUSE PVT LTD

VIKAS® PUBLISHING HOUSE PRIVATE LIMITED
E-28, Sector-8, Noida-201301 (UP), India
Phone: +91-120-4078900 • Fax: +91-120-4078999
Registered Office: Vikas Publishing House Private Limited, A-27, 2nd Floor, Mohan Co-operative Industrial Estate, New Delhi-110044
E-mail: helpline@vikaspublishing.com • Website: www.vikaspublishing.com

SALES AND BRANCH OFFICES OF VIKAS® AND S CHAND AND COMPANY LIMITED

Chennai : Ph: 044-2363 2120, chennai@schandpublishing.com
Guwahati : Ph: 0361-2738 811, 2735 640, guwahati@schandpublishing.com
Hyderabad : Ph: 040-4018 6018, hyderabad@schandpublishing.com
Jalandhar : Ph: 0181-4645 630, jalandhar@schandpublishing.com
Kolkata : Ph: 033-2335 7458, 2335 3914, kolkata@schandpublishing.com
Lucknow : Ph: 0522-4003 633, lucknow@schandpublishing.com
Mumbai : Ph: 022-2500 0297, mumbai@schandpublishing.com
Patna : Ph: 0612-2260 011, patna@schandpublishing.com

Introduction to Artificial Neural Networks
ISBN: 978-81259-1425-9

Product Code: V3ANN50COMP10ENAA0XR

First Published 2003
Reprinted in 2005, 2014, 2021
First Reprint 2022

PRINTED IN INDIA
By Vikas Publishing House Private Limited, Plot 20/4, Site-IV, Industrial Area Sahibabad, Ghaziabad-201010 and Published by Vikas Publishing House Private Limited, E-28, Sector-8, Noida-201301

Preface

This book is written to introduce the subject artificial neural networks to the undergraduate students of engineering and other related courses. The majority of books on this subject require a level of expertise to understand the material. This book presents a large variety of standard neural networks with architecture, algorithms and applications. Simple examples are used to illustrate the applications of the neural networks. This book presumes that the readers are familiar with calculus, matrix notations and operations.

Dr. S. N. Sivanandam wishes to thank Mr. V. Rajan, Managing Trustee, PSG Institutions, Mr. C. R. Swaminathan, Chief Executive, and Dr. P. Radhakrishnan, Principal, PSG College of Technology, Coimbatore, for their whole-hearted cooperation and great encouragement given in this successful endeavour.

He is grateful for the encouragement and support received from the staff members of the Electrical and Electronics Engineering Department and Computer Science and Engineering Department of his college.

Dr. M. Paulraj wishes to express his gratitude to his wife Hema Paulraj, Manager, Information Systems, TNEB, for her advice and patient proofreading. He also expresses his sincere thanks to his son Vishnu Vardhan for his patience.

He expresses his gratitude to Y. Bhd. Tan Sri Profesor Datuk Seri Dr Abu Hassan bin Othman, Vice-Chancellor, Universiti Malaysia Sabah, Kota Kinabalu, East Malaysia, for his generous support in developing this book. He is deeply indebted to Prof. Madya. Dr. Sazali Yaacob, Dean, Prof. Dr. R. Nagarajan and Dr. G. Sainarayanan, School of Engineering and Information Technology, Universiti Malaysia Sabah, Kota Kinabalu, for their support and suggestions.

He also wishes to thank Dr. S. Arumugam, Principal, College of Technology, Coimbatore, for his constant encouragement and support. He is highly indebted to Dr. M. Rangasamy, Professor and Head, Department of Electronics and Instrumentation Engineering, Dr. A. Ebenezer Jeyakumar, Professor and Head, Department of Electrical and Electronics Engineering, Dr. P. Rajendran, Professor of Chemistry, and Dr. R. Sundararajan, Professor of Civil Engineering, College of Technology, Coimbatore for their guidance, inspiring advice and continuous encouragement. He also wishes to thank Prof. S. Palaniswami, Dr. M. Rajaram, Dr. N. Devarajan and Prof. P. K. Jayadev, Assistant Professors, College of Technology, Coimbatore, for their valuable suggestions and timely help.

Both the authors are thankful to Mr. M. Krishnamoorthy, Hewlett Packard, and Mrs. S. Shanmugapriya, Tata Consulting Services, for their invaluable help.

The authors wish to thank their students Vipin Vijaykumar, B. Madan, R. Rajiv, P. Subburaj, S. Shiv Kumar, R. Bharani, M. Gopalakrishnan, K. Srinivasan and R. Archish for their support. The authors also express their profound gratitude to K. Nanjundi Karthick, C. Karthikeyan and K. Deepak for typing and editing the manuscripts. The authors express their sincere thanks to D. Somasundareswari and P. Geeth Priya for proofreading the manuscript.

The authors would like to thank Mr. P. K. Madhavan and Ms. G. Vinaya of Vikas Publishing House Pvt Ltd for their encouragement and professional interactions.

S. N. Sivanandam

M. Paulraj

Contents

Chapter 2

HEBB NET, ADALINE, MADALINE AND PERCEPTRON

Chapter 3

Associative Memory

Chapter 4

Self-organizing Maps: Topological Preserving Nets

Chapter 5

BACKPROPAGATION NETWORK

Chapter 6

Adaptive Resonance Theory

Chapter 7

Special Networks

Chapter 8

Control Networks

CHAPTER

1 Introduction

1.1 INTRODUCTION [B37]

Ever imagined how our brain works! It was more than 2000 years ago that our ancestors had started to discover the architecture and behavior of human brain. Ramon Y.Cajal and Hebb continued the work of Aristotle and tried to build the artificial "thinking machine". Based on the information about the functions of the brain and the quest for obtaining a mathematical model for our learning habits, a new technology Artificial Neural Networks was started. Our brain can process information quickly and accurately. You can recognize your friend's voice in a noisy railway station. How is the brain able to process the voice signal added with the noise and retrieve the original signal? Amazing, isn't it? Can we duplicate this amazing process through a machine? Can we make a machine to duplicate some learning habits of a human? Can a machine be made to learn from experience? The following sections in this chapter reveal the answers to these questions.

1.2 WHAT IS A NEURAL NETWORK

An artificial neural network is an information processing system that has been developed as a generalization of the mathematical model of human cognition (*faculty of knowing*). A neural network is a network of interconnected neurons, inspired from the studies of the biological nervous system. In other words, neural network functions in a way similar to the human brain. The function of a neural network is to produce an output pattern when presented with an input pattern.

Neural network is the study of networks consisting of nodes connected by adaptable weights, which store experimental knowledge from task examples through a process of learning. The nodes of the brain are adaptable; they acquire knowledge through changes in the node weights by being exposed to samples.

1.3 BRAIN—THE ORIGINAL NEURAL NETWORK

Neural network architectures are motivated by models of the human brain and nerve cells. Our current knowledge of the human brain is limited to its anatomical and physiological information. Neuron (from Greek, meaning nerve cell) is the fundamental unit of the brain. The neuron is a complex biochemical and electrical signal processing unit that receives and combines signals from many other neurons through filamentary input paths, the dendrites (Greek: tree links). A neuron in the human brain is shown in Figure 1.1.

A biological neuron has three types of components namely dendrites, soma and axon. Dendrites are bunched into highly complex "dendritic trees", which have an enormous total surface area. The dendrites receive signals from other neurons. Dendritic trees are connected with the main body of the neuron called the soma (Greek: body). The soma has a pyramidal or cylindrical shape. The soma sums the incoming signals. When sufficient input is received, the cell fires. The output area of the neuron is a long fibre called axon. The impulse signal triggered by the cell is transmitted over the axon to other cells. The connecting point between a neuron's axon and another neuron's dendrite is called a synapse (Greek: contact). The impulse signals are then transmitted across a synaptic gap by means of a chemical process. A single neuron may have 1000 to 10000 synapses and may be connected with around 1000 neurons. There are 100 billion neurons in our brain, and each neuron has 1000 dendrites.

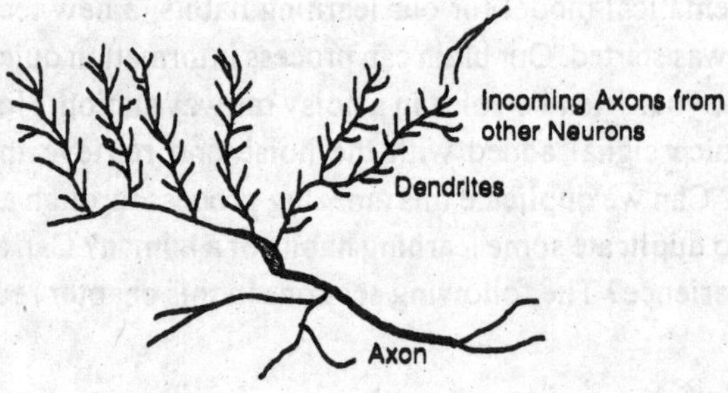

Figure 1.1 *A Biological Nerve Cell*

1.4 ARTIFICIAL NEURON

The artificial neuron (also called processing element or node) mimes the characteristics of the biological neuron. A processing element possesses a local memory and carries out localized information processing operations. The artificial neuron has a set of '*n*' inputs x_i, each representing the output of another neuron (the subscript i takes values between 1 and n and indicates the source of the vector input signal). The inputs are collectively referred to as X. Each input is weighed before it reaches the main body of the processing element by the connection strength or the weight factor (or simply weight) analogous to the synaptic strength. The amount of information about the input that is required to solve a problem is stored in the form of *weights*. Each signal is multiplied with an associated weight $w_1, w_2, w_3, \ldots, w_n$ before it is applied to the summing block. In addition, the artificial neuron has a bias term w_0, a threshold value 'θ' that has to be reached or extended for the neuron to produce a signal, a nonlinear function 'F' that acts on the produced signal 'net' and an output 'y' after the nonlinearity function. The basic model of a neuron is shown in Figure 1.2. It should be noted that the input to the bias neuron is assumed to be 1.

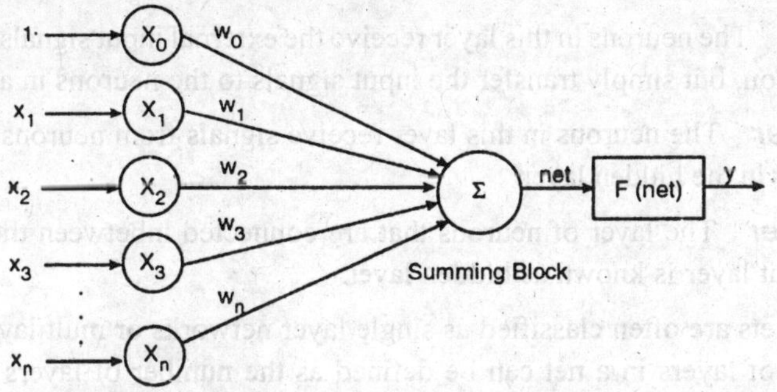

Figure 1.2 *Basic Neuron Model*

The following relation describes the transfer function of the basic neuron model.

$$y = F(\text{net}) \tag{1.1}$$

where

$$\text{net} = w_0 + x_1 w_1 + x_2 w_2 + x_3 w_3 + \ldots\ldots + x_n w_n \tag{1.2}$$

or

$$\text{net} = w_0 + \sum_{i=0}^{n} x_i w_i \tag{1.3}$$

and the neuron firing condition is:

$$\sum_{i=0}^{n} x_i w_i \geq \theta \text{ [for linear activation function]}, x_0 = 1$$

or

$$F(\text{net}) \geq \theta \text{ [for nonlinear activation function]}$$

1.5 CLASSIFICATION OF ARTIFICIAL NEURAL NETWORKS

Artificial neural networks can be classified on the basis of:

1. Pattern of connection between neurons, (architecture of the network)
2. Activation function applied to the neurons
3. Method of determining weights on the connection (training or learning method)

1.6 ARCHITECTURE OF A NEURAL NETWORK

The neurons are assumed to be arranged in layers, and the neurons in the same layer behave in the same manner. All the neurons in a layer usually have the same activation function. Within each layer, the neurons are either fully interconnected or not connected at all. The neurons in one layer can be connected to neurons in another layer. The arrangement of neurons into layers and the connection pattern within and between layers is known as network architecture.

Input layer The neurons in this layer receive the external input signals and perform no computation, but simply transfer the input signals to the neurons in another layer.

Output layer The neurons in this layer receive signals from neurons either in the input layer or in the hidden layer.

Hidden layer The layer of neurons that are connected inbetween the input layer and the output layer is known as hidden layer.

Neural nets are often classified as single layer networks or multilayer networks. The number of layers in a net can be defined as the number of layers of weighted interconnection links between various layers. While determining the number of layers, the input layer is not counted as a layer, because it does not perform any computation. The architecture of a single layer and a multilayer neural network is shown in Figures 1.3 and 1.4.

1.6.1 Single Layer Network

A single layer network consists of one layer of connection weights. The net consists of a layer of units called input layer, which receive signals from the outside world and a layer of units called output layer from which the response of the net can be obtained. This type of network can be used for pattern classification problems.

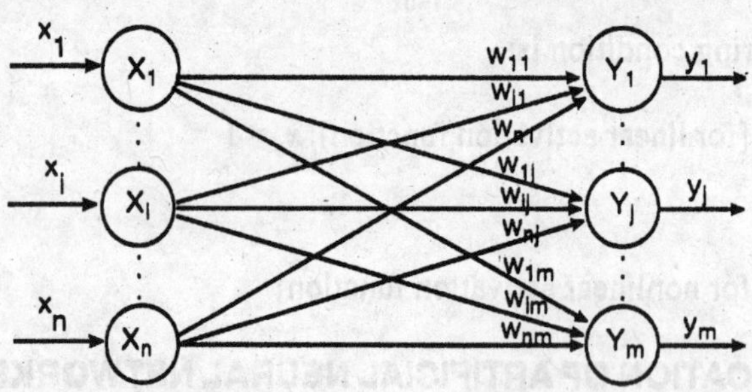

Figure 1.3 *Single Layer Neural Network*

1.6.2 Multilayer Network

A multilayer network consists of one or more layers of units (called hidden layers between the input and output layers. Multilayer networks may be formed by simply cascading a group of layers; the output of one layer provides the input to the subsequent layer. A multilayer net with nonlinear activation function can solve any type of problem. However training a multilayer neural network is very difficult.

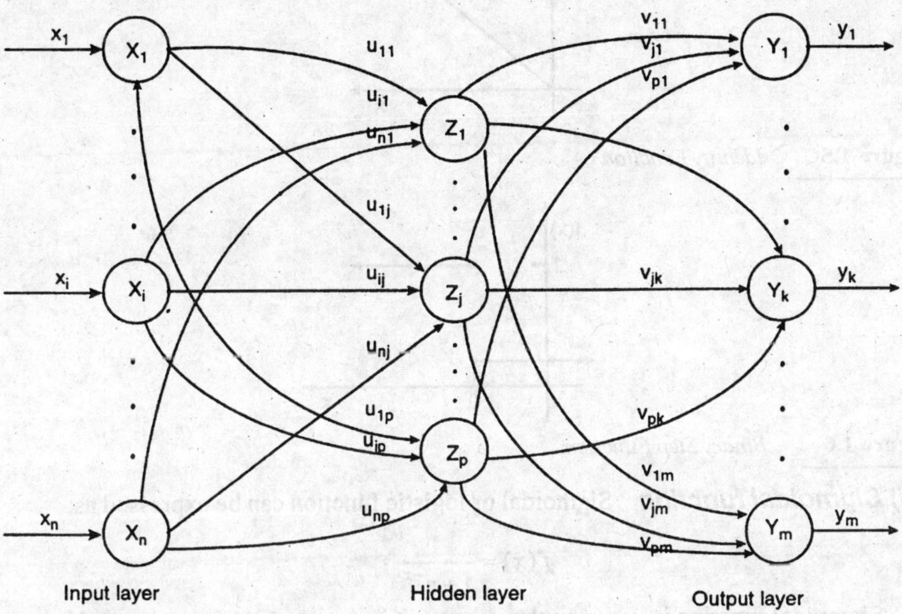

Figure 1.4 *Multilayer Neural Network*

1.7 ACTIVATION FUNCTIONS

The purpose of nonlinear activation function is to ensure that the neuron's response is bounded - that is, the actual response of the neuron is conditioned or damped, as a result of large or small activating stimuli and thus controllable. Further, in order to achieve the advantages of multilayer nets compared with the limited capabilities of single layer networks, nonlinear functions are required. Different nonlinear functions are used, depending upon the paradigm and the algorithm used for training the network. The various activation functions are depicted pictorially in Figures 1.5 to1.8.

(i) Identity function (Linear function) Identity function can be expressed:

$f(x) = x$ for all x.

(ii) Binary step function Binary step function is defined as:

$$f(x)=\begin{cases}1 & \text{if } x\ge\theta\\ 0 & \text{if } x<\theta\end{cases}$$

where θ is the threshold value.

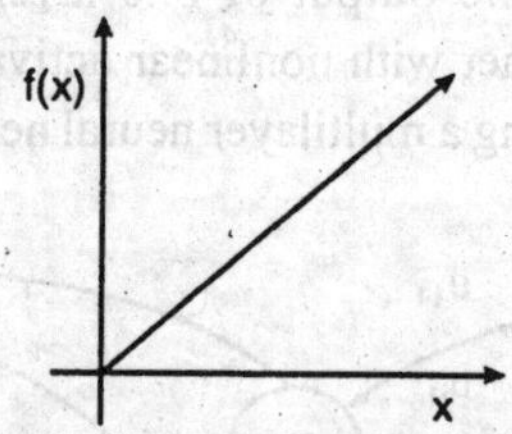

Figure 1.5 *Identity Function*

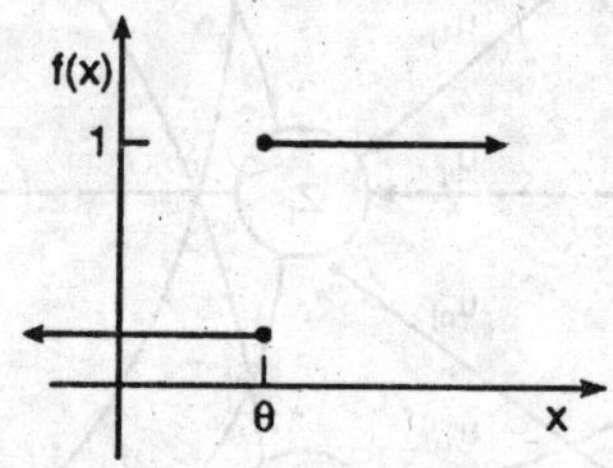

Figure 1.6 *Binary Step Function*

(iii) Sigmoidal function Sigmoidal or logistic function can be expressed as:

$$f(x)=\frac{1}{1+e^{-x}}$$

Sigmoidal function is very popular because it is monotonous, bounded and has a simple derivative, $f'(x)=f(x)\,[1-f(x)]$.

A logistic or a binary sigmoid function with a range from 0 to 1 is shown in Figure 1.7.

(iv) Bipolar sigmoid function Bipolar sigmoid is used as an activation function when the desired range of output value is between −1 and +1. Bipolar activation function can be expressed as:

$$f(x)=\frac{2}{1+e^{-x}}-1$$

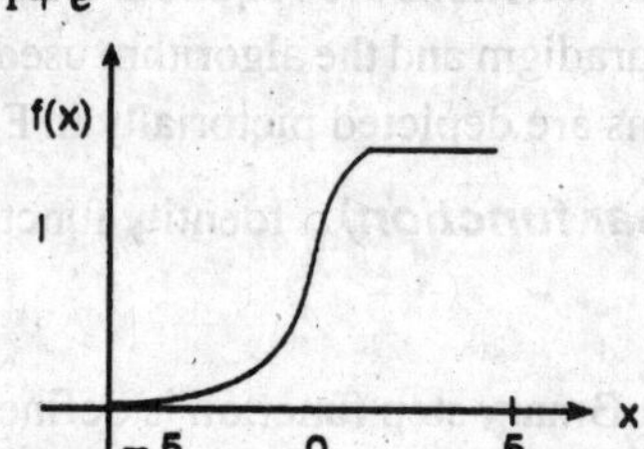

Figure 1.7 *Binary Sigmoidal Function*

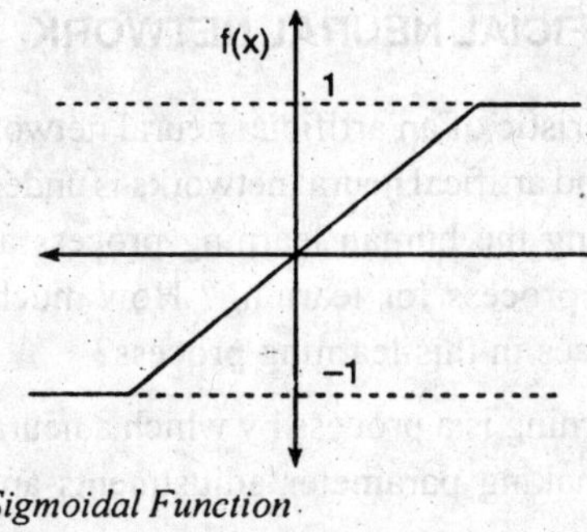

Figure 1.8 *Bipolar Sigmoidal Function*

Example 1.1 For the network shown in Figure 1.9, find the output of the neuron Y when the activation function is

(a) binary sigmoidal

(b) bipolar sigmoidal

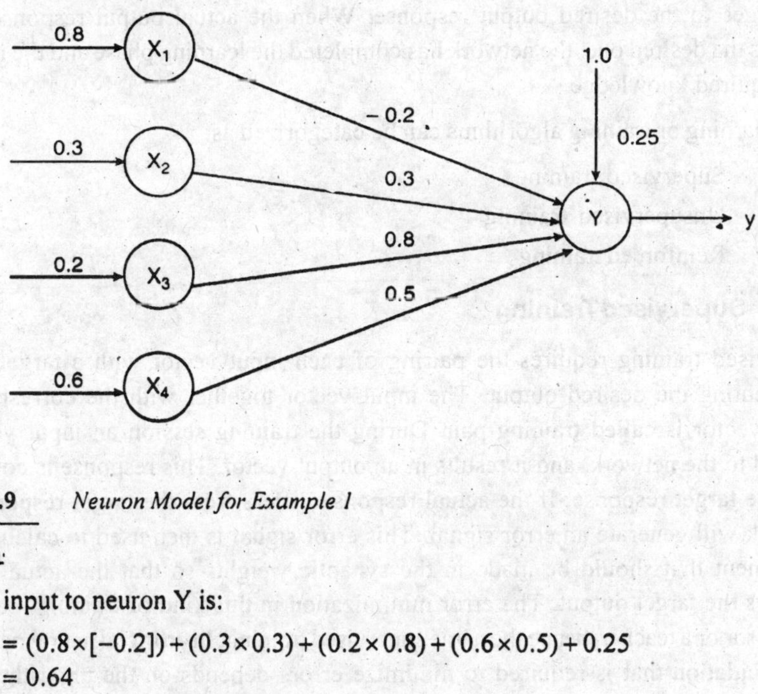

Figure 1.9 *Neuron Model for Example 1*

Solution

Net input to neuron Y is:

$$y_{in} = (0.8 \times [-0.2]) + (0.3 \times 0.3) + (0.2 \times 0.8) + (0.6 \times 0.5) + 0.25$$
$$= 0.64$$

(a) For binary sigmoidal activation function,

$$y = f(y_{in}) = \frac{1}{1 + e^{-0.64}} = 0.6548$$

(b) For bipolar sigmoidal activation function,

$$y = f(y_{in}) = \frac{2}{1 + e^{-0.64}} - 1 = 0.3095$$

1.8 TRAINING AN ARTIFICIAL NEURAL NETWORK

The most important characteristic of an artificial neural network is its ability to learn. Learning in both biological and artifical neural networks is undergoing intense research. The basic questions regarding the human learning process are: How do we learn? Which is the most efficient process for learning? How much and how fast can we learn? What are the hindrances in this learning process?

Generally speaking, learning is a process by which a neural network adapts itself to a stimulus by properly making parameter adjustments and producing a desired response.

Learning is also a continuous process of the output stimuli. If the input stimuli is not recognized by the network, then the network develops a new classification.

Learning (training) is a process in which the network adjusts its parameters the (synaptic weights) in response to input stimuli so that the actual output response converges to the desired output response. When the actual output response is the same as the desired one, the network has completed the learning phase and the network has acquired knowledge.

Learning or training algorithms can be categorized as:

1. Supervised training
2. Unsupervised training
3. Reinforced training

1.8.1 Supervised Training

Supervised training requires the pairing of each input vector with a target vector representing the desired output. The input vector together with the corresponding target vector is called training pair. During the training session an input vector is applied to the network, and it results in an output vector. This response is compared with the target response. If the actual response differs from the target response, the network will generate an error signal. This error signal is then used to calculate the adjustment that should be made in the synaptic weights so that the actual output matches the target output. The error minimization in this kind of training requires a supervisor or a teacher, hence the name supervised training. In artificial neural networks, the calculation that is required to minimize errors depends on the algorithm used, which is normally based on the optimization techniques. Figure 1.10 illustrates the supervised training method. Supervised training methods is used in to perform nonlinear mapping in pattern classification nets, pattern association nets and multilayer neural nets.

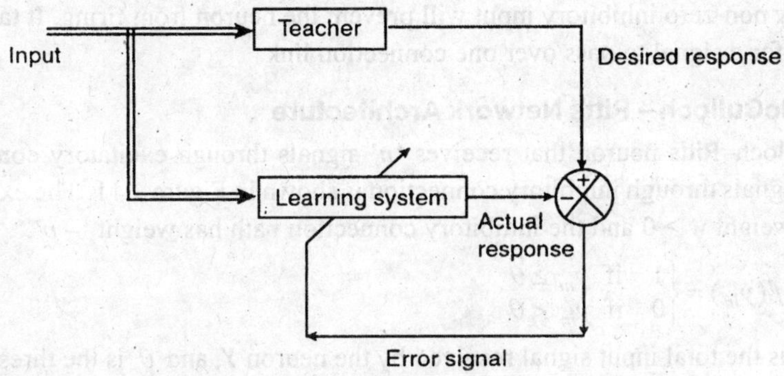

Figure 1.10 *Block Diagram of Supervised Learning*

1.8.2 Unsupervised Training

Unsupervised training is employed in self-organizing neural nets. In contrast to supervised learning, unsupervised training does not require a teacher. In this method of training, the input vectors of similar types are grouped without the use of training data to specify how a typical member of each group looks or to which group a member belongs. During training the neural network receives input patterns and organizes these patterns into categories. When new input pattern is applied, the neural network provides an output response indicating the class to which the input pattern belongs. If a class cannot be found for the input pattern, a new class is generated.

Even though unsupervised training does not require a teacher, it requires certain guidelines to form groups. Grouping can be done based on colour, shape or any other property of the object. If no guidelines are given grouping may or may not be successful.

1.8.3 Reinforced Training

Reinforced training is similar to supervised training. In this method, the teacher does not indicate how close is the actual output to the desired output, but yields only a pass or a fail indication. Thus, the error signal generated during reinforced training is binary.

1.9 McCULLOCH – PITTS NEURON MODEL

Warren McCulloch and Walter Pitts presented the first mathematical model of a single idealized biological neuron in 1943. This model is known as McCulloch – Pitts model.

This model is quite simple because it does not require learning or adoption. The neurons are binary activated. If the neuron fires, it has an activation of 1; if the neuron does not fire, it has an activation of 0. The neurons are connected by directed weighted paths. The connection paths may be excitatory or inhibitory. Excitatory connection has positive weights, and inhibitory connection has negative weights. All the excitatory connections in a particular neuron have the same weight. Each neuron has a fixed threshold such that if the net input to the neuron is greater than the threshold the neuron should fire. The threshold is set such that the inhibition is absolute. This means any non-zero inhibitory input will prevent the neuron from firing. It takes one time step for a signal to pass over one connection link.

1.9.1 McCulloch – Pitts Network Architecture

A McCulloch–Pitts neuron that receives 'n' signals through excitatory connection and 'm' signals through inhibitory connection is shown in Figure 1.11. The excitatory path has weight $w > 0$ and the inhibitory connection path has weight '$-p$'.

$$f(y_{in}) = \begin{cases} 1 & \text{if } y_{in} \geq \theta \\ 0 & \text{if } y_{in} < \theta \end{cases}$$

where y_{in} is the total input signal received by the neuron Y, and θ is the threshold.

The condition for absolute inhibition is $\theta > nw - p$.

Neuron Y will fire if it receives k or more excitatory signals and no inhibitory inputs, i.e. $kw \geq \theta > (k-1)w$.

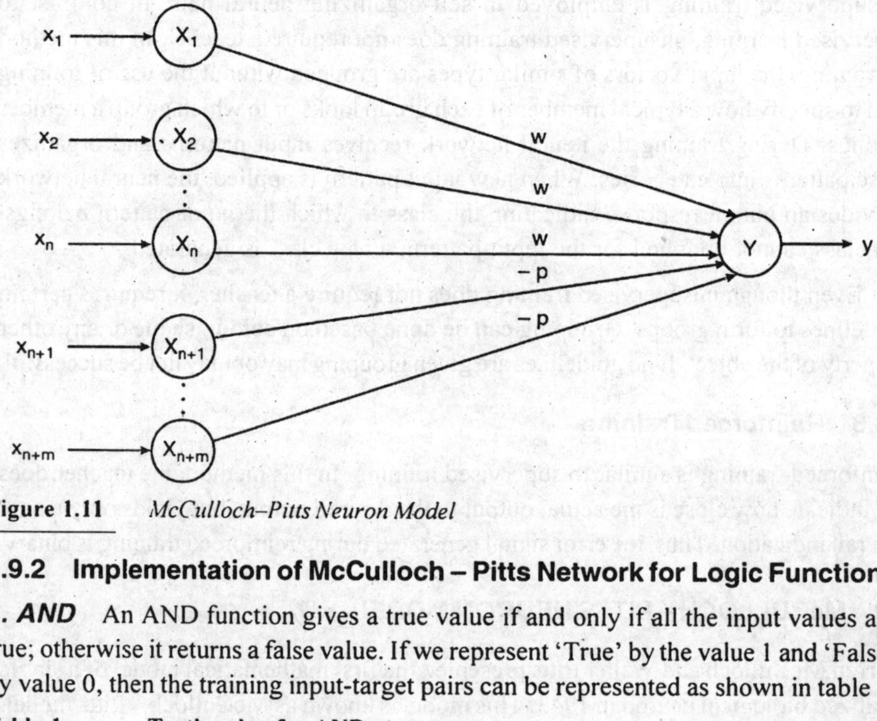

Figure 1.11 *McCulloch–Pitts Neuron Model*

1.9.2 Implementation of McCulloch – Pitts Network for Logic Functions

1. AND An AND function gives a true value if and only if all the input values are true; otherwise it returns a false value. If we represent 'True' by the value 1 and 'False' by value 0, then the training input-target pairs can be represented as shown in table 1.

Table 1 **Truth value for AND**

x_1	x_2	y
0	0	0
0	1	0
1	0	0
1	1	1

A McCulloch–Pitts neuron to implement AND function is shown in Figure 1.12. The threshold for the neuron y is 2.

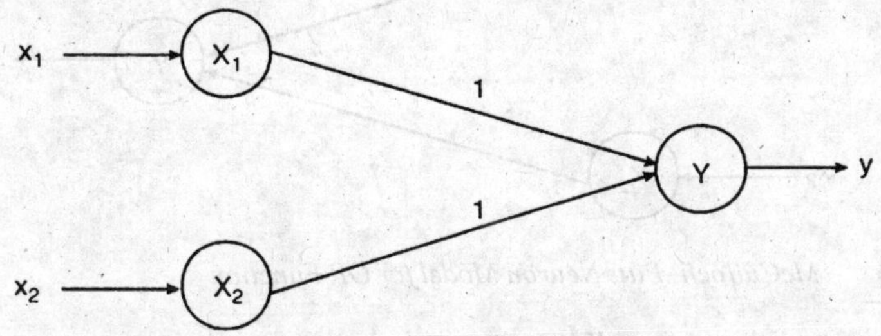

Figure 1.12 *McCulloch–Pitts Neuron Model for AND Function*

The output of the neuron Y can be written as:

$$y = f(y_{in}) = \begin{cases} 1 & \text{if } y_{in} \geq 2 \\ 0 & \text{if } y_{in} < 2 \end{cases}$$

where $y_{in} = x_1 + x_2$

From Figure 1.12,

(a) if $x_1 = x_2 = 1$
then yin = 2
$y = f(y_{in}) = 1$

(b) if $x_1 = 1, x_2 = 0$
then $y_{in} = 1$
$y = f(y_{in}) = 0$

2. OR A OR function returns a true value if any one of the input values is true and returns a false value if all the input values are false. The truth value representation of OR is shown in Table 2. A McCulloch–Pitts neuron to implement OR is shown in Figure1.13. The threshold for the neuron y is 2.

Table 2 **Truth value for OR**

x_1	x_2	y
0	0	0
0	1	1
1	0	1
1	1	1.

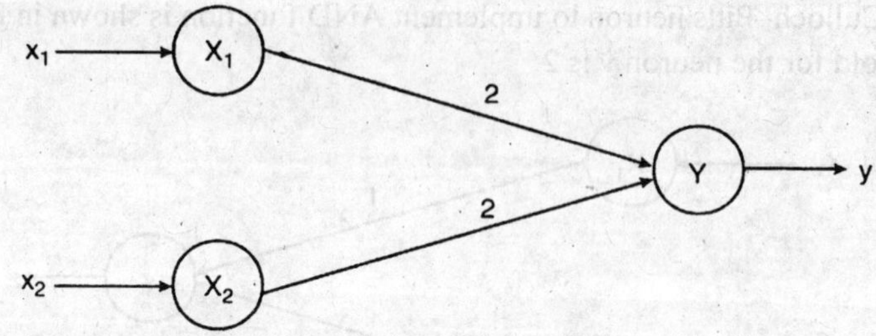

Figure 1.13 *McCulloch-Pitts Neuron Model for OR Function*

The output of the neuron Y is written as:

$$y = f(y_{in}) = \begin{cases} 1 & \text{if } y_{in} \geq 2 \\ 0 & \text{if } y_{in} < 2 \end{cases}$$

where $y_{in} = 2x_1 + 2x_2$

From Figure 1.13,

(a) if $x_1 = x_2 = 1$
then $y_{in} = 4$
$y = f(y_{in}) = 1$

(b) if $x_1 = 1, x_2 = 0$
then $y_{in} = 2$
$y = f(y_{in}) = 1$

(c) if $x_1 = 0, x_2 = 0$
then $y_{in} = 0$
$y = f(y_{in}) = 0$

3. NOT NOT returns a true value if the input is false and returns a false if the input is true. The truth value representation of NOT is shown in Table 3. A McCulloch–Pitts neuron to implement NOT is shown in figure 1.14. The threshold value for the output neuron is 1. The output of the neuron y is:

$$y = f(y_{in}) = \begin{cases} 1 & \text{if } y_{in} < 1 \\ 0 & \text{if } y_{in} \geq 1 \end{cases}$$

where $y_{in} = x_1$

Table 3 **Truth value for NOT**

x_1	y
1	0
0	1

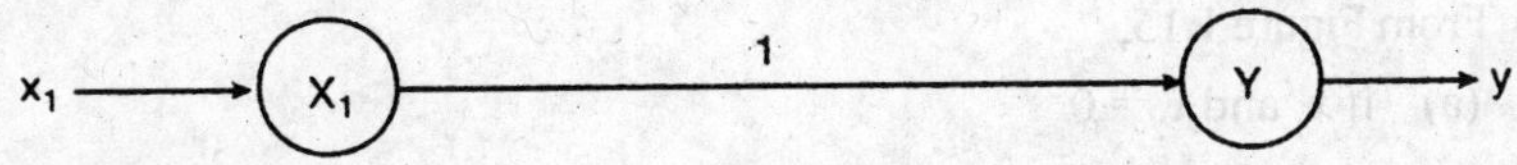

Figure 1.14 *McCulloch–Pitts Neuron Model for NOT Function*

From Figure 1.14,

(a) if $x_1 = 1$

then $y_{in} = 1$

$y = f(y_{in}) = 0$

(b) If $x_1 = 0$

then $y_{in} = 0$

$y = f(y_{in}) = 1$

4. AND NOT AND NOT returns a true value if the first input value is true and the second input value is false; The truth value representation of an AND NOT logical function is shown in Table 4 and the corresponding McCulloch-Pitts model neuron is shown in Figure 1.15. The threshold value for the output neuron is 2.

Table 4 **Truth value for AND NOT**

x_1	x_2	y
0	0	0
0	1	0
1	0	1
1	1	0

The output of the neuron Y is:

$$y = f(y_{in}) = \begin{cases} 1 & \text{if } y_{in} > 1 \\ 0 & \text{if } y_{in} \le 1 \end{cases}$$

where $y_{in} = 2x_1 - x_2$.

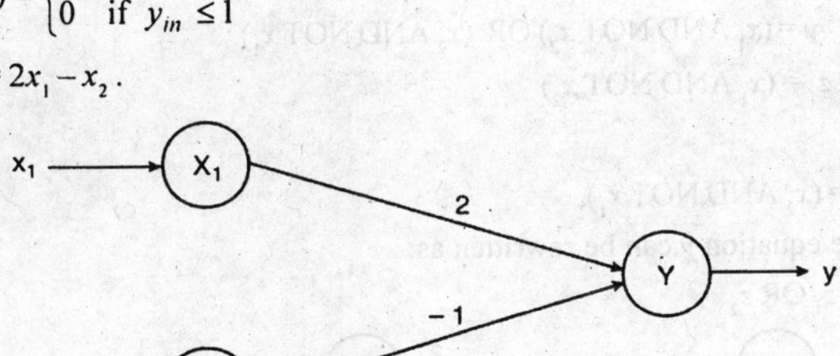

Figure 1.15 *McCulloch–Pitts Neuron Model for AND NOT Function*

From Figure 1.15,

(a) if x_1 and $x_2 = 0$
then $y_{in} = 0$
and $y = f(y_{in}) = 0$

(b) if $x_1 = 0$ and $x_2 = 1$
then $y_{in} = -1$
and $y = f(y_{in}) = 0$

(c) if $x_1 = 1$ and $x_2 = 0$
then $y_{in} = 2$
and $y = f(y_{in}) = 1$

(d) if $x_1 = 1$ and $x_2 = 1$
then $y_{in} = 1$
and $y = f(y_{in}) = 0$

5. XOR XOR returns a true value if exactly one of the input values is true; otherwise it returns a response as false. The truth value representation of XOR is shown in Table 5. A McCulloch–Pitts neuron model to implement XOR is shown in Figure 1.16.

Table 5 **Truth value for XOR**

x_1	x_2	y
0	0	0
0	1	1
1	0	1
1	1	0

The XOR function can be written as:

$$y = (x_1 \text{ AND NOT } x_2) \text{ OR } (x_2 \text{ AND NOT } x_1).$$

Let $z_1 = (x_1 \text{ AND NOT } x_2)$

and

$z_2 = (x_2 \text{ AND NOT } x_1)$,

The equation y can be rewritten as:

$y = z_1 \text{ OR } z_2$

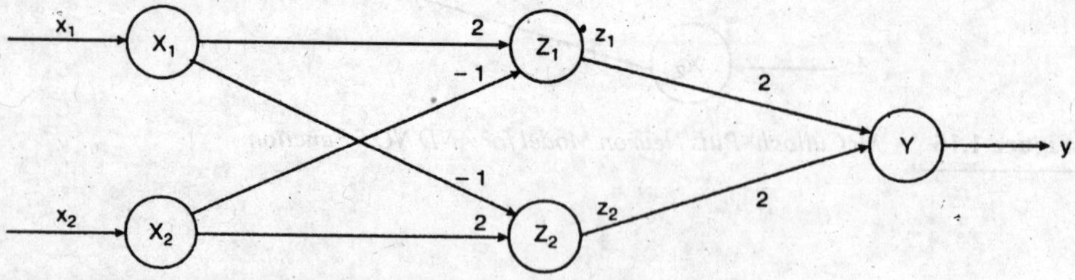

Figure 1.16 *McCulloch–Pitts Neuron Model for XOR Function*

The output of the neuron z_i $(i=1, 2)$ is:

$$z_i = f(z_{ini}) = \begin{cases} 1 & \text{if } z_{ini} \geq 2 \\ 0 & \text{if } z_{ini} < 2 \end{cases}$$

The output of the neuron Y is:

$$y = f(y_{in}) = \begin{cases} 1 & \text{if } y_{in} \geq 2 \\ 0 & \text{if } y_{in} < 2 \end{cases}$$

where $zin_1 = 2x_1 - x_2$,

$zin_2 = 2x_2 - x_1$.

and $y_{in} = 2z_1 + 2z_2$.

If $x_1 = 1$ and $x_2 = 0$

then

$$\begin{aligned} z_{in1} &= 2x_1 - x_2 = 2*1 - 0 = 2 \\ z_1 &= f(z_{in1}) = 1 \\ z_{in2} &= 2x_2 - x_1 = 2*0 - 1 = -1 \\ z_1 &= f(z_{in1}) = 0 \\ z_{in} &= 2z_1 + z_2 = 2*1 + 2*0 = 2 \\ y &= f(y_{in}) = 1 \end{aligned}$$

Similarly, the results for the other three input pair can be verified.

1.10 APPLICATIONS OF NEURAL NETWORKS

There have been many impressive demonstrations of artificial neural networks. A few areas where neural networks are currently applied are mentioned below.

1.10.1 Classification

A neural network can discover the distinguishing features needed to perform a classification task. Classification is the assignment of each object to a specific class, which is an important aspect in image classification. Neural networks have been used successfully in a large number of classification tasks which includes:

(a) Recognition of printed or handwritten characters.

(b) Classification of SONAR and RADAR signals.

1.10.2 Signal Processing

In digital communication systems, distorted signals cause inter-signal interference. One of the first commercial applications of neural networks was to suppress noise cancellation and it was implemented by Widrow using ADALINE. The ADALINE is trained to remove the noise from the telephone line signal.

1.10.3 Speech Recognition

In recent years, speech recognition has received enormous attention. It involves three modules namely, the front end which samples the speech signals and extracts the data, the word processor which is used for finding the probability of words in the vocabulary that match the features of spoken words and the sentence processor which determines if the recognized word makes sense in the sentence. Real time speech recognition system is crucial since it requires a large vocabulary database and large RAM is also required. Kohonen's "Phonetic Typewriter" was an early application in speech recognition, which automatically recognized vocabulary and converted it to text. Neural networks remove the noise inherent in the speech.

1.10.4 Medicine

Anderson [1980] developed an autoassociative network (Brain-State-in-a-Box) to store large amount of medical records, each of which includes information on the symptoms, diagnosis and treatment of a particular case. When a trained network is presented with a set of symptoms, the net finds the best diagnosis and treatment.

1.10.5 Intelligent Control

A problem of concern in industrial motor control is the ability to predict system failure. Motor failure depends on specific motor parameters, transient currents and motor positioning. Neural networks are employed to learn the motor-current variants as well as installation characteristics. 80% to 90% accurate prediction rate has been reported. Many of the neural network applications merge in Robotics. The simplest tasks performed are arm movement, object recognition and object manipulation. Neural networks have been used in many vehicular applications including trains and automatic gear transmission in cars.

Neural networks had been used in steel rolling machines to control the strip thickness within very tight tolerances.

1.10.6 Function Approximation

Many computational models can be described as functions mapping the input vectors to numerical outputs. Neural networks are employed to construct the function that generates approximately the same output for a given input vector based on the available training data.

1.10.7 Financial Forecasting

One of the most sought after applications of neural networks have been in financial applications. The idea that if one dealer can predict market values or assess risk better than his competitors even by a very small amount, leads to an expectation of huge financial benefit. Much of the work in this area is based on the so called 'time series predictions'.

In contrast with the time series prediction, neural networks have also been used in financial modelling which aims at testing theories about the dynamics of market.

1.10.8 Condition Monitoring

The ability of neural nets to receive input from a large number of sensors and to learn to assess the significance of these is a major advantage in condition monitoring. The sensitivity to novelty is almost an emergent property of most neural systems. This has obvious applications in the detection of departures from normality. Time dependent behaviour of nets can also be used in predicting the occurrence of malfunction ahead of time. Applications under this range from health monitoring of turbo machinery to gear boxes, jets and internal combustion engines.

1.10.9 Process Monitoring and Control

Neurocontrol principles can be applied to various areas of the process control industry. Neural techniques come into their own when the link between the measurement and operation parameter selection cannot be obtained by analysis. These techniques can be applied in processes such as chemical and biochemical, pharmaceutical, water purification, food and beverage production, power distribution and oil and gas industries.

1.10.10 Neuro Forecasting

A major application of neural nets is the prediction of prospective long term foreign exchange rates. Neural networks provide greater flexibility in this regard compared to the traditional methods.

1.10.11 Pattern Analysis [B35]

This application works in various areas such as online industrial plant monitoring, smart sensor systems and industrial image analysis as may be required in inspection and control tasks. Other classical problems of pattern analysis such as real time audio bandwidth systems, images and data management can also be tackled with the help of neural networks.

1.11 COMPARISON OF ARTIFICIAL NEURAL NETWORKS AND BIOLOGICAL NETWORKS

1.11.1 NN Speed Processing

Artificial Neural Networks	Biological Networks
Sequential processing is possible and high processing speeds results in neural networks.	Parallelism is possible and low processing speeds results in biological networks.
Artificial systems are usually slow to converge and usually require hundreds or thousands of training presentations for learning to take place.	Biological systems have property of being able to learn with as little as one training presentation. A face that is viewed once, can be recognized again.

Artificial systems focus on learning a single task.	Biological systems have broad capabilities and can address many different types of tasks.
Synchronous updating is possible in discrete time steps.	The updating is asynchronous and when impulse arrives, the parameter decays between intervals

1.11.2 Storage

Artificial Neural Networks	Biological Networks
The memory has an organized behaviour and data retrieved follows an ordered sequence.	The memory follows a pattern of distributed representations and data retrieval depends on retention capacity of the brain.
Artificial neural systems in contrast have usually been limited to 10,000 units with hundreds of connections per unit.	The human brain is extremely large for a neural network containing 10^{11} neurons with as many as 10^4 interconnections each.
Long-term memory resides in the synapses or weights and short-term memory corresponds to the signals sent by the neurons.	This system leads to more possible neural assemblies and activity patterns that could in principle be used in neural function.

1.11.3 Fault Tolerance

Artificial Neural Networks	Biological Networks
Learning takes place by a formulated set of rules and hence the system is less faulty. The processing elements receive many signals and sum up the weighted inputs. These networks can be retrained in case of significant damage (i.e. loss of data).	Learning takes place arbitrarily and hence the system is bound for failure. Biological networks are fault tolerable and even in a traumatic loss, other neurons can take over the function of damaged cells.
Redundancy can increase the reliability of the system, allowing it to function even when some of the neural units are destroyed.	Redundancy is used. When some cells die, the nervous system appears to perform the same. It can counteract sources of noise in biological systems.
Generalization of pattern is more difficult. Back propagation organizes feature detectors in middle layers of systems with three or more layers.	Generalization becomes easier in biological networks. This system extracts an abstract of special features from sensory inputs corresponding to feature detectors.

1.11.4 Control Mechanism

Artificial Neural Networks	Biological Networks
The strength of the neuron depends on whether it is active or inactive and have relatively simpler interconnections.	The strength of the neuron depends on active chemicals present and connections are stronger or weaker as a result of structure layer rather than individual synapses.
Artificial neural network can transfer precise scalar values from unit to unit.	Biological impulse transmission takes place at any time and its timing is determined by incoming signals.
Artificial networks have fully interconnected slabs and are often layered.	Biological systems generally have predetermined wiring at the system level.

1.12 SUMMARY

There has been a resurgence of interest in artificial neural networks over the last few years, as researchers from diverse backgrounds have produced a firm theoretical foundation and demonstrated numerous applications of this rich field of study. An artificial neural network is an information processing system that has been developed as a generalization of the mathematical models of human cognition. These networks are based on and are motivated by models of our brain and nerve cells. The biological neuron constitutes three main features namely the cell body or soma, the axon and the dendrites. In the case of artificial net, the neuron is a node or processing element, which processes weighted inputs and produces outputs which might be used as inputs to other nodes. These ANN models are classified based on the network, the activation function applied and the method of training.

A neural network consists of layers; neurons in any particular layer behave similarly. Based on the number of layers the net is classified as Single layer or Multilayer network. A single layer net consists of one layer of connection weights whereas a multilayer net consists of more than one layer. Activation functions are used to bring about a response that is bounded. There are various activation functions namely the identity function, sigmoid function, step function, bipolar sigmoidal and Gaussian function. Training or learning is a process by which a net adapts itself to a stimulus by properly making parameter adjustments. Learning is of three types namely supervised, unsupervised and reinforced training. Supervised training is one in which the net is presented with an input stimulus and target output pair. In the case of unsupervised training, the net is excited with input stimuli and the inputs are clustered into groups by the net itself. Reinforced training is similar to supervised training but the teacher in this case responds with a pass or fail alone.

The first mathematical model of a single idealized biological neuron was the McCulloch–Pitts model. The neurons of this model are binary activated. They have a threshold value and if the neuron is above this value, the neuron fires (output 1) else the output is zero. Artificial neural networks have widespread applications in diverse fields like pattern recognition, classification, signal processing, medicine, control systems and business.

SHORT QUESTIONS AND ANSWERS

1. What are artificial neural networks?

   An artificial neural network is an information processing system that has certain performance characteristics in common with Biological Neural Networks.

2. What are the assumptions made in artificial neural networks?

   - Information processing occurs in many simple elements called neurons.
   - Signals are passed between neurons over connection links.
   - Each connection link has an associated weight, which in a typical neural net multiplies the signal transmitted.
   - Each neuron applies an activation function to its net input in order to determine its output signal.

3. How is a neural network characterized?

   A neural network is characterized by

   - its pattern of connections between the neurons,
   - its method of determining the weights on the connections and
   - its activation function.

4. Define feature detectors in the hidden layer.

   Feature detectors are the units that respond to a particular feature that may appear in the input pattern.

5. What are the applications of neural networks?

   Neural networks offer possibilities for solving problems that require pattern recognition, pattern mapping dealing with noisy data, pattern completion, associative look-ups and systems that learn or adapt during use. It is also used in signal processing, speech production and recognition, image processing and analysis, SONAR and seismic signal classification and adaptive controls, medicine and business.

6. Give the advantages and disadvantages of hidden neurons.

   The presence of a hidden unit together with the nonlinear activation function gives it the ability to solve many problems that cannot be solved by a net with only input and output units.

   The major difficulty with hidden units is that the net becomes difficult to train.

7. What are the main components of a biological neuron?

The three main components of a biological neuron are:

a. dendrites

b. soma

c. axon

8. Where are the neural networks implemented?

Implementation of neural networks is through software simulators, computer programs that simulate the operations of the neural network. Such a simulation might be done on a Von Neumann machine. The speed of the simulation depends on the speed of the hardware upon which the simulation is executed.

9. Define net architecture and give its classification.

The arrangement of neurons into layers and the connection patterns within and between layers is called the net architecture. It can be a single layer, multilayer or competitive net.

10. Distinguish between supervised and unsupervised training.

In supervised training, a sequence of training vectors or patterns each with an associated target vector is presented to the net. The weights are adjusted according to the learning algorithm. An example for such training is the backpropagation networks used for pattern classification and association. In unsupervised training, a sequence of input vectors is provided but no target values are specified. The net modifies the weight so that the most similar input vectors are assigned to the output unit. An example for such training is the self-organizing nets like Kohonen's Self-organizing Map and Adaptive Resonance Theory.

11. What is the other name for weight?

The other name for weight is connection strength.

12. What do you infer when the error gets diverged instead of getting converged during the consecutive process of training?

When the error gets diverged rather than converged during the consecutive process of training, it represents that the network has started memorizing.

13. List the common activation functions.

1. Identity function

$f(x) = x$; for every x

2. Binary step function

$f(x) = 1;$ if $x \geq \theta$

$\quad\quad 0;$ if $x < \theta$

3. Binary sigmoidal function

$$f(x) = \frac{1}{1+e^{-x}}$$

4. Bipolar sigmoidal function

$$f(x) = \frac{2}{1+e^{-x}} - 1$$

14. **What is the basic difference between a digital computer and a neural network?**

The basic difference between a digital computer and a neural network is that a neural network does not process information based on the sequential algorithm whereas a digital computer processes information based on the sequential algorithm.

15. **What are the features inherited by ANN from biological neurons?**

Several key features of the processing elements of ANN are suggested by the properties of biological neurons as given below.

- Processing element receives many signals.
- Signals are modified by weights at the receiving synapse.
- Processing element sums the weighted input.
- Neuron fires under appropriate conditions.
- Output is transmitted to many other neurons.
- Information processing is local.
- Memory is distributed.
- A synapse's strength may be modified through experience.
- Neurotransmitters may be excitatory or inhibitory.

16. **What are the two types of memories? Where are they stored?**

Memory may be short-term or long-term. Long-term memory resides in the neuron's synapse or weight. Short-term memory corresponds to the signals sent by the neuron.

17. **What does firing rule mean?**

A firing rule determines how one calculates whether the node should fire for any input pattern. It relates to all input patterns, not only the ones on which the node was trained.

18. **What does "generalization of a node" mean?**

The difference between the truth value representation before and after application of the firing rule is called the "generalization of the node" due to that particular firing rule.

19. **Explain briefly what feedforward and feedback nets mean.**

A feedforward net is one in which there are no closed loops.

A feedback net is one where information can find its way around a loop from the output back to the input.

20. Explain Fault Tolerance.

Artificial neural networks can be designed to identify signals even when in corrupted or incomplete form. Also they can be made such that they are insensitive to small damage to the network and the net can be retained in case of significant damage. These two properties are referred to as fault tolerance.

REVIEW QUESTIONS

1. What is a neural network?
2. Compare and contrast the biological neuron and the artificial neuron.
3. Define synapse.
4. Give a portrayal of a biological neuron with all its parts.
5. Draw the basic neuron model.
6. Explain briefly the function of each layer of a neuron model.
7. Graphically represent the various activation functions.
8. Give the basic equations of the various activation functions.
9. Differentiate the three types of training networks.
10. How can an ANN be applied in business? Give few applications.
11. What is the difference between pattern recognition and classification? How is ANN applied in both?
12. Explain briefly about Intelligent Control. Give few applications in industries.

CHAPTER

2

HEBB Net, ADALINE, MADALINE and Perceptron

2.1 INTRODUCTION

A neuron is considered to be an adaptive element. Its weights can be modified depending on the input signal it receives, its output value and the associated teacher response. In some cases, if teacher signal is not available, the neuron will modify its weight based on the input and/or output.

2.2 AMARI'S GENERAL LEARNING RULE

Consider a single layer feedforward neural network consisting of n input neurons and m output neurons (Fig. 2.1). It is convenient to consider the weights to be elements of a matrix, **W** such that **W**= R^{n*m}.

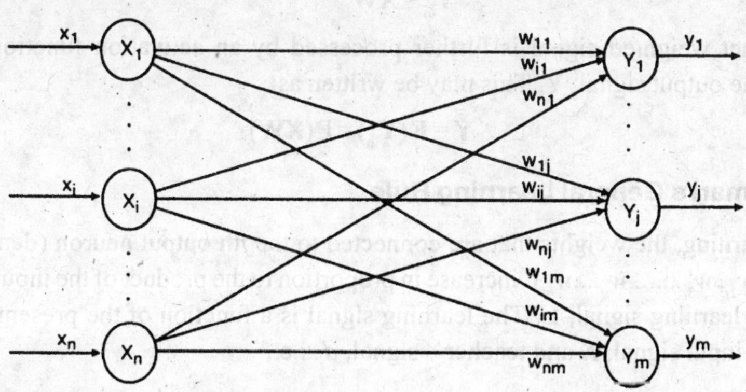

Figure 2.1 *Single Layer Neural Network*

The dimensions of the weight matrix **W** are n rows and m columns. For example, the weight connecting the second input neuron to the fourth output neuron would be w_{24}. In general, the weight matrix can be represented as:

$$\mathbf{W} = \begin{bmatrix} w_{11} & w_{12} & \dots & w_{1j} & \dots & w_{1m} \\ w_{21} & w_{22} & \dots & w_{2j} & \dots & w_{2m} \\ \dots & \dots & \dots & \dots & \dots & \dots \\ w_{i1} & w_{i2} & \dots & w_{ij} & \dots & w_{im} \\ \dots & \dots & \dots & \dots & \dots & \dots \\ w_{n1} & w_{n2} & \dots & w_{nj} & \dots & w_{nm} \end{bmatrix}$$

Note: The elements of the weight matrix are given in lower case letters and the weight matrix, **W**, is given in upper case and bold letters.

Let

$\mathbf{X} = [x_1 \cdot x_2\, x_3 \dots x_i \dots x_n]$ denote the input vector,

$\mathbf{Y_{in}} = [y_{in1}\, y_{in2}\, y_{in3} \dots y_{inj} \dots y_{inm}]$ denote the net weighted input vector,

$\mathbf{Y} = [y_1\, y_2\, y_3 \dots y_j \dots y_m]$ denote the output vector.

Note: The elements of the input vector, x_i ($i = 1,2,3\dots,n$) represent the input signals applied to the artificial neurons. The elements of the output vector, y_j ($j = 1, 2,\dots m$) represent the output signals after processing by the activation function, $F(.)$.

The net weighted input signals at the jth output neuron can be written as:

$$Y_{inj} = x_1 w_{ij} + x_2 w_{2j} + \dots + x_n w_{nj}$$

$$= \sum_{i=1}^{n} x_i w_{ij} \tag{2.1}$$

In general, the net weighted input signal can be given as the product of the input and weighted vector. It can be represented as:

$$\mathbf{Y_{in}} = \mathbf{XW}$$

The net weighted signal is further processed by an activation function, **F**, to produce the output signal, **Y**. This may be written as:

$$\mathbf{Y} = \mathbf{F}(\mathbf{Y_{in}}) = \mathbf{F}(\mathbf{XW})$$

2.2.1 Amari's General Learning Rule

During learning, the weights that are connected to the jth output neuron (denoted by $\mathbf{w_j} = [w_{1j}, w_{2j}, w_{3j}, \dots\dots, w_{ij} \dots w_{nj}]^T$ increase in proportion to the product of the input vector, **X** and the learning signal, **L**. The learning signal is a function of the present weight values, $\mathbf{w_j}$ input signal, **X** and teacher's signal, d_i. i.e.,

$$\Delta \mathbf{w}_j = \mathbf{c} * \mathbf{L}(w_j, \mathbf{X}, d_j)\mathbf{X}^T \tag{2.2}$$

where Δw_j is the change in weight and

c is a positive learning constant.

The adopted new weight vector is

$$\mathbf{w}_j(\text{new}) = \mathbf{w}_j(\text{old}) + \Delta \mathbf{w}_j \tag{2.3}$$

Note: w_j is a column vector.

2.3 HEBB LEARNING RULE

In the brain, learning is particularly done by the change in the synaptic gap (strength). The first person to comment upon this was the psychologist Donald Hebb in 1949.

Hebb's original statement was:

"When an axon of cell *A* is near enough to excite a cell *B* and repeatedly or persistently takes place in firing it, some growth process or metabolic change takes place in one or both cells such that *A*'s efficiency, as one of the cells firing *B*, is increased."

To put it in a more accurate manner, Hebb's hypothesis may be stated as:

"Increase the value of weight if the output is active when the input associated with that weight is also active."

If we assume the input *x* and the output *y* have binary values, the weight value will be incremented only when the output is "1" and the corresponding input is "1".

Stent [1973] rephrased the Hebb's hypothesis as:

1. If two neurons on either side of a synapse (connection) are activated simultaneously, then the strength of that synapse is selectively increased.
2. If two neurons on either side of a synapse are activated asynchronously, then synapse is selectively weakened or eliminated.

For Hebbian rule, the weight vector increases proportional to the product of input and the learning signal, where the learning signal is equal to the neuron's output.

2.3.1 Hebb Net

Based on Hebbian Learning rule, McClelland and Rumelhart (1988) developed the Hebb net. This net consists of a single layer feedforward neural network. This net has a fixed bias value of 1). The input and the output patterns must be of bipolar form.

The Hebb net does not learn if the input-output patterns are in binary form. This is the extreme limitation of Hebb net.

Fig. 2.2 shows a simple Hebb net.

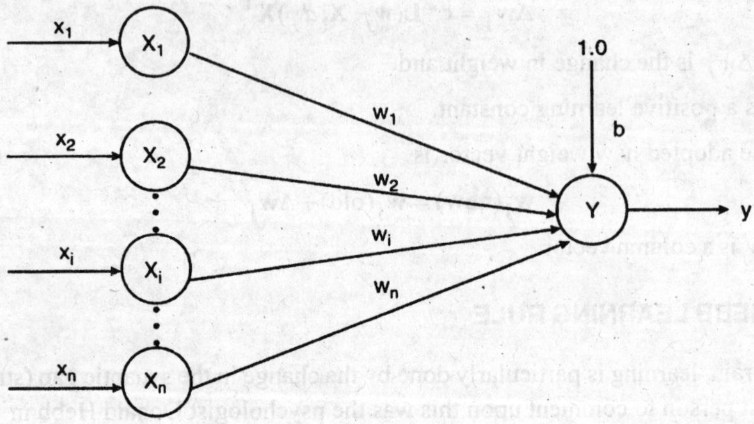

Figure 2.2 *A Simple Hebb Net*

2.3.2 Algorithm to Train Hebb Net

Step 1: Initialize all weights to zero, $w_i = 0$ (for $i = 1,2,3,...,n$)

where n is the number of input neurons.

Initialize the bias value to zero, $b = 0$.

Step 2: For each input vector, target output pair $S{:}t$, do steps 3 to 6.

Step 3: Set activations for input units with the input vector.

$$x_i = s_i \quad (\text{for } i = 1,2,3,...,n)$$

Step 4: Set the corresponding output value to the output neuron.

$$y = t$$

Step 5: Apply Hebb rule and modify weights.

$$w_i\,(\text{new}) = w_i\,(\text{old}) + x_i y \quad (\text{for } i = 1,2,3,..,n)$$

Step 6: Adjust the bias.

$$b\,(\text{new}) = b\,(\text{old}) + y$$

The above algorithm requires only one pass through the training set. The weight update can be written in the vector form as:

$$\mathbf{W}(\text{new}) = \mathbf{W}(\text{old}) + \mathbf{X}^T y$$

Note:

W is a column vector.

X is a row vector.

y is a scalar.

2.3.3 Linear Separability

The intension of training a network is to find the weights that will respond correctly when the net is presented with an input pattern that is similar to one of the training pattern.

The activation function of the output neuron is a step function. Consider a sample neural net with n input neurons and one output neuron. If the response of the output neuron is 1 for an input pattern then the input pattern is a member of the class. If the response of the output is –1 then the input pattern does not belong to the class.

The net input to the output neuron can be written as $Y_{in} = w_0 + \sum x_i w_i$

Using the above equation, the decision boundary between the region where yin > 0 and $y_{in} < 0$ can be determined. Depending on the number of input neurons in the network, this equation represents a line or a plane or a hyper plane.

If it is possible to find the weights so that all of the training input vectors for which the correct response is 1 lie on one side of the boundary, and all of the training patterns for which the correct response is –1 lie on the either side of the boundary, then thc problem is linearly separable otherwise the problem is linearly non separable.

Example 2.1 Design a Hebb net to implement logical AND function using bipolar input-output patterns. The following example is illustrated below:

Solution The training pattern for an AND logic function is shown below

Training Patterns

	Input				**Target**
	x_1	x_2	b		y
$\mathbf{X}_1$	–1	–1	1	y_1	–1
$\mathbf{X}_2$	–1	1	1	y_2	–1
$\mathbf{X}_3$	1	–1	1	y_3	–1
$\mathbf{X}_4$	1	1	1	y_4	1

A single layer network with 2 input neurons, one bias and one output neuron is considered. The initial weights are set to zero.

$$\mathbf{W}(\text{old}) = [0 \quad 0 \quad 0]^T$$

Case I :

For the first input, $\mathbf{X}_1 = [-1 \ -1 \ \ 1]$ and the target, $y_1 = [-1]$ the updated weight is:

$$\begin{aligned}\mathbf{W}(\text{new}) &= \mathbf{W}(\text{old}) + \mathbf{X}_1{}^T y_1 \\ &= [0 \ \ 0 \ \ 0]^T + [-1 \ -1 \ \ 1]^T [-1] \\ &= [0 \ \ 0 \ \ 0]^T + [1 \ \ 1 \ -1]^T \\ &= [1 \ \ 1 \ -1]^T\end{aligned}$$

Case II :

On applying the second input vector, $\mathbf{X}_2 = [-1 \ \ 1 \ \ 1]$ and the corresponding target, $y_2=[-1]$ the new weight vector is :

$$\begin{aligned}\mathbf{W}(\text{new}) &= \mathbf{W}(\text{old}) + \mathbf{X}_2^{\,T} y_2 \\ &= [1 \ \ 1 \ \ -1]^T + [-1 \ \ 1 \ \ 1]^T[-1] \\ &= [1 \ \ 1 \ -1]^T + [1 \ \ -1 \ -1]^T \\ &= [2 \ 0 \ -2]^T\end{aligned}$$

Case III:

For the third input pattern, $\mathbf{X}_3 = [1 \ -1 \ \ 1]$ and the corresponding target, $y_3 = [-1]$ the new weight vector is:

$$\begin{aligned}\mathbf{W}(\text{new}) &= \mathbf{W}(\text{old}) + \mathbf{X}_3^{\,T} y_3 \\ &= [2 \ 0 \ -2]^T + [1 \ \ -1 \ \ 1]^T[-1] \\ &= [2 \ 0 \ -2]^T + [-1 \ \ 1 \ -1]^T \\ &= [1 \ 1 \ -3]^T\end{aligned}$$

Case IV:

Applying the fourth input pattern, $\mathbf{X}_4 = [1 \ \ 1 \ \ 1]$ and the corresponding target, $y_4 = [1]$ the final weight vector is:

$$\begin{aligned}\mathbf{W}(\text{new}) &= \mathbf{W}(\text{old}) + \mathbf{X}_4^{\,T} y_4 \\ &= [1 \ 1 \ -3]^T + [1 \ \ 1 \ \ 1]^T[1] \\ &= [1 \ \ 1 \ -3]^T + [1 \ \ 1 \ \ 1]^T \\ &= [2 \ \ 2 \ -2]^T\end{aligned}$$

The Hebb net architecture with the final weight vector is shown in Fig. 2.3.

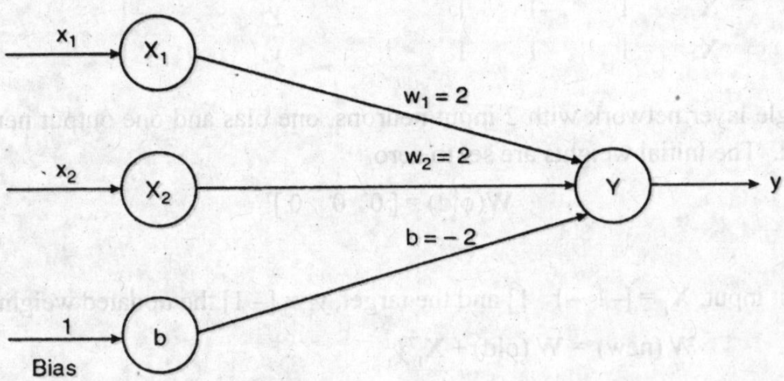

Figure 2.3 *Hebb Net for AND Function*

The given AND function can be represented as a classification problem between inputs that produce a '1' as output and those that produce '−1' as output. The function can be represented by means of pattern space in which the inputs represent the coordinate system for that space and the set of co-ordinates gives the position of the feature in that space.

Fig. 2.4 shows the two input variables labelled x_1 and x_2 on the pattern space diagram. The four points (–1,–1), (–1,1), (1,–1) and (1,1) represent the positions in the pattern space. At each point, the value of the output of the function, $y = x_1$ AND x_2 is marked as either a dot (for –1) or a cross (for 1).

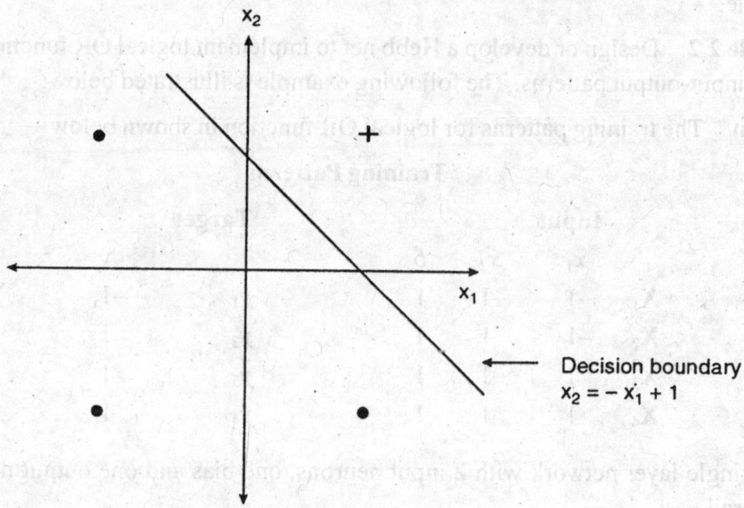

Figure 2.4 *Decision Boundary for AND Function*

In this example, we have considered the separation of the input space into regions where the response is negative. The values of x_1 and x_2 for which the net gives a positive response and the values for which it gives a negative response is known as the separating line,

$$x_1 w_1 + x_2 w_2 + b = 0.$$

Using the final weight values, the equation for the boundary line is $2x_1 + 2x_2 - 2 = 0$ or $x_2 = -x_1 + 1$. The straight line $x_2 = -x_1 + 1$, separates the pattern space into two regions such that for unit input response the points lie on one side of the boundary while for all the other three input patterns, [(–1, –1), (–1,1), (1, –1)] for which the output response is '–1', the points lie on the other side of the boundary. Since a straight line separates the two classes, this problem is referred to as a linearly separable problem.

Note:

In general, for an n input network, the relation that determines the decision boundary is given by

$$b + \sum_{i=1}^{n} x_i w_i = 0$$

Depending on the number of output neurons in the network, the equation will represent either a line, plane or a hyper-plane.

If there are weights and a bias so that all of the training input vectors for which the correct response is '+1' lie on one side of the decision boundary and all of the training input vectors for which the correct response is '-1' lie on other side of the decision boundary, then the problem is linearly separable, otherwise it is known as linearly non-separable.

Example 2.2 Design or develop a Hebb net to implement logical OR function using bipolar input-output patterns. The following example is illustrated below:

Solution The training patterns for logical OR function in shown below.

Training Patterns

	Input				**Target**
	x_1	x_2	b		y
$\mathbf{X}_1$	−1	−1	1	y_1	−1
$\mathbf{X}_2$	−1	1	1	y_2	1
$\mathbf{X}_3$	1	−1	1	y_3	1
$\mathbf{X}_4$	1	1	1	y_4	1

A single layer network with 2 input neurons, one bias and one output neuron is considered.

The initial weights are set to zero.

$\mathbf{W}(\text{old}) = [0 \;\; 0 \;\; 0]^T$

Case I :

For the first input, $\mathbf{X}_1 = [-1 \; -1 \;\; 1]$ and the target, $y_1 = [-1]$ the updated weight is:

$$\begin{aligned}\mathbf{W}(\text{new}) &= \mathbf{W}(\text{old}) + \mathbf{X}_1^T y_1\\ &= [0 \;\; 0 \;\; 0]^T + [-1 \; -1 \;\; 1]^T \, [-1]\\ &= [0 \;\; 0 \;\; 0]^T + [1 \;\; 1 \; -1]^T\\ &= [1 \;\; 1 \; -1]^T\end{aligned}$$

Case II :

On applying the second input vector, $\mathbf{X}_2 = [-1 \;\; 1 \;\; 1]$ and the corresponding target, $y_2 = [1]$ the new weight vector is :

$$\begin{aligned}\mathbf{W}(\text{new}) &= \mathbf{W}(\text{old}) + \mathbf{X}_2^T y_2\\ &= [1 \; 1 \; -1]^T + [-1 \;\; 1 \;\; 1]^T [1]\\ &= [1 \;\; 1 \; -1]^T + [-1 \;\; 1 \;\; 1]^T\\ &= [0 \;\; 2 \;\; 0]^T\end{aligned}$$

Case III:

For the third input pattern, $\mathbf{X}_3 = [1 \ \ -1 \ \ 1]$ and the corresponding target, $y_3 = [1]$ the new weight vector is :

$$\mathbf{W}(\text{new}) = \mathbf{W}(\text{old}) + \mathbf{X}_3{}^T y_3$$
$$= [0 \ 2 \ 0]^T + [1 \ -1 \ 1]^T [1]$$
$$= [0 \ 2 \ 0]^T + [1 \ -1 \ 1]^T$$
$$= [1 \ 1 \ 1]^T$$

Case IV:

Applying the fourth input pattern, $\mathbf{X}_4 = [1 \ 1 \ 1]$ and the corresponding target, $y_4 = [1]$ the final weight vector is :

$$\mathbf{W}(\text{new}) = \mathbf{W}(\text{old}) + \mathbf{X}_4{}^T y^4$$
$$= [1 \ 1 \ 1]^T + [1 \ 1 \ 1]^T [1]$$
$$= [1 \ 1 \ 1]^T + [1 \ 1 \ 1]^T$$
$$= [2 \ 2 \ 2]^T$$

The final weights are marked in the Hebb net and shown in Fig. 2.5.

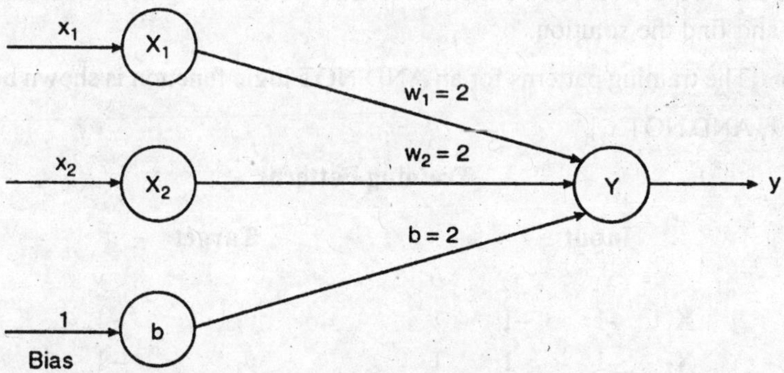

Figure 2.5 *Hebb Net for OR Function*

Using the final weights, the equation for the boundary line is $2x_1 + 2x_2 + 2 = 0$ or $x_2 = -x_1 - 1$.

The decision region for the net is shown in Figure 2.6. From Figure 2.6, it can be observed that the straight line $x_2 = -x_1 - 1$, separates the pattern space into two regions.

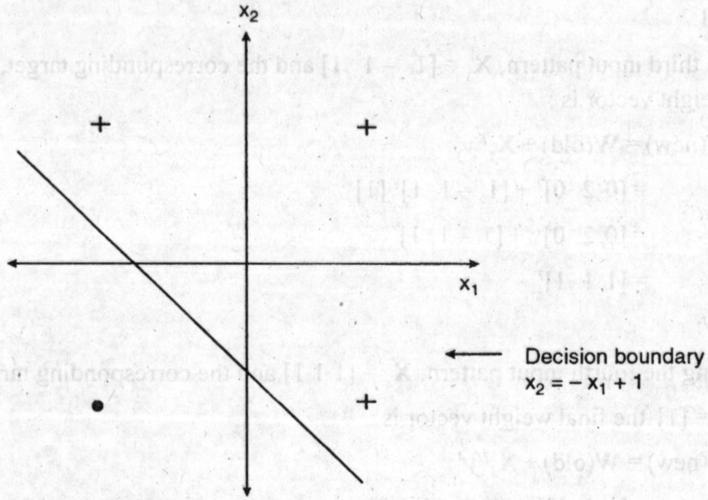

Figure 2.6 *Decision Boundary for OR Function*

The input patterns [(− 1,1), (1, − 1), (1,1)] for which the output response is '1', lie on one side of the boundary and the input pattern (− 1, − 1) for which the output response is '− 1', lie on the other side of the boundary.

Example 2.3 Apply Hebb rule method to train patterns that define the AND NOT function and find the solution.

Solution The training patterns for an AND NOT logic function is shown below:

[$y = x_1$ AND NOT x_2]

Training Patterns

	Input			Target	
	x_1	x_2	b		y
$\mathbf{X}_1$	−1	−1	1	y_1	−1
$\mathbf{X}_2$	−1	1	1	y_2	−1
$\mathbf{X}_3$	1	−1	1	y_3	1
$\mathbf{X}_4$	1	1	1	y_4	−1

A single layer network with 2 input neurons, one bias and one output neuron is considered.

The initial weights are set to zero.

$$\mathbf{W}\,(\text{old}) = [0 \quad 0 \quad 0]^T$$

Case I:

For the first input vector, $\mathbf{X}_1 = [-1 \ \ -1 \ \ 1]$ and the target, $y_1 = [-1]$ the updated weight is:

$$\mathbf{W}(\text{new}) = \mathbf{W}(\text{old}) + \mathbf{X}_1^T y_1$$
$$= [0\ \ 0\ \ 0]^T + [-1\ -1\ \ 1]^T\,[-1]$$
$$= [0\ \ 0\ \ 0]^T + [1\ \ \ 1\ -1]^T$$
$$= [1\ \ 1\ -1]^T$$

Case II:

On applying the second input vector, $\mathbf{X}_2 = [-1\ \ 1\ \ 1]$ and the corresponding target, $y_2 = [-1]$ the new weight vector is :

$$\mathbf{W}(\text{new}) = \mathbf{W}(\text{old}) + \mathbf{X}_2^T y_2$$
$$= [1\ \ 1\ -1]^T + [-1\ \ 1\ \ 1]^T[-1]$$
$$= [1\ \ 1\ -1]^T + [1\ -1\ -1]^T$$
$$= [2\ \ 0\ \ -2]^T$$

Case III:

For the third input pattern, $\mathbf{X}_3 = [1\ \ -1\ \ \ 1]$ and the corresponding target, $y_3 = [1]$ the new weight vector is :

$$\mathbf{W}(\text{new}) = \mathbf{W}(\text{old}) + \mathbf{X}_3^T y_3$$
$$= [2\ \ 0\ -2]^T + [1\ -1\ \ \ 1]^T[1]$$
$$= [2\ \ 0\ -2]^T + [1\ -1\ \ 1]^T$$
$$= [3\ -1\ -1]^T$$

Case IV:

Applying the fourth input pattern, $\mathbf{X}_4 = [1\ \ \ 1\ \ 1]$ and the corresponding target,

$y_4 = [-1]$ the final weight vector is :

$$\mathbf{W}(\text{new}) = \mathbf{W}(\text{old}) + \mathbf{X}_4^T y_4$$
$$= [3\ -1\ \ -1]^T + [1\ \ 1\ \ 1]^T[-1]$$
$$= [3\ \ -1\ -1]^T + [-1\ -1\ -1]^T$$
$$= [2\ -2\ \ -2]^T$$

The final weights are marked in the Hebb net and shown in Fig. 2.7.

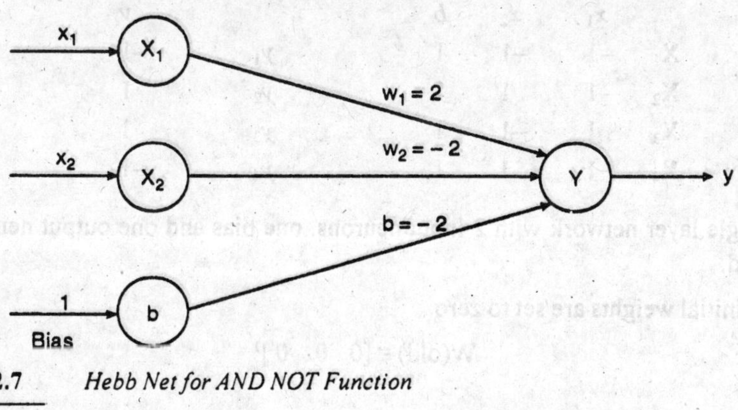

Figure 2.7 *Hebb Net for AND NOT Function*

Using the final weights the equation for the boundary line is $2x_1 - 2x_2 - 2 = 0$ or $x_2 = x_1 - 1$.

The decision region for the net is shown in Figure 2.8. From Figure 2.8, it can be observed that the straight line $x_2 = x_1 - 1$, separates the pattern space into two regions.

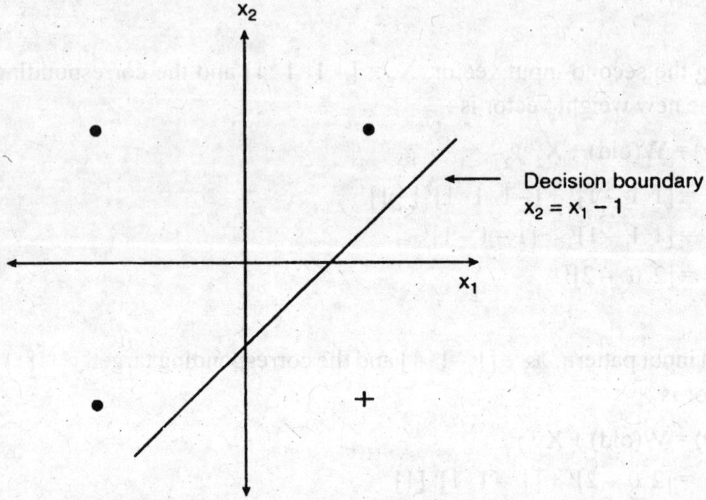

Figure 2.8 *Decision Boundary for AND NOT Function*

The input patterns [(− 1, 1), (− 1, − 1), (1, 1)] for which the output response is '− 1', lie on one side of the boundary and the input pattern (1, − 1) for which the output response is '1', lie on the other side of the boundary.

Example 2.4 Apply Hebb rule method to training patterns that define the XOR function and find the solution.

Solution The training patterns for an XOR logic function is shown below: [$y = x_1$ XOR x_2]

Training Patterns

	Input			Target	
	x_1	x_2	b		y
$\mathbf{X}_1$	−1	−1	1	y_1	−1
$\mathbf{X}_2$	−1	1	1	y_2	1
$\mathbf{X}_3$	1	−1	1	y_3	1
$\mathbf{X}_4$	1	1	1	y_4	−1

A single layer network with 2 input neurons, one bias and one output neuron is considered.

The initial weights are set to zero.

$$\mathbf{W}(\text{old}) = [0 \quad 0 \quad 0]^T$$

Case I:

For the first input vector, $\mathbf{X}_1 = [-1\ \ -1\ \ 1]$ and the target, $y_1 = [-1]$ the updated weight is:

$$\begin{aligned}\mathbf{W}(\text{new}) &= \mathbf{W}(\text{old}) + \mathbf{X}_1^T y_1 \\ &= [0\ \ 0\ \ 0]^T + [-1\ \ -1\ \ 1]^T\ [-1] \\ &= [0\ \ 0\ \ 0]^T + [1\ \ 1\ \ -1]^T \\ &= [1\ \ 1\ \ -1]^T\end{aligned}$$

Case II:

On applying the second input vector, $\mathbf{X}_2 = [-1\ \ 1\ \ 1]$ and the corresponding target, $y_2 = [1]$ the new weight vector is :

$$\begin{aligned}\mathbf{W}(\text{new}) &= \mathbf{W}(\text{old}) + \mathbf{X}_2^T y_2 \\ &= [1\ \ 1\ \ -1]^T + [-1\ \ 1\ \ 1]^T [1] \\ &= [1\ \ 1\ \ -1]^T + [-1\ \ 1\ \ 1]^T \\ &= [0\ \ 2\ \ 0]^T\end{aligned}$$

Case III:

For the third input pattern, $\mathbf{X}_3 = [1\ \ -1\ \ 1]$ and the corresponding target, $y_3 = [1]$ the new weight vector is :

$$\begin{aligned}\mathbf{W}(\text{new}) &= \mathbf{W}(\text{old}) + \mathbf{X}_3^T y_3 \\ &= [0\ \ 2\ \ 0]^T + [1\ \ -1\ \ 1]^T [1] \\ &= [0\ \ 2\ \ 0]^T + [1\ \ -1\ \ 1]^T \\ &= [1\ \ 1\ \ 1]^T\end{aligned}$$

Case IV:

Applying the fourth input pattern, $\mathbf{X}_4 = [1\ \ 1\ \ 1]$ and the corresponding target,

$y_4 = [-1]$ the final weight vector is:

$$\begin{aligned}\mathbf{W}(\text{new}) &= \mathbf{W}(\text{old}) + \mathbf{X}_4^T y_4 \\ &= [1\ \ 1\ \ 1]^T + [1\ \ 1\ \ 1]^T [-1] \\ &= [1\ \ 1\ \ 1]^T + [-1\ -1\ -1]^T \\ &= [0\ \ 0\ \ 0]^T\end{aligned}$$

The final weights do not give the correct output for all input patterns. Fig. 2.9 shows that the input patterns are linearly non-separable. The XOR function is a classical example of a pattern classification problem that is not linearly separable.

The graph of the four input pairs cannot be divided by a single line to separate it into two categories.

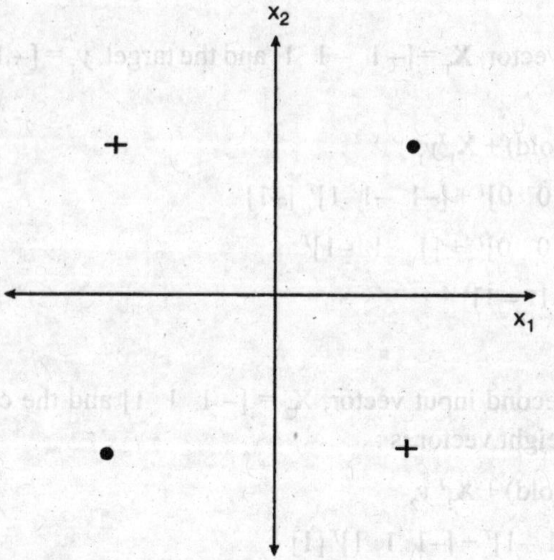

Figure 2.9 *Decision Boundary for Exclusive-OR Function*

Example 2.5 Classify the two-dimensional input patterns (representing letters) using Hebb rule. i.e. (the T-C Problem).

Solution The T-C problem is fairly simple pattern-recognition identification. It is required to distinguish between the letters 'T' and 'C'. Fig. 2.10(a), shows the data representation scheme for the T-C problem in which each letter is super-imposed on a 3 × 3 grid and the filled grid squares are represented by '1'. Each input vector consists of 9 elements.

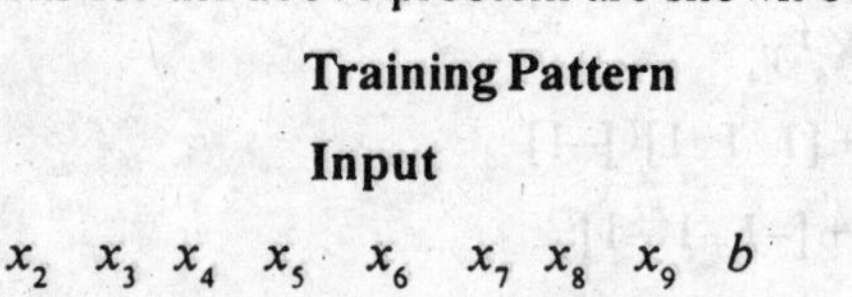

Figure 2.10(a) *T-C Data Representation*

The training patterns for the above problem are shown below.

Training Pattern

Pattern	**Input**										**Target**
	x_1	x_2	x_3	x_4	x_5	x_6	x_7	x_8	x_9	b	y
T	1	1	1	-1	1	-1	-1	1	-1	1	1
C	1	1	1	1	-1	-1	1	1	1	1	-1

A single layer neural network with 9 input neurons, one bias and one output neuron is considered. The initial weight values are set to zero.

W(old) = $[0\,0\,0, 0\,0\,0, 0\,0\,0, 0]^T$

Case I:

For the first training pair, $\mathbf{X}_1 = [1\ 1\ 1, -1\ 1\ -1, -1\ 1\ -1, 1]^T$ and the target value,

$y_1 = [1]$ the new weight vector is:

$$\mathbf{W}(\text{new}) = \mathbf{W}(\text{old}) + \mathbf{X}_1^T y_1$$
$$= [1\ 1\ 1, -1\ 1\ -1, -1\ 1\ -1, 1]^T$$

Case II:

On applying the second training pair, $\mathbf{X}_2 = [1\ 1\ 1,\ 1\ -1\ -1,\ 1\ 1\ 1,\ 1]^T$ and the target value, $y_2 = [-1]$ the new weight vector is:

$$\mathbf{W}(\text{new}) = \mathbf{W}(\text{old}) + \mathbf{X}_2^T y_2$$
$$= [1\ 1\ 1, -1\ 1\ -1, -1\ 1\ -1, 1]^T + [1\ 1\ 1,\ 1\ -1\ -1,\ 1\ 1\ 1,\ 1]^T [-1]$$
$$= [0\ 0\ 0, -2\ 2\ 0, -2\ 0\ -2, 0]^T$$

The final weights are marked in Hebb net and shown in Fig. 2.10 (b).

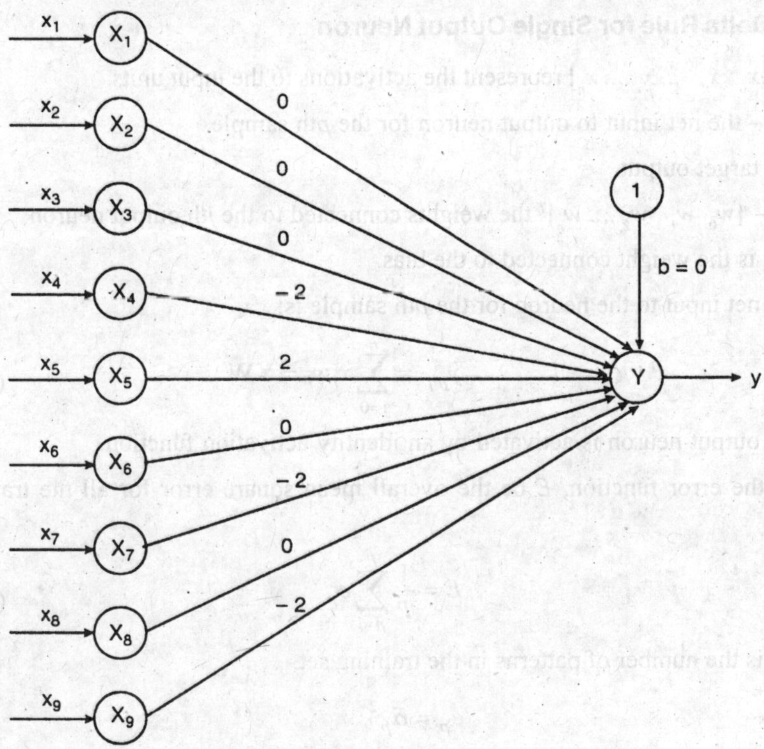

Figure 2.10 (b) *Hebb Net for T-C Problem*

2.4 DELTA RULE

The Delta rule is also referred to as Widrow-Hoff rule or Least Mean Square (LMS) rule. This rule is applicable for the supervised training of neural networks. According to this rule, the change in weight is directly proportional to the error signal $(t_j - y_j)$ and the input. The error signal is equal to the difference between the desired output value and the actual output value of the neuron.

The change in weight vector, $\Delta \mathbf{W}_j$ (weights that are connected to jth neuron) can be represented as:

$$\Delta \mathbf{W}_j = c(t_j - \mathbf{X}\mathbf{W}_j)\mathbf{X}^T \tag{2.4}$$

Note:

c - Learning constant.

t_j - desired value at the jth output neuron.

$\mathbf{W}$, $\Delta \mathbf{W}_j$ - column vector,

$\mathbf{X}$ - row vector.

For this learning rule, weights can be initialized to any value.

2.4.1 Delta Rule for Single Output Neuron

Let $\mathbf{X} = [x_0 \ \ x_1 \ \ ... x_i .... x_n]$ represent the activations to the input units.

y_{inp} – the net input to output neuron for the pth sample.

t – target output.

$\mathbf{W}_j$ – $[w_0 \ \ w_1 \ \ w_2 .... w_n]^T$ the weights connected to the jth output neuron.

Note: w_0 is the weight connected to the bias.

The net input to the neuron for the pth sample is:

$$y_{inp} = \sum_{i=0}^{n} x_i w_i = \mathbf{XW} \tag{2.5}$$

The output neuron is activated by an identity activation function.

Let the error function, E be the overall mean square error for all the training patterns.

$$E = \frac{1}{P}\sum_{p=1}^{P} e_p \tag{2.6}$$

where P is the number of patterns in the training set.

$$e_p = \delta_p^{\ 2} \tag{2.7}$$

where $\delta_p = t_p - y_{inp}$

$$Y_{inp} = t_p - y_{inp} \tag{2.8}$$

$$E = \frac{1}{P}\sum_{p=1}^{P}[t_p - \sum_{i=0}^{n} x_i w_i]^2 \tag{2.9}$$

The quickest way of finding minima is to use a gradient descendent method, where the adjustments of parameters (weights in this case) are proportional to the derivative of the error function with respect to the weights but opposite in sign.

i.e.
$$\Delta w_i = -\alpha \frac{\partial E}{\partial w_i} \tag{2.10}$$

where α - Learning constant.

$$\frac{\partial E}{\partial w_i} = \frac{1}{P}\sum_{p=1}^{P}\frac{\partial e_p}{\partial w_i} \tag{2.11}$$

$$\frac{\partial E}{\partial w_i} = \frac{1}{P}\sum_{p=1}^{P}\frac{\partial e_p}{\partial w_i}$$

$$e_p = \delta^2{}_p$$

$$\therefore \frac{\partial e_p}{\partial \delta_p} = 2\delta_p \tag{2.12}$$

$$\frac{\partial \delta_p}{\partial w_i} = \frac{\partial \delta_p}{\delta y_{inp}}\frac{\partial y_{inp}}{\delta w_i} \tag{2.13}$$

$$\delta_p = t_p - y_{inp} \tag{2.14}$$

Differentiating Equation 2.14 with respect to y_{inp},

$$\therefore \frac{\partial \delta_p}{\partial y_{inp}} = -1$$

$$y_{inp} = x_0 w_0 + x_1 w_1 + \ldots + x_i w_i + \ldots + x_n w_n \tag{2.15}$$

$$\therefore \frac{\partial E}{\partial w_i} = x_i \tag{2.16}$$

$$\therefore \frac{\partial E}{\partial w_i} = \frac{1}{P}\sum_{p=1}^{P} -2\delta_p x_i$$

$$\therefore \frac{\partial E}{\partial wi} = \frac{-2}{P}\sum_{p=1}^{P}\delta_p x_i$$

$$\therefore \Delta w_i = \frac{2\alpha}{P}\sum_{p=1}^{P}\delta_p x_i$$

Adjusting the weights by an amount proportional to the values of $x\delta$ minimizes the mean squared error. The training consists of finding the mean values of $x\delta$ for each of the inputs over the whole training set. Then the weights are adjusted by this amount of α.

Note:

1. The weights are set to small random values.
2. The bias weight, w_0 is adjusted in the same way as other weights and the corresponding input, x_0 is always set to 1.

3. The value of the learning constant may be set as $\alpha = 1/(n+1)$, where n is the number of inputs.
4. Ideally, the mean value of $x\delta$ should be taken from the whole training set after training. In practice, the weights are nearly always adjusted using the values of $x\delta$ at each training pattern.

2.4.2 Generalized Delta Rule

In the original form of delta rule, the activation function for the output units are identity functions. The generalized delta rule allows for an arbitrary differentiable activation function.

The squared error for a pattern is

$$E = (t_j - y_j)^2$$

where t_j is the target output and y_j is the actual output at the jth output neuron. The gradient of the error function consists of the partial derivative of E with respect to the weights. By adjusting the weight w_{ij} (connected between the ith input neuron and the jth output neuron) in the direction of $-\dfrac{\partial E}{\partial w_{ij}}$, the error can be reduced.

The error function can be written as: $\dfrac{\partial E}{\partial w_{ij}} = (t_j - y_j)^2$

where $y_i = f(y_i n_j)$

$$y_i = \sum_{i=1}^{n} x_i w_{ij}$$

$$\frac{\partial E}{\partial w_{ij}} = -2(t_j - y_j)\frac{\partial_f (y_{inj})}{\partial w_{ij}}$$

$$= -2(t_j - y_j) f'(y_{inj})\frac{\partial f(y_{inj})}{\partial w_{ij}}$$

$$= -2(t_j - y_j) x_1 f'(y_{inj})$$

The weight adjustment can be written as

$$\Delta w_{ij} = \alpha(t_j - y_j) f'(y_{inj}) x_i$$

where α (learning rate) is a positive constant.

2.5 ADALINE [B2]

The ADAptive LInear NEuron Model was developed by Widrow-Hoff [1960]. This network is trained by Delta rule. The activation function for this network is identity function. This network consists of a single neuron in the output layer, which receives signal from n input units. It also has a bias whose activation is always '1'. A single ADALINE is shown in Fig. 2.11.

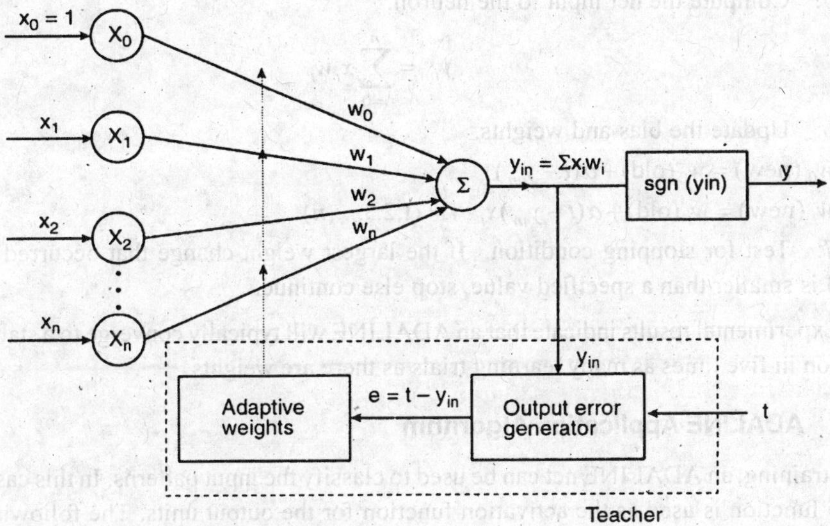

Figure 2.11 *Adaline Model with Teacher*

The input to the neuron, **X** is represented as:

$\mathbf{X} = [x_0 \ \ x_1 \ \ ... x_i .... x_n]$.

Note: $x_0 = \text{bias} = 1$

$\mathbf{W} = [w_0 \ \ w_1 \ \ w_2 ... w_i \ w_n]^T$ represents the weight vector.

$y_{in} = \mathbf{XW}$ = output of the neuron before the nonlinearity.

$y = \text{sgn}(y_{in}) = \text{sgn}\ (\mathbf{XW})$ = output from the neuron after the nonlinearity.

t = target signal.

$\delta = t - y_{in}$ = output error used during training.

Initially, the weights are assigned some random values between '–1' and '1'. The weighted sum of the inputs including a bias term is calculated and it is compared with the target output and based on the delta rule, the weights are adjusted. To teach a ADALINE model, the following learning algorithm is used.

2.5.1 ADALINE Learning Algorithm

Step 1: Assign random synaptic weight values in the range – 1 to +1.

Step 2: While stopping condition is false, do steps 3 to 7.

Step 3: For each bipolar training pair S:t, do steps 4 to 7.

Step 4: Set activations to the input units:

$x_0 = 1$, and

$x_i = s_i \ (i = 1,2,3, ...,n)$.

Step 5: Compute the net input to the neuron.

$$y_{in} = \sum_{i=0}^{n} x_i w_i$$

Step 6: Update the bias and weights.

$$w_0\,(\text{new}) = w_0\,(\text{old}) + \alpha(t - y_{in})$$

$$w_i\,(\text{new}) = w_i\,(\text{old}) + \alpha(t - y_{in})x_i \quad i = (1,2,3,\ldots,n)$$

Step 7: Test for stopping condition. If the largest weight change that occurred in step 3 is smaller than a specified value, stop else continue.

Experimental results indicate that an ADALINE will typically converge to a stable solution in five times as many learning trials as there are weights.

2.5.2 ADALINE Application Algorithm

After training, an ADALINE net can be used to classify the input patterns. In this case, a step function is used as the activation function for the output units. The following algorithm is used to classify the output pattern after training the ADALINE.

Step 1: Initialize weights.

Step 2: For each bipolar input vector x, do steps 3 to 5.

Step 3: Compute net input to output units.

$$y_{in} = \sum_{i=0}^{n} x_i w_i$$

Step 4: Apply the activation function.

$$y = \begin{cases} 1 & \text{if } y_{in} \geq 0 \\ -1 & \text{if } y_{in} < 0 \end{cases}$$

Example 2.6 Using ADALINE model, find the weights after the first epoch to perform the following classifications. Vectors (1 1 1 1) and (−1 −1 −1 −1) are members of the first class and the vectors (1 1 1 −1) and (1 −1 −1 1) are members of the second class. Assume a learning rate of 0.5 and initial weights of 0.

Solution The results of the first epoch are tabulated below.

x_1	x_2	x_3	x_4	t	y_{in}	$t-y_{in}$	Δw_1	Δw_2	Δw_3	Δw_4	w_1	w_2	w_3	w_4
1	1	1	1	1	0	1	0.5	0.5	0.5	0.5	0.5	0.5	0.5	0.5
−1	1	−1	−1	1	−1	2	−1	1	−1	−1	−0.5	1.5	−0.5	−0.5
1	1	1	−1	−1	1	2	−1	−1	−1	1	−1.5	0.5	−1.5	0.5
1	−1	−1	1	−1	0	−1	−0.5	0.5	0.5	−0.5	−2	1	−1	0

Note: Further training is required to reach the final correct weight values for minimizing the total squared error. Computer simulations approximate the final weights as [−1 1 0 1].

2.6 MADALINE SYSTEM NETWORK

The MADALINE system has a layer of ADALINE units that are connected to a layer of MADALINE units. A simple MADALINE architecture is shown in Figure 2.12. Figure 2.12 shows 'n' units in the input layer, 'm' units in the ADALINE layer and one unit in the MADALINE layer. Each unit in the ADALINE and MADALINE layer has a bias of excitation '1'.

All the weights that are connected from the ADALINE layer to the MADALINE are fixed, positive and have equal values.

The unit sample employs a majority vote rule on the outputs of the ADALINE layer. If more than half of the ADALINE output is '+1', then the output of the MADALINE is +1 else –1. The weights connected from the input layer to the ADALINE layer are adjusted during training process.

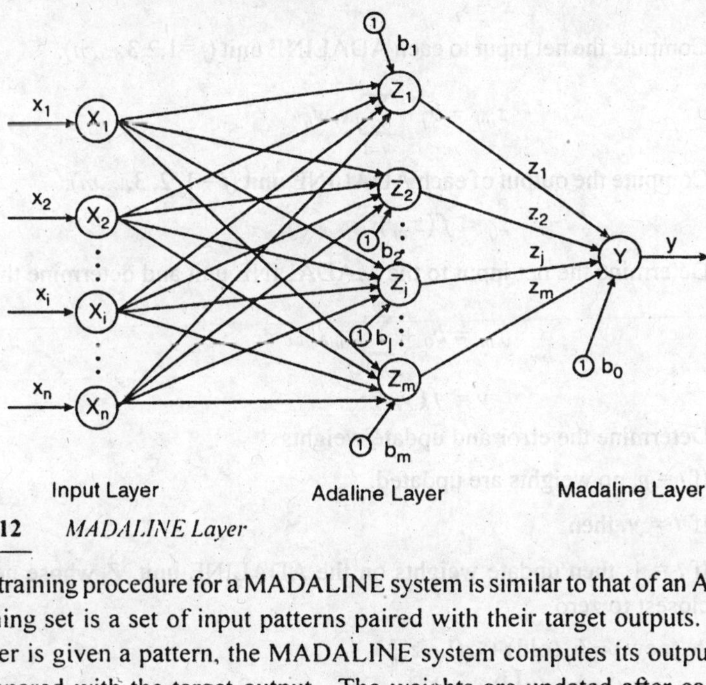

Figure 2.12 *MADALINE Layer*

The training procedure for a MADALINE system is similar to that of an ADALINE. The training set is a set of input patterns paired with their target outputs. After the input layer is given a pattern, the MADALINE system computes its output which is then compared with the target output. The weights are updated after each pattern presentation.

During the updating procedure, the MADALINE output is first compared to target output. Since each is +1 or –1, there is either a match or not a match. Learning takes place only when the MADALINE has given an incorrect answer. Thus, if there is a match, nothing is changed. If there is no match, then some of the weights are updated. Specifically, the ADALINE unit whose sum was closest to zero in the wrong direction is adopted, if the corresponding target value is 1. If there is a match and the target value is '–1', then all the weights connected to the ADALINE units that have positive net input are adopted.

2.6.1 Training Algorithm for MADALINE

Note: For simplicity only one unit is assumed in the MADALINE layer.

The activation functions for the ADALINE and MADALINE units are:

$$f(x) = \begin{cases} +1 & \text{if } x \geq 0 \\ -1 & \text{if } x < 0 \end{cases}$$

Step 1: The ADALINE weights are set to random values. Set all the MADALINE weight values equal to v and $v \geq 0$ and set the learning rate, α a small positive value greater than 0.

Step 2: While stopping condition is false, do steps 3 to 9.

Step 3: For each bipolar training pair $S{:}t$, do steps 4 to 8.

Step 4: Set the activations for the input units ($i = 1,2,3,\ldots,n$).

$$x_i = s_i$$

Step 5: Compute the net input to each ADALINE unit ($j = 1,2,3,\ldots,m$).

$$z_{inj} = b_j + \sum_{i=1}^{n} x_i w_{ij}$$

Step 6: Compute the output of each ADALINE unit ($j = 1, 2, 3,\ldots,m$).

$$z_j = f(z_{inj})$$

Step 7: Determine the net input to the MADALINE unit and determine the output.

$$y_{in} = b_0 + \sum_{j=1}^{m} z_{inj}$$

$$y = f(y_{in})$$

Step 8: Determine the error and update weights.

If $t = y$, no weights are updated.

If $t \neq y$, then

If $t = 1$, then update weights on the ADALINE unit, Z_j whose net input is closest to zero.

$$b_j(\text{new}) = b_j(\text{old}) + \alpha(1 - z_{inj})$$

$$w_{ij}(\text{new}) = w_{ij}(\text{old}) + \alpha(1 - z_{inj})x_i \qquad i = 1,2,3,\ldots,n.$$

If $(t \neq y)$ and $(t = -1)$, then update weights on all units Z_k, that have positive net input.

$$b_k(\text{new}) = b_k(\text{old}) + \alpha(1 - z_{ink})$$

$$w_{ik}(\text{new}) = w_{ik}(\text{old}) + \alpha(1 - z_{ink})x_i \qquad i = 1,2,3,\ldots,n.$$

Step 9: Test for stopping condition.

If there are no weight changes (or weight change has reached an acceptable level) or a specified maximum number of weight update iterations have been performed then stop, or else continue.

2.6.2 Applications of ADALINE / MADALINE

Widrow and his colleagues applied ADALINE/MADALINE and studied applications such as weather forecasting, speech recognition, vector cardiographic diagnosis and image classification. They have also built an adaptive filter using an ADALINE.

Figure 2.13 shows the basic idea for the configuration of an adaptive filter developed by Widrow.

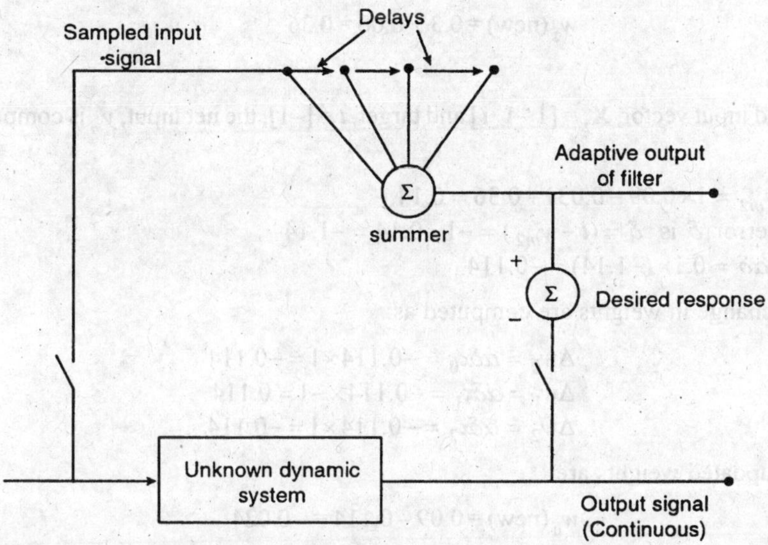

Figure 2.13 *Adaptive Filter to Model on Unknown Dynamics*

A signal enters at the top left and is sampled over an interval of time to provide inputs to the processing unit (summer). The unit performs a weighted sum, compares its output with a target signal and then weight adjustments are made. This system allows an adaptive filter to model an unknown dynamic system whose input and output are available.

Example 2.7 Apply ADALINE method to implement AND NOT logical function with the initial weights as [0.15 0.25 0.3]. Find the new weights after first pass of the entire sample. Assume a learning rate of 0.1. (Use bipolar input-output patterns.)

Solution

Case I:

For the first input vector, $\mathbf{X}_1 = [1\ -1\ -1]$ and target, $t = [-1]$, the net input, y_{in} is computed as:

$$y_{in1} = 1 \times 0.15 - 0.25 - 0.3 = -0.4$$

The error δ is : $\delta = (t - y_{in1}) = -1 + 0.4 = -0.6$

$$\alpha\delta = 0.1 \times (-0.6) = -0.06.$$

The change in weights are computed as:

$$\Delta w_0 = \alpha\delta x_0 = -0.06 \times 1 = -0.06$$
$$\Delta w_1 = \alpha\delta x_1 = -0.06 \times 1 = -0.06$$
$$\Delta w_2 = \alpha\delta x_2 = -0.06 \times 1 = -0.06$$

The updated weights are:

$$w_0\,(\text{new}) = 0.15 - 0.06 = 0.09$$
$$w_1\,(\text{new}) = 0.25 + 0.06 = 0.31$$
$$w_2\,(\text{new}) = 0.3 + 0.06 = 0.36$$

Case II:

For second input vector, $\mathbf{X}_2 = [1\ -1\ \ 1]$ and target, $t = [-1]$, the net input, y_{in} is computed as:

$$y_{in2} = 1 \times 0.09 - 0.031 + 0.36 = 0.14$$

The error, δ is : $\delta = (t - y_{in2}) = -1 - 0.14 = -1.14$

$$\alpha\delta = 0.1 \times (-1.14) = -0.114$$

The change in weights are computed as:

$$\Delta w_0 = \alpha\delta x_0 = -0.114 \times 1 = -0.114$$
$$\Delta w_1 = \alpha\delta x_1 = -0.114 \times -1 = 0.114$$
$$\Delta w_2 = \alpha\delta x_2 = -0.114 \times 1 = -0.114$$

The updated weights are:

$$w_0\,(\text{new}) = 0.09 - 0.114 = -0.024$$
$$w_1\,(\text{new}) = 0.31 + 0.114 = 0.424$$
$$w_2\,(\text{new}) = 0.36 - 0.114 = 0.246$$

Case III:

For the third input vector, $\mathbf{X}_3 = [1\ 1\ -1]$ and target, $t = [1]$, the net input, y_{in} is computed as:

$$y_{in3} = -0.024 \times 1 + 0.424 \times 1 - 0.246 = 0.154$$

The error, δ is : $\delta = t - y_{in3} = 1 - 0.154 = 0.846$

$$\alpha\delta = 0.1 \times 0.846 = 0.0846$$

The change in weights are computed as:

$$\Delta w_0 = \alpha\delta x_0 = 0.0846 \times -1 = -0.0846$$
$$\Delta w_1 = \alpha\delta x_1 = 0.0846 \times 1 = 0.0846$$
$$\Delta w_2 = \alpha\delta x_2 = 0.08466 \times (-1) = -0.0846$$

The updated weights are:

$$w_0\,(\text{new}) = 0.024 - 0.0846 = 0.0606$$
$$w_1\,(\text{new}) = 0.424 + 0.0846 = 0.5086$$
$$w_2\,(\text{new}) = 0.246 - 0.0846 = 0.1614$$

Case IV:

For fourth input vector, $X_4 = [1\ 1\ 1]$ and target, $t = [-1]$, the net input, y_{in} is computed as:

$$y_{in4} = 0.0606 + 0.5086 + 0.1614 = 0.7306$$

The error, δ is : $\delta = t - y_{in4} = -1 - 0.7360 = -1.7306$

$$\alpha\delta = 0.1 \times (-1.7306) = -1.7306$$

The change in weights are computed as:

$$\alpha\delta x_0 = \alpha\delta x_1 = \alpha\delta x_2 = -0.17306$$

The above steps are summarized in the Table shown below:

x_0	x_1	x_2	w_0	w_1	w_2	y_{in}	T	$L = (t-y_{in})$	KLx_0	KLx_1	KLx_2
1	-1	-1	0.15	0.25	0.3	-0.4	-1	-0.6	0.06	0.06	0.06
1	-1	1	0.09	0.31	0.36	0.14	-1	-1.14	-0.114	0.114	-0.114
1	1	-1	-0.24	0.424	0.246	0.154	1	0.846	0.0846	0.0846	-0.0846
1	1	1	0.0606	0.5086	0.1614	0.162	-1	-0.173	-0.173	-0.173	-0.173

The updated weights are:

$$w_0(\text{new}) = 0.0606 - 0.17306 = -0.11246$$

$$w_1(\text{new}) = 0.5086 - 0.17306 = 0.33554$$

$$w_2(\text{new}) = 0.1614 - 0.17306 = -0.01166$$

The new weight values are $[-0.11246\ \ 0.33554\ \ -0.01166]$.

2.7 PERCEPTRON LAYER NETWORK [B2]

Perceptron, the first adaptive network architecture was invented by Frank Rosenblatt in 1957. Rosenblatt's research was oriented towards modeling the brain in an attempt to understand memory, learning and cognitive processes. The Mark1 Perceptron model developed by Rosenblatt is shown in Fig. 2.14.

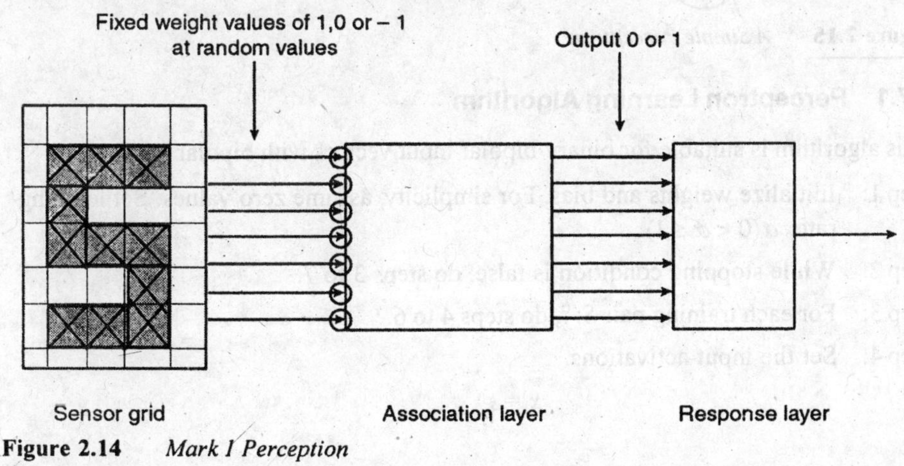

Figure 2.14 *Mark I Perception*

Block (1962) model employs binary activations for the sensory and associatory units and an activation of 1, 0 or –1 for the response units. The signal sent from associator units to the output unit is a binary signal (0 or 1).

The activation function for the response unit is:

$$y = f(y_{in})$$

$$f(y_{in}) = \begin{cases} 1 & \text{if } y_{in} > \theta \\ 0 & \text{if } -\theta \le y_{in} \le \theta \\ -1 & \text{if } y_{in} < \theta \end{cases}$$

The weights that are connected between the association layer and response layer are adjusted during training. After presenting each training input vector, the net calculates the net input to the perceptron and then the output response of the perceptron. The output signal is compared with the target value to determine whether an error has occurred. If an error has occurred, then only the weights on the connections from units that sent a non-zero signal to the output unit will be adjusted.

$$\text{i.e. } w_i(\text{new}) = w_i(\text{old}) + \alpha x_i t$$

where t is the target value 1 or –1 and α is the learning rate.

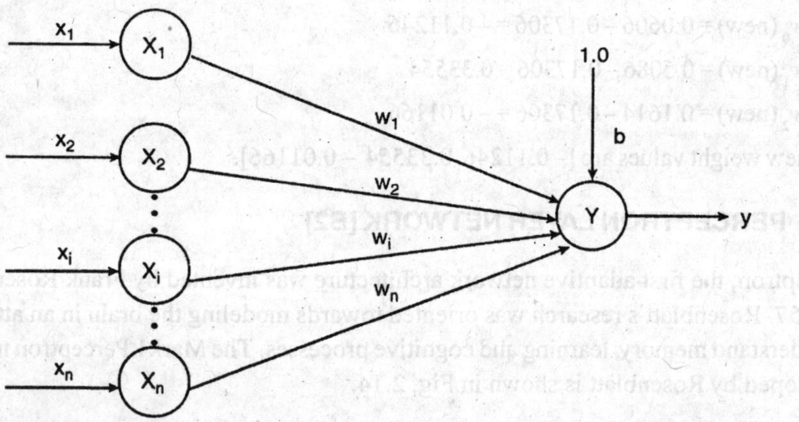

Figure 2.15 *A Simple Perceptron*

2.7.1 Perceptron Learning Algorithm

This algorithm is suitable for binary/bipolar input vectors with bipolar target.

Step 1: Initialize weights and bias. For simplicity, assume zero values. Set learning rate, $\alpha (0 < \alpha \le 1)$.

Step 2: While stopping condition is false, do steps 3 to 7.

Step 3: For each training pair S: t, do steps 4 to 6.

Step 4: Set the input activations.

$$x_i = s_i$$

Step 5: Compute net input to the perceptron and the output response of the perceptron.

$$y_{in} = b + \sum_{i=1}^{n} x_i w_i$$

$$y = \begin{cases} 1 & y_{in} > \theta \\ 0 & -\theta \le y_{in} \le \theta \\ -1 & y_{in} < \theta \end{cases}$$

Step 6: Update the bias and weights if the target is not equal to the output response.

if $t \neq y$
if $xi \neq 0$
$w_i(\text{new}) = w_i(\text{old}) + \alpha x_i t \quad i = 1,2,3,\ldots,n$
else no change in weights.
$b(\text{new}) = b(\text{old}) + \alpha t$

Step 7: Test for stopping condition. If no weight change in step 3 stop else continue.

Note:

1. Weights connecting active input units are updated. i.e. $x_i \neq 0$.
2. Weights are updated for patterns that do not produce the correct output value.

2.7.2 Perceptron Application Algorithm

Step 1: Apply Perceptron Training Algorithm to train the weights.

Step 2: For each input vector *x* to be classified, do steps 3 to 4.

Step 3: Set activations of input units.

Step 4: Compute net input and output of perceptron.

$$y_{in} = b + \sum_{i=1}^{n} x_i w_i$$

$$y = \begin{cases} 1 & y_{in} > \theta \\ 0 & -\theta \le y_{in} \le \theta \\ -1 & y_{in} < -\theta \end{cases}$$

2.7.3 Perceptron Training Algorithm with Several Output Classes

Step 1: Initialize weights and bias.

Step 2: While stopping condition is false, do steps 3 to 7.

Step 3: For each bipolar pair *S*: *t*, do steps 4 to 6.

Step 4: Set the activations of input units.

$$x_i = s_i \qquad i = 1,2,3,\ldots,n$$

Step 5: Compute the output of each unit. $j = 1,2,3,\ldots m$

$$y_{inj} = b + \sum_{i=1}^{n} x_i w_{ij}$$

$$y_j = \begin{cases} 1 & y_{inj} > \theta \\ 0 & -\theta \le y_{inj} \le \theta \\ -1 & y_{inj} < -\theta \end{cases}$$

Step 6: Update bias and weights ($j = 1,2,3,...,m$, $i = 1,2,3,...,n$).

If $t_j \neq y_j$

then $b_j(\text{new}) = b_j(\text{old}) + \alpha t_j$

$w_{ij}(\text{new}) = w_{ij}(\text{old}) + \alpha x_i t_j$

else bias and weight values remain unchanged.

Step 7: Test for stopping condition. If no weight changes in step 3, stop else continue.

Note:

1. Weights connecting active input units are updated. i.e. $x_i \neq 0$.
2. Weights are updated for patterns that do not produce the correct output value.

Example 2.8 Develop a Perceptron network to implement an AND function.

Solution For the first input sample, $x_0 = 1$; $x_1 = 1$; $x_2 = 1$; $t = 1$, the net input to the output neuron, y_{in} is:

$$y_{in} = w_0 + \sum_{i=1}^{n} x_i w_i$$

$$y_{in} = 0 + (1 \times 0) + (1 \times 0)$$

$$y_{in} = 0$$

Applying the activation function,

$$y = \begin{cases} 1 & y_{inj} > 0 \\ 0 & -0 \le y_{in} \le 0 \\ -1 & y_{inj} < -0 \end{cases}$$

the output of the perceptron, $y = 0$.

Since $y \neq t$, the new weights are calculated as:

$$w_0(\text{new}) = w_0(\text{old}) + \alpha.t$$

$$= 0 + (1 \times 1) = 1$$

$$w_i(\text{new}) = w_i(\text{old}) + \alpha\, x_1\, t$$

$$w_1(\text{new}) = w_1(\text{old}) + \alpha\, x_1\, t$$

$$= 0 + (1 \times 1 \times 1) = 1$$

$$w_2(\text{new}) = w_2(\text{old}) + \alpha\, x_2\, t$$

$$= 0 + (1 \times 1 \times 1) = 1$$

The weight matrix after presenting the first sample, **W** = [1 1 1].

For the second input sample, $x_0 = 1; x_1 = -1; x_2 = 1; t = -1$, the net input to the output neuron, y_{in} is:

$$y_{in} = w_0 + \sum_{i=1}^{n} x_i\, w_i$$

$$y_{in} = 1 + (-1 \times 1) + (1 \times 1)$$

$$y_{in} = 1$$

The output of the perceptron is $y = 1$.

Since $y \neq t$, the new weights are calculated as:

$$w_0(\text{new}) = w_0(\text{old}) + \alpha t$$
$$= 1 + (1 \times -1) = 0$$
$$w_i(\text{new}) = w_i(\text{old}) + \alpha\, x_i\, t$$
$$w_1(\text{new}) = w_1(\text{old}) + \alpha\, x_1\, t$$
$$= 1 + (1 \times -1 \times -1) = 2$$
$$w_2(\text{new}) = w_2(\text{old}) + \alpha\, x_2\, t$$
$$= 1 + (1 \times 1 \times -1) = 0$$

The weight matrix after presenting the second sample, **W** = [0 2 0].

For third input sample, $x_0 = 1; x_1 = 1; x_2 = -1; t = -1$, the net input to the output neuron, y_{in} is:

$$y_{in} = w_0 + \sum_{i=1}^{n} x_i\, w_i$$

$$y_{in} = 0 + (1 \times 2) + (-1 \times 0)$$

$$y_{in} = 2$$

The output of the perceptron is $y = 1$.

Since $y \neq t$, the new weights are calculated as:

$$w_0(\text{new}) = w_0(\text{old}) + \alpha t$$
$$= 0 + (1 \times -1) = -1$$
$$w_i(\text{new}) = w_i(\text{old}) + \alpha\, x_i\, t$$
$$w_1(\text{new}) = w_1(\text{old}) + \alpha\, x_1\, t$$
$$= 2 + (1 \times 1 \times -1) = 1$$
$$w_2(\text{new}) = w_2(\text{old}) + \alpha\, x_2\, t$$
$$= 0 + (1 \times -1 \times -1) = 1$$

The weight matrix after presenting the third sample, **W** = [–1 1 1].

For fourth input sample, $x_0 = 1; x_1 = -1; x_2 = -1; t = -1$, the net input to output neuron, y_{in} is:

$$y_{in} = w_0 + \sum_{i=1}^{n} x_i \, w_i$$

$$y_{in} = -1 + (-1 \times 1) + (-1 \times 1)$$

$$y_{in} = -3$$

The output of the perceptron is $y = -1$.

Since $y = t$, no change in weight occurs.

The weight matrix after presenting the fourth sample, **W** = [–1 1 1].

Example 2.9 Develop a Perceptron network to implement an OR function.

Solution Let the initial weights be zero.

For the first input sample, $x_0 = 1; x_1 = 1; x_2 = 1; t = 1$, the net input to the output neuron, y_{in} is:

$$y_{in} = w_0 + \sum_{i=1}^{n} x_i \, w_i$$

$$y_{in} = 0 + (1 \times 0) + (1 \times 0)$$

$$y_{in} = 0$$

Applying the activation function,

$$y = \begin{cases} 1 & y_{inj} > 0 \\ 0 & -0 \le y_{in} \le 0 \\ -1 & y_{inj} < -0 \end{cases}$$

the output of the perceptron, y = 0.

Since $y \neq t$, the new weights are calculated as:

$$w_0(\text{new}) = w_0(\text{old}) + \alpha t$$
$$= 0 + (1 \times 1) = 1$$
$$w_i(\text{new}) = w_i(\text{old}) + \alpha x_i t$$
$$w_1(\text{new}) = w_1(\text{old}) + \alpha x_1 t$$
$$= 0 + (1 \times 1 \times 1) = 1$$
$$w_2(\text{new}) = w_2(\text{old}) + \alpha x_2 t$$
$$= 0 + (1 \times 1 \times 1) = 1$$

The weight matrix after presenting the first sample, W = [1 1 1].

For second input sample, $x_0 = 1; x_1 = -1; x_2 = 1; t = 1$, the net input to the output neuron, y_{in} is:

$$y_{in} = w_0 + \sum_{i=1}^{n} x_i w_i$$

$$y_{in} = 0 + (-1 \times 1) + (1 \times 1)$$

$$y_{in} = 1$$

The output of the perceptron is $y = 1$.

Since $y = t$, no change in weight occurs.

For third input sample, $x_0 = 1; x_1 = 1; x_2 = -1; t = 1$, the net input to the output neuron, y_{in} is:

$$y_{in} = w_0 + \sum_{i=1}^{n} x_i w_i$$
$$y_{in} = 1 + (1 \times 1) + (-1 \times 1)$$
$$y_{in} = 1$$

The output of the perceptron is $y = 1$.

Since $y = t$, no change in weight occurs.

For fourth input sample, $x_0 = 1; x_1 = -1; x_2 = -1; t = -1$, the net input to the output neuron, y_{in} is:

$$y_{in} = w_0 + \sum_{i=1}^{n} x_i w_i$$
$$y_{in} = 1 + (-1 \times 1) + (-1 \times 1)$$
$$y_{in} = -1$$

The output of the perceptron is $y = -1$.

Since $y = t$, no change in weight occurs.

The weight matrix after presenting the fourth sample, **W** = [1 1 1].

Example 2.10 Develop a Perceptron network to implement an AND NOT function.

Solution Let the initial weights be zero.

For first input sample, $x_0 = 1; x_1 = 1; x_2 = 1; t = -1$, the net input to output neuron, y_{in} is:

$$y_{in} = w_0 + \sum_{i=1}^{n} x_i w_i$$
$$y_{in} = 0 + (1 \times 0) + (1 \times 0)$$
$$y_{in} = 0$$

Applying the activation function,

$$y = \begin{cases} 1 & y_{inj} > 0 \\ 0 & -0 \le y_{in} \le 0 \\ -1 & y_{inj} < -0 \end{cases}$$

the output of the perceptron, $y = 0$.

Since $y \neq t$, the new weights are calculated as:

$$w_0(\text{new}) = w_0(\text{old}) + \alpha t$$
$$= 0 + (1 \times 1) = 1$$

$$w_i(\text{new}) = w_i(\text{old}) + \alpha\, x_i\, t$$
$$w_1(\text{new}) = w_1(\text{old}) + \alpha\, x_1\, t$$
$$= 0 + (1 \times 1 - 1) = -1$$
$$w_2(\text{new}) = w_2(\text{old}) + \alpha\, x_2\, t$$
$$= 0 + (1 \times 1 \times -1) = -1$$

The weight matrix after presenting the first sample, $\mathbf{W} = [1\ -1\ -1]$.

For second input sample, $x_0 = 1; x_1 = -1; x_2 = 1; t = -1$, the net input to the output neuron, y_{in} is:

$$y_{in} = w_0 + \sum_{i=1}^{n} x_i\, w_i$$
$$y_{in} = 1 + 1 - 1 = 1$$
$$y = 1$$

The output of the perceptron is $y = 1$.

Since $y \neq t$, the new weights are calculated as:

$$w_0(\text{new}) = w_0(\text{old}) + \alpha\, t$$
$$= 1 + (1 \times -1) = 0$$
$$w_i(\text{new}) = w_i(\text{old}) + \alpha\, x_i\, t$$
$$w_1(\text{new}) = w_1(\text{old}) + \alpha\, x_1\, t$$
$$= -1 + (1 \times -1 \times -1) = 0$$
$$w_2(\text{new}) = w_2(\text{old}) + \alpha\, x_2\, t$$
$$= -1 + (1 \times 1 \times -1) = -2$$

The weight matrix after presenting the second sample, $\mathbf{W} = [0\ 0\ -2]$.

For third input sample, $x_0 = 1; x_1 = 1; x_2 = -1; t = 1$, the net input to the output neuron, y_{in} is:

$$y_{in} = w_0 + \sum_{i=1}^{n} x_i\, w_i$$
$$y_{in} = 0 + (1 \times 0 + -1 \times -2)$$
$$y_{in} = -2$$

The output of the perceptron is $y = +1$.

Since $y = t$, no change in weight occurs.

For fourth input sample, $x_0 = 1; x_1 = -1; x_2 = -1; t = -1$, the net input to the output neuron, y_{in} is:

$$y_{in} = w_0 + \sum_{i=1}^{n} x_i w_i$$
$$y_{in} = 0 + (-1 \times 0) + (-1 \times -2)$$
$$y_{in} = 2$$

The output of the perceptron is $y = 1$.

Since $y \neq t$, the new weights are calculated as:

$$w_0(\text{new}) = w_0(\text{old}) + \alpha t$$
$$= 0 + (1 \times -1) = -1$$
$$w_i(\text{new}) = w_i(\text{old}) + \alpha x_i t$$
$$w_1(\text{new}) = w_1(\text{old}) + \alpha x_1 t$$
$$= 0 + (1 \times -1 \times -1) = 1$$
$$w_2(\text{new}) = w_2(\text{old}) + \alpha x_2 t$$
$$= -2 + (1 \times -1 \times -1) = -1$$

The weight matrix after presenting the fourth sample, $\mathbf{W} = [-1\ 1\ -1]$.

Example 2.11 Implement the T-C Problem using a Perceptron.

Solution Let the initial weights be zero.

$\mathbf{X}_1 = [\ 1\ 1\ 1\ -1\ 1\ -1\ -1\ 1\ -1\ 1];\ t = 1$

$\mathbf{X}_2 = [1\ 1\ 1\ \ 1\ -1\ -1\ \ 1\ 1\ 1\ \ 1];\ t = -1$

For first input sample, the net input to the output neuron, y_{in} is:

$$y_{in} = w_0 + \sum_{i=1}^{n} x_i w_i$$
$$y_{in} = 0 + (1 \times 0) + (1 \times 0) + (1 \times 0) + (-1 \times 0) + (1 \times 0) + (-1 \times 0)$$
$$+ (-1 \times 0) + (1 \times 0) + (-1 \times 0)$$
$$y_{in} = 0$$

Applying the activation function,

$$y = \begin{cases} 1 & y_{inj} > 0 \\ 0 & -0 \le y_{in} \le 0 \\ -1 & y_{inj} < -0 \end{cases}$$

the output of the perceptron, $y = 0$.

Since $y \neq t$, the new weights are calculated as:

$$w_0(\text{new}) = w_0(\text{old}) + \alpha t$$
$$= 0 + (1 \times 1) = 1$$
$$w_i(\text{new}) = w_i(\text{old}) + \alpha x_i t$$
$$w_1(\text{new}) = w_i(\text{old}) + \alpha x_1 t$$
$$= 0 + (1 \times 1 \times 1) = 1$$
$$w_2(\text{new}) = w_2(\text{old}) + \alpha x_2 t$$
$$= 0 + (1 \times 1 \times 1) = 1$$
$$w_3(\text{new}) = w_3(\text{old}) + \alpha x_3 t$$
$$= 0 + (1 \times 1 \times 1) = 1$$

$$w_4(\text{new}) = w_4(\text{old}) + \alpha x_4 t$$
$$= 0 + (1 \times -1 \times 1) = -1$$
$$w_5(\text{new}) = w_5(\text{old}) + \alpha x_5 t$$
$$= 0 + (1 \times 1 \times 1) = 1$$
$$w_6(\text{new}) = w_6(\text{old}) + \alpha x_6 t$$
$$= 0 + (1 \times -1 \times 1) = -1$$
$$w_7(\text{new}) = w_7(\text{old}) + \alpha x_7 t$$
$$= 0 + (1 \times -1 \times 1) = -1$$

For second input sample, the net input to output neuron, y_{in} is:

$$y_{in} = w_0 + \sum_{i=1}^{n} x_i w_i$$
$$y_{in} = 1 + (1 \times 1) + (1 \times 1) + (1 \times 1) + (-1 \times 1) + (1 \times -1)$$
$$+ (-1 \times -1) + (-1 \times 1) + (1 \times 1) + (-1 \times 1)$$
$$y_{in} = 2$$

The output of the perceptron is $y = 1$.

Since $y \neq t$, the new weights are calculated as:

$$w_0(\text{new}) = w_0(\text{old}) + \alpha t$$
$$= 1 + (1 \times -1) = 0$$
$$w_i(\text{new}) = w_i(\text{old}) + \alpha x_i t$$
$$w_1(\text{new}) = w_1(\text{old}) + \alpha x_1 t$$
$$= 1 + (1 \times 1 \times -1) = 0$$
$$w_2(\text{new}) = w_2(\text{old}) + \alpha x_2 t$$
$$= 1 + (1 \times 1 \times -1) = 0$$
$$w_3(\text{new}) = w_3(\text{old}) + \alpha x_3 t$$
$$= 1 + (1 \times 1 \times -1) = 0$$
$$w_4(\text{new}) = w_4(\text{old}) + \alpha x_4 t$$
$$= -1 + (1 \times 1 \times -1) = -2$$
$$w_5(\text{new}) = w_5(\text{old}) + \alpha x_5 t$$
$$= 1 + (1 \times -1 \times -1) = 2$$
$$w_6(\text{new}) = w_6(\text{old}) + \alpha x_6 t$$
$$-1 + (1 \times -1 \times -1) = 0$$
$$w_7(\text{new}) = w_7(\text{old}) + \alpha x_7 t$$
$$= -1 + (1 \times 1 \times -1) = -2$$
$$w_8(\text{new}) = w_8(\text{old}) + \alpha x_8 t$$
$$= 1 + (1 \times 1 \times -1) = 0$$
$$w_9(\text{new}) = w_9(\text{old}) + \alpha x_9 t$$
$$= -1 + (1 \times 1 \times -1) = -2$$

2.8 SUMMARY

In Artificial Neural Network, a neuron learns by itself or by a teacher and it can be called as an adaptive element. The learning rule is an important criteria to be incorporated in Artificial Neural Networks. At first, Amari proposed a learning rule for a single layer network. This rule leads to Donald's Hebb rule. Based on Hebbian Learning Rule, McClelland and Rumelhart (1988) developed a net called Hebb net. This Hebb net suffers with the binary input pattern and it is better in case of bipolar input, which is considered to be an extreme limitation of this net.

Further Widrow-Hoff developed a rule based on the error signal (Delta Rule) which is applicable for the supervised training of Artificial Neural Networks. The Delta Rule deals with the Least Mean Squared error and the weight change is done directly with the error signal $(t_j - y_j)$ and input values.

In 1960, Widrow-Hoff developed a network called ADALINE (ADAptive LInear NEuron) which is trained by the Delta Rule. The activation function for the ADALINE is an identity function. The network has single output neuron and leads to the development of Multilayer Feedforward Networks.

The MADALINE is a multilayer network system having a layer of ADALINE units that are connected to a layer of MADALINE units. Both ADALINE and MADALINE have the application of adaptive echo cancellation in most of the communication systems.

Frank Rosenblatt (1957) invented an adaptive architecture for a net called Perceptron. Perceptron layered network generally have a supervised training algorithm, which changes its weights when there is no match of target value and the output value from the network. This network does not have the ability to handle the linearly separable problems. The learning rules discussed in this chapter are the fundamental rules in Artificial Neural Network and these rules will be used extensively in the forth- coming chapters for the design of Modern Networks.

SHORT QUESTIONS AND ANSWERS

1. Draw the basic model of a neuron.

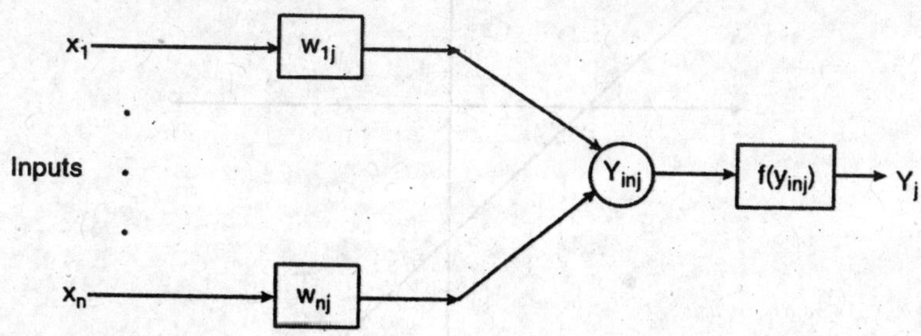

Figure 2.16 *Basic Model of a Neuron*

2. **What is meant by stability and plasticity in Artificial Neural Networks?**

   The learning system to remain plastic or adaptable enough to learn new inputs whenever they might appear and yet remain stable enough to preserve the pre-stored information is called stability and plasticity in Artificial Neural Networks.

3. **Name three different layers of a neural network.**

   The three different layers of a neural network are the Input, Hidden and Output layers.

4. **Give the sigmoid functions used in Artificial Neural Networks and their significance.**

   The sigmoid functions used in Artificial Neural Networks are

   Binary sigmoid function, $f(x) = \dfrac{1}{1+e^{-x}}$

   Bipolar sigmoid function, $f(x) = \dfrac{2}{1+e^{-x}} - 1$

   Significance:

   1. It is monotonic.
   2. It is bounded.
   3. It has simple derivatives.

5. **Draw a decision boundary line for OR function using bipolar inputs and targets.**

Input (x_1, x_2)	Output (t)
1, 1	1
1, −1	1
−1, 1	1
−1, −1	−1

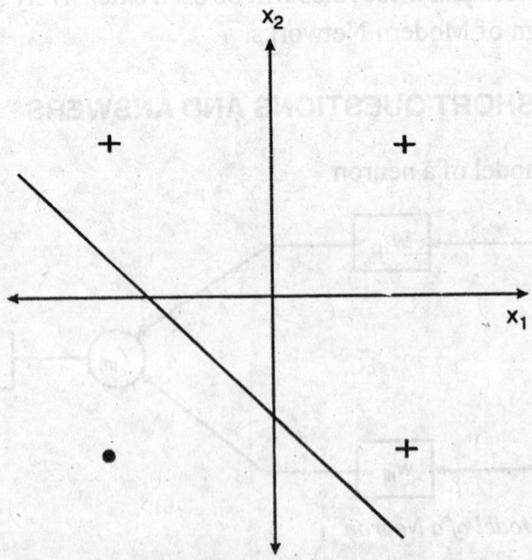

Figure 2.17 *Decision Boundary for OR Function*

6. What is the fundamental model of a neuron in Artificial Neural Networks?

McCulloch Pitt's model is the fundamental model of a neuron in Artificial Neural Networks.

7. Define Hebb rule.

Hebb stated that "when an axon of cell A is near enough to excite a cell B and repeatedly or persistently takes place in firing it, some growth process or metabolic change takes place in one or both cells such that A's efficiency, as one of the cells firing B, is increased".

8. What is the limitation of Hebb net?

The Hebb net does not learn if the input and output patterns are in the binary form. This is the limitation of Hebb net.

9. What is a perceptron layer?

The weights on the output layer which are trainable in the perceptron architecture is called perceptron layer.

10. What are the limitations of perceptron?

The main limitations of perceptron are:

1. It failed to be linearly separable and it could not differentiate between two linearly separable sets of pattern.
2. Different sets of input patterns have to be trained.

11. Does the perceptron require supervised learning? If not, what does it require ?

Perceptron requires the supervised learning.

12. What are the applications of perceptron network?

The applications of perceptron network include:

1. Pattern Classification.
2. Pattern Recognition.
3. Image Processing.

13. Define delta rule.

Delta rule states that, "The change in weights is directly proportional to the error signal, $(t_j - y_j)$ and input signal."

14. Define the error function for delta rule.

The error function for the delta rule is given by:

$$\text{Error function, } E = \frac{1}{P}\sum_{p=1}^{P}\left(t_p - \sum_{i=0}^{n} x_i\, w_i\right)^2$$

where p is the number of patterns in the training set.

15. What is the drawback using delta rule or optimization algorithm?

The drawback of using delta rule or optimization algorithm is that they may find local minima during the process of weight updating.

16. What is ADALINE?

ADAptive LInear NEuron model is trained by delta rule with an identity function as activation function. This network has single unit in output layer which receives signal from '*n*' input units and also has a bias term whose activation is always '1'.

17. Draw the ADALINE model with teacher.

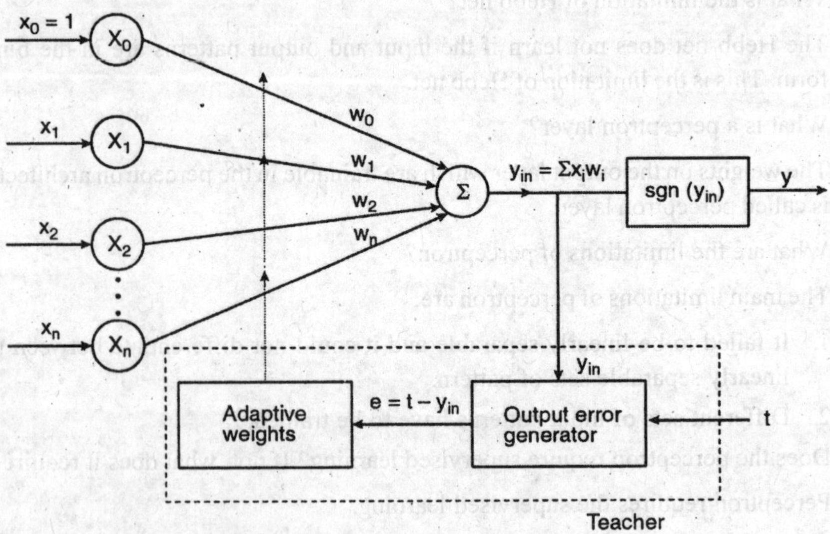

Figure 2.18 *Adaline Model with Teacher*

18. What is MADALINE?

The MADALINE model uses many ADALINEs in parallel with a single output unit that has a value based on some priority or selecting rules.

19. What are the characteristics of weights that are connected between ADALINE and MADALINE layers?

The weights that are connected between ADALINE and MADALINE layers must be fixed, positive and have equal values.

20. What is the net input to MADALINE unit, when the output of the MADALINE unit is '+1' in majority vote rule?

The net input to MADALINE unit is greater than or equal to 2p+b0 to get the output '+1' in majority vote rule.

21. How is the MADALINE trained in majority vote rule?

The weights from ADALINE to MADALINE units are fixed. The input patterns are given and compared with the target value. If the target is not getting matched, the weights must be updated. If the target is '+1' and not matched, then the weights which are nearer are adjusted to zero. If the target is '−1' and **not** matched, then the weights which have positive values are adjusted.

22. List out some of the applications of ADALINE and MADALINE.

The applications of ADALINE and MADALINE are:

1. Call Processing System in Communication Systems.
2. Adaptive Echo Cancellation Systems in Signal Processing.
3. Truck-Backer-Upper Control, etc.

REVIEW QUESTIONS

1. Explain briefly Amari's General learning rule.
2. Draw the architecture of a simple net.
3. Define decision boundary.
4. Differentiate between linearly separable and non-linearly separable problems.
5. What is gradient descent method?
6. Give a few applications of ADALINE/MADALINE.
7. Draw the architecture of a simple perceptron.
8. Explain briefly perceptron learning algorithm.
9. Explain briefly perceptron application algorithm.
10. Define perceptron learning rule.
11. Why is Delta rule called the least mean square rule?
12. Briefly explain perceptron learning rule convergence theorem.
13. Draw the architecture of ADALINE/MADALINE.
14. Explain the process of overcoming linear separability limitation.
15. Explain the structure of McCulloch and Pitts model of a neuron.

CHAPTER

3

Associative Memory

3.1 INTRODUCTION

In 1982, John Hopfield published a very influential paper which drew the attention to the associative properties of a class of neural nets. The analysis is based on a definition of 'energy' in the net and a proof that the net operates by minimizing this energy when settling into suitable patterns of operation.

It is based on the properties of interconnected cells of simple linear devices such that the system has stable states. Its states can be created by changing the strength of the interconnection between cells.

Associative memories belong to a class of neural networks that learns according to the input/output patterns. Neural network usually acquire prior information, and their connectivity matrices most often need to be formed in advance. Associative memory usually enables a parallel search within a stored data file. The purpose of the search is to output one or all stored data items that match the given search argument and to retrieve it entirely or partially. It is also believed that biological memory operates according to associative memory principles. No memory locations have addresses; storage is distributed over a large, densely interconnected assembly of neurons.

Retrieving information is content addressability, which for a computer system can be sequential or indexed. Sequential is similar to looking for name in jumbled up telephone directory; every entry would have to be scanned until correct one was found. Indexed is a similar process except that the telephone book would be in correct order.

The Artificial Neural Networks plays the role of an associative memory in which data is collectively stored in the form of a weight matrix or memory, and the process of developing the weight matrix is referred to as learning or storing the desired patterns, while retrieval or recall refers to the generation of output pattern when an input is presented to the network.

3.2 AUTOASSOCIATIVE MEMORY

An autoassociative memory requires suppression of the output noise at memory output. This can be done by thresholding the output and by recycling the output followed by a feedforward pass through a neural network. Such a network has a feedback, nonlinear mapping in the form of thresholding and dynamical.

3.2.1 Ideal Characteristics of Autoassociative Memory

The ideal characteristics of a autoassociative memory are given below:

1. Many associated pattern pairs should be stored.
2. This storage should be accomplished through a self-organizing process.
3. The information should be stored in a distributed manner.
4. The appropriate output response should be generated on receipt of the associated input pattern.
5. The correct output response should be generated even if the input pattern is distorted or incomplete.
6. It should be able to add new associations to the existing memory.

3.2.2 Autoassociative Net

For an autoassociative net, the training input and target output vectors should be identical. The process of training is often called storing the vectors, which may be binary or bipolar. A stored vector can be retrieved from distorted partial (noisy) input, if the input is sufficiently similar to it. The performance of the net is judged by its ability to reproduce a stored pattern from noisy input; performance is in general better for bipolar vectors than binary vectors.

3.2.3 Architecture

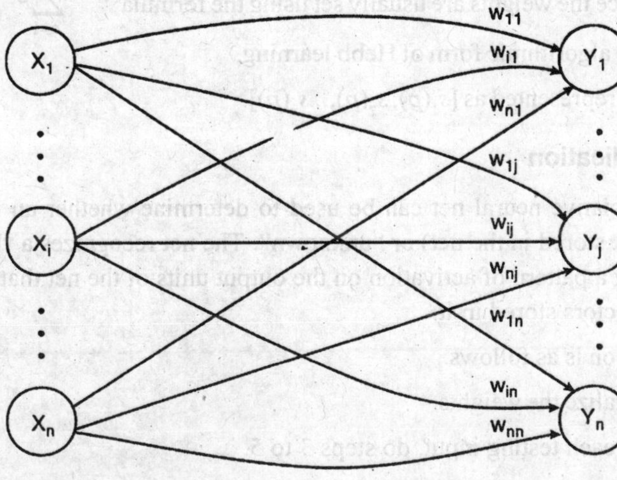

Figure 3.1 *Autoassociative Network*

3.2.4 Nomenclature

$s(p)$: Sample vector $(s_1(p), s_2(p), \ldots s_n(p))$

X : Input vector $(x_1(p), x_2(p), \ldots x_n(p))$

Y : Output vector $(y_1(p), y_2(p), \ldots y_n(p))$

w_{ij} : weights between ith input unit and jth output unit

3.2.5 Algorithm

For mutually orthogonal vectors, the Hebb rule can be used for setting weights in an autoassociative net because the input and output vectors are perfectly correlated component by component (i.e. they are the same). There are same numbers of output units as input units.

Step 1: Initialise all the weights $i, j = 1, 2, \ldots, n$.

$w_{ij} = 0$

Step 2: For each vector to be stored, do steps 3 to 5.

Step 3: Set activation for each input unit, $i = 1, 2, \ldots, n$.

$x_i = s_i$

Step 4: Set activation for each output unit, $j = 1, 2, \ldots, n$.

$y_j = s_j$

Step 5: Adjust the weights, $i = 1, 2, \ldots, n$ and $j = 1, 2, \ldots, n$.

$w_{ij}\text{(new)} = w_{ij}\text{(old)} + x_i y_j$

In practice the weights are usually set using the formula $w = \sum_{p=1}^{P} s^T(p)s(p)$ rather than from the algorithmic form of Hebb learning,

where $s(p)$ is represented as $[s_1(p), s_2(p), ...s_n(p)]$.

3.2.6 Application

An autoassociative neural net can be used to determine whether an input vector is "known" (i.e. stored in the net) or "unknown". The net recognizes a "known" vector by producing a pattern of activation on the output units of the net that is the same as one of the vectors stored in it.

The application is as follows:

Step 1: Initialize the weights.

Step 2: For each testing input, do steps 3 to 5.

Step 3: Set the activations of the input units equal to the input vector.

Step 4: Compute the net input to each output unit, $j = 1, 2, ..., n$.

$$y_{inj} = \sum_i x_i w_{ij}$$

Step 5: Apply activation function, $j = 1,2, ... ,n$.

$$y_j = f(y_{inj}) = \begin{cases} 1 & \text{if } y_{inj} > 0 \\ -1 & \text{if } y_{inj} \le 0 \end{cases}$$

3.2.7 Advantages

The autoassociative net has the power of recurrent neural processing within a parallel architecture. The recurrences through the thresholding layer of processing neurons tend to eliminate gradually noise superimposed on the initialising input vector. This coerces the incorrect pattern bits toward one of the stored memories. The network's computational ability makes it possible to apply it in speech processing, database retrieval, image processing, pattern classification and other fields.

3.2.8 Limitations

The associative memories whether designed by Hebbian learning rule or by a modified rule suffer from substantial capacity limitations. Capacity limitations cause diversified symptoms. It can amount to convergence of spurious memories and difficulties with recovery of stored patterns if they are close to each other in Hamming distance sense. Overload memory may not be able to recover data stored or may recall spurious outputs. Another inherent problem is that the memory convergences to stored pattern complements.

Example 3.1 Use an autoassociative network to store a vector $s(p) = [1\ -1\ \ 1\ \ 1]$. Examine whether the associative net accurately retrieves the input vector $[1\ -1\ -1\ \ 1]$.

Solution The weight matrix $\boldsymbol{W}$ is obtained as:

$\boldsymbol{W} = \boldsymbol{s}^T(p)\,\boldsymbol{s}(p)$

$$\boldsymbol{W} = \boldsymbol{s}^T(p)\boldsymbol{s}(p)$$

$$= \begin{bmatrix} 1 \\ -1 \\ 1 \\ 1 \end{bmatrix} [1\ -1\ 1\ 1]$$

$$\boldsymbol{W} = \begin{bmatrix} 1 & -1 & 1 & 1 \\ -1 & 1 & -1 & -1 \\ 1 & -1 & 1 & 1 \\ 1 & -1 & 1 & 1 \end{bmatrix}$$

For testing the input pattern

$$\boldsymbol{X} = [1 -1 -1\ 1]$$

$$Y_{in} = \boldsymbol{X}\boldsymbol{W}$$

$$Y_{in} = [1 -1 -1\ 1] \begin{bmatrix} 1 & -1 & 1 & 1 \\ -1 & 1 & -1 & -1 \\ 1 & -1 & 1 & 1 \\ 1 & -1 & 1 & 1 \end{bmatrix}$$

$$Y_{in} = [2 -2\ 2\ 2]$$

$$Y = f(Y_{in}) = [1 -1\ 1\ 1].$$

Since the response vector Y is same as the stored vector, we can say that the input vector is recognized as a known vector.

3.3 ITERATIVE AUTOASSOCIATIVE NET

In some cases, the net does not respond immediately to an input signal with a stored target pattern, but the response may be enough like a stored pattern at least in the sense of having more nodes committed to the values of +1 or –1 and fewer nodes with the unsure response of 0 to suggest using this first response as input to the net again.

3.3.1 Discrete Hopfield Net

An iterative autoassociative net has been developed by Hopfield [1982]. The net is fully interconnected in the sense that each unit is connected to every other unit. The net has symmetric weights with no self-connections, i.e. $w_{ij} = w_{ji}$ and $w_{ii} = 0$.

The small difference between this network and the autoassociative net with the threshold function is that it can have significant effect in terms of whether or not the nets converge for a particular input pattern. The limitations that are in the Hopfield net are presented here.

- only one unit updates its activation at a time (based on the signal it receives from each other unit) and
- each unit continues to receive an external signal in addition to the signal from other units in the net.

The asynchronous updating of the unit allows a function, known as energy or Lyapunov function, to be found on the net. The existence of such a function enables us to provide a net that will converge to a stable set of activations rather than oscillating. The original formulation of discrete Hopfield net showed the usefulness of the net as content addressable memory. Later, extensions for continuous-valued activations can be used either for pattern association or constrained optimization.

3.3.2 Architecture

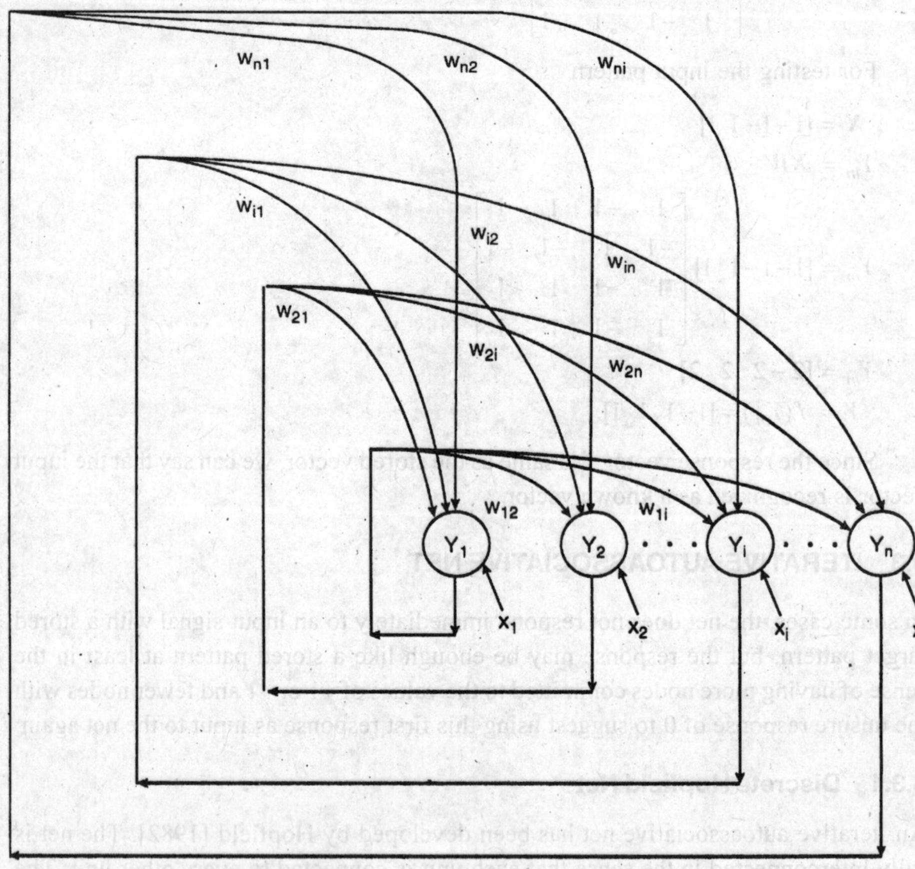

Figure 3.2 *Discrete Hopfield Net*

3.3.3 Activation Function

In Hopfield network, the activation function is a simple threshold. The output of a neuron is one, if the weighted sum of the outputs of other neurons is greater than a threshold θ; otherwise it is zero.

It is calculated as:

$$\text{net}_j = \sum_{i \neq j} w_{ij} y_i + x_j$$

$$y_j = \begin{cases} 1 & \text{if net}_j > \theta_j \\ 0 & \text{if net}_j < \theta_j \\ y_j & \text{unchanged if net}_j = \theta_j \end{cases}$$

The state of a network is simply the set of the current values of the output signals from all neurons. The state of each neuron is changed at discrete random times. When a new input vector is applied, the network moves from one vector to another until it stabilizes.

Energy Hopfield has made an analogy between training the neural network and minimizing a value which has been interpreted as its global 'energy'.

A neuron that has a large positive weight associated with it is likely to fire when the input to the neuron is one, i.e., a large positive weight means that the neuron fires easily with a stimulus on one of its inputs. On the other hand, an input with a small positive value will probably not be able to make the neuron fire on its own. In this case, a lot of stimulus or energy is required. Finally, inputs with negative weights will inhibit the neuron and so even more energy is required on the inputs to cause the neuron to fire.

From the above discussion, it is evident that energy in a neural net is related to the negative sum of all the weighted inputs of the neurons. For a single neuron, the energy at a particular time is defined as:

$$E = -y[x_2 w_2 + x_3 w_3 + \dots + x_n w_n + \theta + x_1] \tag{3.1}$$

Energy function Extending the above discussion, the energy function for the Hopfield network shown in Fig. 3.2 can be written as:

$$E = -\frac{1}{2}\sum_{i \neq j}\sum_{j} y_i y_j w_{ij} - \sum_i x_i y_i + \sum_i \theta_i y_i \tag{3.2}$$

The change in energy is due to a change in the state of the neuron i is ΔE. This can be calculated using the following equation.

$$\Delta E = -\left[\sum_j y_i w_{ij} + x_i \theta_i\right]\Delta y_i$$

$$= (\text{net}_i - \theta_i)\Delta y_i \tag{3.3}$$

where Δy_i is the change in the output of the neuron i.

To minimize E, we have to make sure that ΔE is always negative.

If the net value of the neuron i is greater than the threshold, the term in the brackets will be positive, and making use of the activation function, it can be further stated that the output of the neuron i must change in the positive direction (or remain constant). This means that Δy_i can be positive or zero and ΔE must be negative; hence the network energy must either decrease or stay constant.

If the net value of the neuron is less than the threshold, then Δy_i can be negative or zero; hence again the energy must decrease or remain constant.

Finally, if the net equals the threshold θ_i, the energy remains unchanged. It can be observed that any change in the system state will either reduce the energy or maintain its current value. As the energy shows a continuous downward trend, eventually it must find a minimum and stop when the network has attained a stable condition.

3.3.4 Algorithm

Hopfield's description of algorithm used binary input vectors.

To store a set of binary patterns $s(p), p = 1, 2, ..., P$,

$$s(p) = (s_1(p) \dots s_i(p) \dots s_n(p))$$

The weight matrix, $w = \{w_{ij}\}$ is given by

$$w_{ij} = \sum_p \left[(2s_i(p)-1)(2s_j(p)-1)\right] \text{ for } i \neq j \text{ and } w_{ii} = 0.$$

The application algorithm is stated for binary pattern; the activation can be modified easily to accommodate bipolar patterns.

3.3.5 Application

A binary Hopfield net can be used to determine whether an input vector is a "known" vector (i.e. one that was stored in the net) or an "unknown" vector. The net recognizes a "known" vector by producing a pattern of activation on the units of the net that is the same as the vector stored on the net. If the input vector is an "unknown" vector, the activation vector produced as the net iterates will converge to an activation vector that is one of the stored patterns; such a pattern is called 'spurious stable state'.

Step 1: Initialize weights to store patterns.

Step 2: While activations are not converged, do steps 3 to 9.

Step 3: For each input vector x, do steps 4 to 8.

Step 4: Set the initial activation of net equal to external input vector, x.

$$y_i = x_i \ (i = 1, 2, \dots, n)$$

Step 5: Do steps 6 to 8 for each unit, y_i.

Step 6: Compute net input.

$$y_{inj} = x_i + \sum_j y_j w_{ji}$$

Step 7: Determine activation (output signal).

$$y_i = \begin{cases} 1 & \text{if } y_{ini} > \theta \\ y_i & \text{if } y_{ini} = \theta \\ 0 & \text{if } y_{ini} < \theta \end{cases}$$

Step 8: Broadcast the value of y_i to all other units. (This updates activation vector.)

Step 9: Test for convergence.

The threshold, θ is usually taken to be zero. The order of update of the units is random, but each unit is updated at the same average rate. Originally, Hopfield used binary activations with no external input after first time step. Later, the external input was allowed to continue during processing. Although typically Hopfield used binary activation, the model was formulated for any two distinct values.

Example 3.2 Design a Hopfield network for 4-bit bipolar patterns. The training patterns are:

I sample = S_1 = [1,–1,–1,–1]

II sample = S_2 = [–1,1,1,–1]

III sample = S_3 = [–1,–1,–1,1]

Find the weight matrix and the energies for the three input samples. Determine the pattern to which the sample S = [–1,1,–1,–1] associates.

Solution

Given

$$X = \begin{bmatrix} 1 & -1 & -1 & -1 \\ -1 & 1 & 1 & -1 \\ -1 & -1 & -1 & 1 \end{bmatrix}$$

$$W = \frac{1}{4}\sum_{i=1}^{4} x_i x_i'$$

$$= X^T X$$

$$= \begin{bmatrix} 1 & -1 & -1 \\ -1 & 1 & -1 \\ -1 & 1 & -1 \\ -1 & -1 & 1 \end{bmatrix} \begin{bmatrix} 1 & -1 & -1 & -1 \\ -1 & 1 & 1 & -1 \\ -1 & -1 & -1 & 1 \end{bmatrix}$$

$$= \begin{bmatrix} 3 & -1 & -1 & -1 \\ -1 & 3 & 3 & -1 \\ -1 & 3 & 3 & -1 \\ -1 & -1 & -1 & 3 \end{bmatrix}$$

Calculating the energy of the networks for each pattern:

$$E = \frac{-1}{2}\sum_{i=1}^{4}\sum_{j=1}^{4} x_i w_{ij} x_j$$

Energy for pattern 1: $S = [1,-1,-1,-1]$

$$E_1 = \frac{-1}{2}[20] = -10$$

Energy for pattern 1: $S = [-1,1,1,-1]$

$$E_1 = \frac{-1}{2}[24] = -12$$

Energy for pattern 1: $S = [-1,-1,-1,1]$

$$E_1 = \frac{-1}{2}[20] = -10$$

Now the test vector given is $S = [-1,1,-1,-1]$.

Energy for test pattern $S = [-1,1,-1,-1]$:

$$E_1 = \frac{-1}{2}[4] = -2$$

$E = -2$ is less than -10 as expected.

By synchronous updating method:

Net input = $S \times \boldsymbol{W}$

$$= [-1\ 1\ -1\ -1]\begin{bmatrix} 3 & -1 & -1 & -1 \\ -1 & 3 & 3 & -1 \\ -1 & 3 & 3 & -1 \\ -1 & -1 & -1 & 3 \end{bmatrix}$$

$$= [-2\ \ 2\ \ 2\ -2]$$

Applying the threshold limit $\theta = 0$.

Therefore output = $[-1\ \ 1\ \ 1 -1]$

Energy $E = -12$ which is the same as pattern 2.

Therefore, pattern $S = [-1\ \ 1\ -1\ -1]$ is associated to pattern 2.

3.4 HETEROASSOCIATIVE MEMORY NEURAL NETWORK

Associative memory neural network are nets in which the weights are determined in such a way that the net can store a set of P pattern associations. Each association is a pair of vectors $(s(p), t(p))$ with $p = 1,2, \ldots ,P$. Each vector $s(p)$ has n-tuples and the vector $t(p)$ has m types. The weights may be found using Hebb rule or Delta rule. The net will find an appropriate output vector that corresponds to an input vector x, that may be either one of the stored patterns $s(p)$ or a new pattern (such as one of the training patterns corrupted by noise).

3.4.1 Architecture

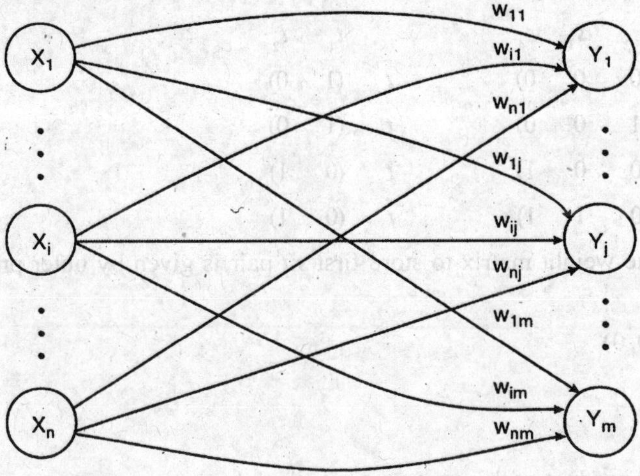

Figure 3.3

3.4.2 Algorithm

Step 1: Initialize weights using either Hebb rule or Delta rule.

Step 2: For each input vector, do steps 3 to 5.

Step 3: Set the activations for input layer units equal to the current input vector, x_i.

Step 4: Compute net input to output units.

$$y_{inj} = \sum_i x_i w_{ij}$$

Step 5: Determine the activation of the output units.

$$y_j = \begin{cases} 1 & \text{if } y_{inj} > 0 \\ 0 & \text{if } y_{inj} = 0 \\ -1 & \text{if } y_{inj} < 0 \end{cases}$$

The output vector y gives the pattern associated with the input vector x. This heteroassociative memory is not iterative.

Other activation functions can also be used. If the target responses of the net are binary, a suitable activation function is given by:

$$f(x) = \begin{cases} 1 & \text{if } x > 0 \\ 0 & \text{if } x \le 0 \end{cases}$$

Example 3.3 Train a heteroassociative net by outer product rule for input row vectors $s = (x_1, x_2, x_3, x_4)$ to output row vectors $t = (t_1, t_2)$:

	s_1	s_2	s_3	s_4		t_1	t_2
s	(1	0	0	0)	t	(1	0)
s	(1	1	0	0)	t	(1	0)
s	(0	0	0	1)	t	(0	1)
s	(0	0	1	1)	t	(0	1)

Solution The weight matrix to store first $s{:}t$ pair is given by outer product of the vector,

$$s = (1, 0, 0, 0)$$

and

$$t = (1, 0).$$

The outer product of this vector pair is given by,

$$\begin{bmatrix} 1 \\ 0 \\ 0 \\ 0 \end{bmatrix} [1 \;\; 0] = \begin{bmatrix} 1 & 0 \\ 0 & 0 \\ 0 & 0 \\ 0 & 0 \end{bmatrix}$$

Similarly, to store the second pair,

$$s = (1, 1, 0, 0)$$

and

$$t = (1, 0)$$

The weight matrix is,

$$\begin{bmatrix} 1 \\ 1 \\ 0 \\ 0 \end{bmatrix} [1 \;\; 0] = \begin{bmatrix} 1 & 0 \\ 1 & 0 \\ 0 & 0 \\ 0 & 0 \end{bmatrix}$$

To store the third pair,

$$s = (0, 0, 0, 1)$$

and

$$t = (0, 1).$$

The weight matrix is:

$$\begin{bmatrix} 0 \\ 0 \\ 0 \\ 1 \end{bmatrix} [0 \;\; 1] = \begin{bmatrix} 0 & 0 \\ 0 & 0 \\ 0 & 0 \\ 0 & 1 \end{bmatrix}$$

And to store the fourth pair,

$s=(0, 0, 1, 1)$

and

$t=(0, 1)$.

The weight matrix is:

$$\begin{bmatrix} 0 \\ 0 \\ 1 \\ 1 \end{bmatrix} [0 \ \ 1] = \begin{bmatrix} 0 & 0 \\ 0 & 0 \\ 0 & 1 \\ 0 & 1 \end{bmatrix}$$

The weight matrix to store all the four patterns is the sum of the weight matrices to store each pattern pair separately, i.e.

$$w = \begin{bmatrix} 1 & 0 \\ 0 & 0 \\ 0 & 0 \\ 0 & 0 \end{bmatrix} + \begin{bmatrix} 1 & 0 \\ 1 & 0 \\ 0 & 0 \\ 0 & 0 \end{bmatrix} + \begin{bmatrix} 0 & 0 \\ 0 & 0 \\ 0 & 0 \\ 0 & 1 \end{bmatrix} + \begin{bmatrix} 0 & 0 \\ 0 & 0 \\ 0 & 1 \\ 0 & 1 \end{bmatrix} = \begin{bmatrix} 2 & 0 \\ 1 & 0 \\ 0 & 1 \\ 0 & 2 \end{bmatrix}$$

3.5 BIDIRECTIONAL ASSOCIATIVE MEMORY [B24, B25]

Bidirectional Associative Memory (BAM) is a heteroassociative content addressable memory consisting of two layers. It uses forward and backward information flow to produce an associative search for stored stimulus-response association. A BAM stores a set of pattern associations by summing bipolar correlation matrices. The architecture of net consists of two layer of neurons connected by directional weighted connections. The net iterates by sending the signal back and forth between the two layers until all neurons reach equilibrium (i.e. until each neuron's activation remains constant for several steps). Bidirectional associative memory neural nets gives response in the *Y* layer if the input is given to *X* layer and vice versa. Because the weights are bidirectional and the algorithm alternates between updating the activations for each layer we shall refer to layers as *X*-layer and *Y*-layer (rather than input and output layers). Three varieties of BAM - binary, bipolar and continuous—are considered. Several other variations exist. However the architecture of them is the same.

3.5.1 Architecture

The single layer nonlinear feedback BAM network (with heteroassociative content addressable memory) has *n* units in *X*-layer and *m* units in the *Y*-layer. The connections between the layers are bidirectional, i.e. if the weight matrix for signals sent from *Y*-layer to *X*-layer is *w*, the weight matrix for signals sent from *Y*-layer to *X*-layer is w^T.

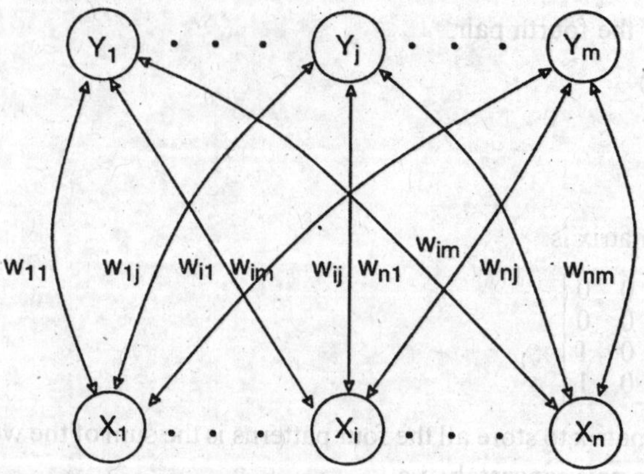

Figure 3.4 *Bidirectional Associative Network*

3.5.2 Discrete BAM

The two bivalent (binary and bipolar) forms of BAM are closely related. In each, the weights are found from the sum of the outer products of the bipolar form of training vector pairs. Also, the activation is a step function with the possibility of non-zero threshold. It has been shown that bipolar vectors improve the performance of the net.

Setting weights The weight matrix to store a set of input and target vectors, $s(p) : t(p), p = 1,2, \ldots ,P$

$$S(p) = (s_1(p) \ldots s_i(p) \ldots s_n(p)) \text{ and}$$

$$t(p) = (t_1(p) \ldots t_j(p) \ldots t_m(p))$$

can be determined by Hebb rule. The formulae for the entries depend on whether the training vectors are binary or bipolar. For binary input vectors, the weight matrix $w = \{w_{ij}\}$ is given by,

$$w_{ij} = \sum_p \left[(2s_i(p)-1)(2s_j(p)-1)\right] \tag{3.4}$$

For bipolar input vectors, the weight matrix $w = \{w_{ij}\}$ is given by,

$$w_{ij} = \sum_p s_i(p)t_j(p) \tag{3.5}$$

Activation function The activation function for a discrete BAM is the appropriate step function, depending on whether binary or bipolar vectors are used.

For binary input vectors, the activation function for the *Y*-layer is:

$$y_j = \begin{cases} 1 & \text{if } y_{inj} > 0 \\ y_j & \text{if } y_{inj} = 0 \\ 0 & \text{if } y_{inj} < 0 \end{cases}$$

and the activation for the *X*-layer is:

$$x_i = \begin{cases} 1 & \text{if } x_{ini} > 0 \\ x_i & \text{if } x_{ini} = 0 \\ 0 & \text{if } x_{ini} < 0 \end{cases}$$

For bipolar input vectors, the activation function for the *Y*-layer is:

$$y_j = \begin{cases} 1 & \text{if } y_{inj} > \theta_j \\ y_j & \text{if } y_{inj} = \theta_j \\ -1 & \text{if } y_{inj} < \theta_j \end{cases}$$

and the activation function for the *X*-layer is:

$$x_i = \begin{cases} 1 & \text{if } x_{ini} > \theta_i \\ x_i & \text{if } x_{ini} = \theta_i \\ -1 & \text{if } x_{ini} < \theta_i \end{cases}$$

Note that if the net value is exactly equal to the threshold value, the activation function "decides" to leave the activation of that unit at its previous value. Signals are sent only from one layer to another at any stage of the process, not simultaneously in both directions.

3.5.3 Algorithm

Step 1: Initialize the weights to store a set of *P* vectors.

Initialize all activations to zero.

Step 2: For each testing input, do steps 3 to 8.

Step 3: Present input pattern *x* to *X*-layer (i.e. set activations of *X*-layer to current input pattern).

Step 4: Present input pattern *y* to *Y*-layer (The input patterns may be zero vector).

Step 5: While activations are not converged, do steps 6 to 8.

Step 6: Update activations of units in *Y*-layer.

Compute net input.

$$y_{inj} = \sum_i x_i w_{ij}$$

Compute activations.

$$y_j = f(y_{inj})$$

Send signal to *X*-layer.

Step 7: Update activations of units in *X*-layer.

Compute net input.

$$x_{ini} = \sum_j y_i w_{ij}$$

$x_i = f(x_{ini})$

Send signal to Y-layer.

Step 8: Test for convergence.

If the activation vectors, X and Y have reached equilibrium then stop; otherwise continue.

3.5.4 Continuous BAM

A continuous BAM transforms input smoothly and continuously into output in the range [0,1] using the logistic sigmoid function as the activation for all units.

For binary input vectors $(s(p), t(p))$, $p = 1, 2, \ldots P$, the weights are determined by the formula

$$w_{ij} = \sum_p \left[(2s_i(p)-1)(2t_j(p)-1)\right] \tag{3.6}$$

The activation function is the logistic sigmoid.

$$f(y_{inj}) = \frac{1}{1+\exp(-y_{inj})}$$

where a bias is included in calculating the net input to any unit

$$y_{inj} = b_j + \sum_i x_i w_{ij}$$

and corresponding formulae apply for units in the X-layer.

Example 3.4 Use a BAM to store the following three pairs of vectors.

$X_1 = (1\ -1\ -1)$ $\qquad Y_1 = (1\ -1)$

$X_2 = (-1\ 1\ -1)$ $\qquad Y_2 = (-1\ 1)$

$X_3 = (-1\ -1\ 1)$ $\qquad Y_3 = (1\ -1)$

Examine the network for the test vector (–1 –1 –1).

Solution The weight vector $W = W_1 + W_2 + W_3$

$$W = X_1^T Y_1 + X_2^T Y_2 + X_3^T Y_3$$

$$W = \begin{bmatrix} 1 \\ -1 \\ -1 \end{bmatrix} [1 -1] + \begin{bmatrix} -1 \\ 1 \\ -1 \end{bmatrix} [-1\ 1] + \begin{bmatrix} -1 \\ -1 \\ 1 \end{bmatrix} [1 -1]$$

$$W = \begin{bmatrix} 1 & -1 \\ -3 & 3 \\ 1 & -1 \end{bmatrix}$$

The output for the test vector $X = (-1\ -1\ -1)$ is:

$$Y = XW = [-1 -1 -1]\begin{bmatrix} 1 & -1 \\ -3 & 3 \\ 1 & -1 \end{bmatrix}$$

$$Y = [1 -1]$$

The test pattern associates with the first pattern.

3.6 STORAGE CAPACITY

Storage capacity of a neural net refers to the quantity of information that can be stored in a network in such a way that it can be retrieved without error. The storage capacity can be measured as:

$$C = \frac{\text{Number of stored patterns}}{\text{Number of neurons in the network}}$$

If a network is not fully connected, then another measure of capacity may be more appropriate such as:

$$C = \frac{\text{Number of stored patterns}}{\text{Number of connection weights in the network}}$$

The storage capacity of an associative memory neural network is the number of patterns or pattern pairs that can be stored before the net begins to forget.

SHORT QUESTIONS AND ANSWERS

1. How does an autoassociative net recognize a "known" vector?

   The network recognizes a "known" vector by producing a pattern of activation on the output units of the net that is same as one of the vectors stored in it.

2. How is the output noise suppressed in autoassociative memory?

   The noise suppression at the output can be done by thresholding the output and by recycling the output followed by a feedforward pass through the neural network. Such a network has feedback, nonlinear mapping in the form of thresholding and dynamical.

3. What are the advantages of associative memory?

   The autoassociative net has the power of recurrent neural processing within a parallel architecture. The recurrences through the thresholding layer of processing neurons tend to eliminate gradually the noise superimposed on the initializing input vector. This coerces the incorrect pattern bits towards one of the stored memories. The network's computational ability makes it possible to apply it in speech processing, database retrieval, image processing, pattern classification and other fields.

4. What are the limitations of associative memory?

The associative memories whether designed by Hebbian learning rule or by a modified rule suffer from substantial capacity limitations. Capacity limitations cause diversified symptoms. It can amount to convergence of spurious memories and difficulties with recovery of stored patterns if they are close to each other in Hamming distance sense. Overloaded memory may not be able to recover data stored or may recall spurious outputs. Another inherent problem is the memory convergence to stored pattern complements.

5. What is a Hopfield net?

The Hopfield net is an iterative autoassociative net. The net is a fully interconnected neural net in the sense that each unit is connected to every other unit. The net has symmetric weights with no self connections, i.e. $w_{ij} = w_{ji}$ and $w_{ii} = 0$.

6. What are the differences between Hopfield net and a normal autoassociative net?

The differences are:

- only one unit updates its activation at a time (based on the signal it receives from each other unit) and
- each unit continues to receive an external signal in addition to the signal from other units in the net.

7. Mention a few applications of Hopfield net.

A binary Hopfield net can be used to determine whether an input vector is a "known" vector (i.e. one that was stored in the net) or an "unknown" vector. The net recognizes a "known" vector by producing a pattern of activation on the units of the net that is the same as the vector stored on the net. If the input vector is an "unknown" vector, the activation vector produced as the net iterates will converge to an activation vector that is one of the stored patterns; such a pattern is called '*spurious stable state*'.

8. What are heteroassociative memory neural network?

Heteroassociative memory neural network are nets in which the weights are determined in such a way that the net can store a set of P pattern associations. Each association is a pair of vectors $(s(p), t(p))$ with $p = 1, 2, ..., P$. Each vector $s(p)$ has m-tuples. The weights may be found using Hebb rule or Delta rule. The net will find an appropriate output vector that corresponds to an input vector, x that may be either one of the stored patterns $s(p)$ or a new pattern (such as one of the training patterns corrupted by noise).

9. What is a Bidirectional Associative Memory?

Bidirectional Associative Memory is a heteroassociative content addressable memory consisting of two layers. It uses forward and backward information flow to produce an associative search for stored stimulus-response association. A BAM stores a set of pattern associations by summing bipolar correlation matrices.

The architecture of net consists of two layer of neurons connected by directional weighted connections. The net iterates by sending the signal back and forth between the two layers until all neurons reach equilibrium (i.e. until each neuron's activation remains constant for several steps). Bidirectional associative memory neural nets can respond to input to either layer.

10. How are weights determined in Bidirectional Associative Memory?

    In bipolar and binary forms of BAM, the weights are found from the sum of the outer products of the bipolar form of training vector pairs. Also, the activation is a step function with the possibility of non-zero threshold. It has been shown that bipolar vectors improve the performance of the net.

11. Mention the activation functions used by Bidirectional Associative Memory.

    The activation function for a BAM is the appropriate step function depending on whether binary or bipolar vectors are used.

    For binary input vectors, the activation function for the *Y*-layer is:

$$y_j = \begin{cases} 1 & \text{if } y_{inj} > 0 \\ y_j & \text{if } y_{inj} = 0 \\ 0 & \text{if } y_{inj} < 0 \end{cases}$$

and the activation for the *X*-layer is:

$$x_i = \begin{cases} 1 & \text{if } X_{ini} > 0 \\ x_i & \text{if } X_{ini} = 0 \\ 0 & \text{if } X_{ini} < 0 \end{cases}$$

For bipolar input vectors, the activation function for the *Y*-layer is:

$$y_j = \begin{cases} 1 & \text{if } y_{inj} > \theta_j \\ y_j & \text{if } y_{inj} = \theta_j \\ -1 & \text{if } y_{inj} < \theta_j \end{cases}$$

and the activation function for the *X*-layer is:

$$x_i = \begin{cases} 1 & \text{if } X_{ini} > \theta_i \\ x_i & \text{if } X_{ini} = \theta_i \\ -1 & \text{if } X_{ini} < \theta_i \end{cases}$$

12. Define storage capacity.

    The storage capacity of a neural net refers to the quantity of information that can be stored in a network in such a way that it can be retrieved without error. The storage capacity can be measured as:

$$C = \frac{\text{Number of stored patterns}}{\text{Number of neurons in the network}}$$

If a network is not fully connected, then another measure of capacity may be more appropriate such as:

$$C = \frac{\text{Number of stored patterns}}{\text{Number of connection weights in the network}}$$

The storage capacity of an associative memory neural network is the number of patterns or pattern pairs that can be stored before the net begins to forget.

REVIEW QUESTIONS

1. What is content addressable memory?
2. Draw the architecture of an associative neural network.
3. Briefly explain the applications of an autoassociative neural net.
4. What is Iterative autoassociative net?
5. Draw the architecture of Discrete Hopfield Network.
6. Mention the types of Bidirectional Associative Memory.
7. Draw the architecture of Bidirectional Associative Memory.
8. Write the formula for calculating the weight matrix of a discrete Bidirectional Associative Memory.
9. What is continuous Bidirectional Associative Memory?
10. Give some advantages of Bidirectional Associative Memory.
11. Differentiate between standard memory and associative memory.
12. Give an application area for Hopfield network.
13. What is the difference between Autoassociation and Heteroassociation?
14. Write the energy function of Hopfield net.
15. Define storage capacity.

CHAPTER

4

Self-organizing Maps: Topological Preserving Nets

4.1 INTRODUCTION

In neural computing, it has been assumed that data is available for both inputs and outputs of the nets. In perceptron systems, the classification of training patterns is provided in the sense that one particular neuron is taught to respond to patterns belonging to one particular class. In error back propagation, the target patterns as well as input patterns are presented so that the system can calculate the errors from which the weight adjustment algorithm operates.

For biological and technical reasons a net can make sense of streams of data without mentioning its classification. It could be argued that living systems have evolved to extract the features through repeated exposures to the environment. The living system has the ability to fire different parts of a neural system while presenting streams of data without the agency of teacher or trainer.

Self-organized clustering may be defined as a mapping through which N-dimensional pattern spaces are mapped into a smaller number of points in an output space. The mapping is achieved autonomously by a system without supervision. In other words, the clustering is achieved in a self-organized manner.

In a self-organizing network, the weights in the neurons represent a class of patterns. Input patterns are presented to all the neurons and each neuron produces an output. The value of the output from each neuron is used as a measure to find how close are the input pattern and the stored pattern. A competitive learning strategy is used to select a neuron whose connection vector matches closely with the input vector and the weights are reinforced.

The term self-organizing refers to the ability to learn and organize information without being given correct answers for the input pattern. Thus, self-organizing networks perform unsupervised learning. This computational model may serve to explain some neuro-biological phenomenon such as how a baby learns since it doesn't know what is correct.

4.2 FIXED WEIGHT COMPETITIVE NETS

When more than one neuron in the output layer fires, an additional structure is included in the network so that the net is forced to make a decision as to which one neuron will fire. This mechanism is termed as competition. When the competition is completed, only one neuron in the completing group will have a non-zero output signal. A specific competitive net that is based on "winner-takes-all" is the Maxnet.

4.2.1 Maxnet

Maxnet is a typical example of a competitive net which is based on the "winner- takes-all" policy. This subnet chooses the node whose input is the largest of all. The n nodes in the net are interconnected completely. This net has symmetric weights. All the weights are fixed and hence, there is no necessity for training the network. The Maxnet operates as a recurrent recall network that operates in an auxiliary mode. The network architecture is given below.

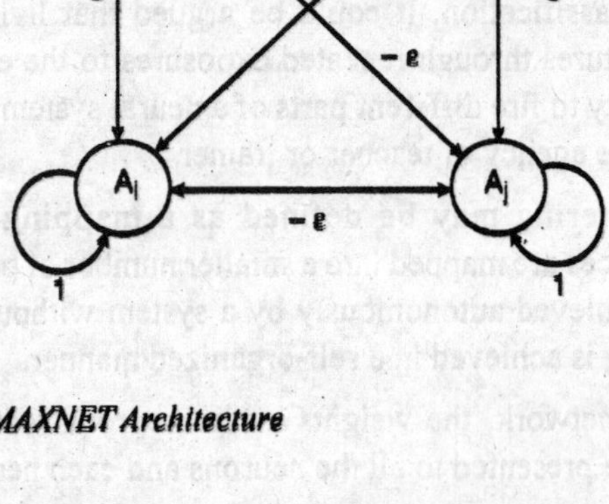

Figure 4.1 ***MAXNET Architecture***

Activation function

$$F(x) = \begin{cases} x & \text{if } x > 0 \\ 0 & \text{otherwise} \end{cases}$$

Algorithm

Step 1: Set activation and weights,

$a_j(0)$ is the input to node, A_j.

$$w_{ij} = \begin{cases} 1 & \text{if } i = j \\ -\varepsilon & \text{if } i \neq j \end{cases}$$

Step 2: While stopping condition is false, do step 3 to 5.

Step 3: Update the activation at each node.

For $j = 1,2,3,...,n$

$$a_j(\text{new}) = f\left[a_j(\text{old}) - \varepsilon \sum_{k \neq j} a_k(\text{old})\right]$$

Step 4: Save activations for use in next iterations.

$a_j(\text{old}) = a_j(\text{new}),\ j = 1,2,3,...,n$

Step 5: Test for stopping conditions.

If more than one node has a non-zero activation, then continue else stop.

Example 4.1 A Maxnet consists of three inhibitory weights as 0.25. The net is initially activated by the input signals [0.1 0.3 0.9]. The activation function of the neuron is

$$F(x) = \begin{cases} x & x > 0 \\ 0 & \text{otherwise} \end{cases}$$

Find the final winning neuron.

Solution

Given

$$a_1(0) = 0.1,\ a_2(0) = 0.3,\ a_3(0) = 0.9$$

Applying the Maxnet algorithm the net signal at the first iteration is:

$$\begin{aligned}
a_1(1) &= f[0.1 - 0.25\ (0.3 + 0.9)] \\
&= f(-0.425) = 0 \\
a_2(1) &= f[0.3 - 0.25(0.1 + 0.9)] \\
&= f(0.05) = 0.05 \\
a_3(1) &= f[0.9 - 0.25(0.3 + 0.1)] \\
&= f(0.8) = 0.8 \\
a_1(2) &= 0 \\
a_2(2) &= f[0.05 - 0.25(0 + 0.8)] \\
&= f(-0.15) = 0 \\
a_3(2) &= f[0.8 - 0.25(0 + 0.05)] \\
&= f(0.7875) = 0.7875
\end{aligned}$$

The third neuron is the winner.

4.2.2 Mexican Hat Network

Mexican hat network is a more general contrast enhancing subnet than the Maxnet. Each neuron is connected to other neurons either through excitatory links or through inhibitory links. Neurons which are in close proximity are connected through excitatory links which have positive weights. These neurons are called "co-operative neighbors". Neurons which are farther away are connected through inhibitory links which have negative weights. They are called "competitive neighbors". In addition, there are some more unconnected neurons present in the net. All these neurons in a particular layer receive an external signal in addition to the interconnection signals. The interconnection pattern for every neuron is similar to the one described above.

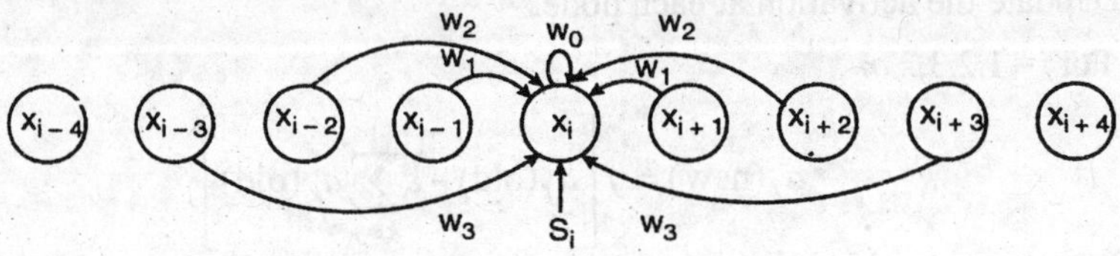

Figure 4.2 *Architecture of Mexican Hat Network*

S_i - Contrast enhancement Signal.

Activation function

$$x_i(t) = f[s_i(t) + \sum_k w_k x_{ik}(t-1)$$

The interconnections for each neuron have 2 symmetrical regions around it. The region near the neuron (x_{i+1}, x_{i-1}, x_{i+2}, x_{i-2}) has positive weights (w_1,w_2). The weight, w_3 between x_i and x_{i+3} and x_{i-3} is negative. Neurons, x_{i+4} and x_{i-4} are not connected with x_i. Thus, in this example, units within the radius of 2 units are positively connected while outside radius 2 units and within a radius of 3 units are negatively connected and those outside radius 3 units are not connected at all.

Terminology

R_1: Radius of positive reinforcement region

R_2: Radius of connecting links ($R_1 < R_2$)

W_k: Weights between x_i, x_{i+k} and x_{i-k}

W_k is positive if $0 \leq k \leq R_1$

W_k is negative if $R_1 \leq k \leq R_2$

X: Vector of activations

x_old: Activation vector at previous time step

t_max: Total number of iterations of contrast enhancement

S: External signal

Algorithm

Step 1: Set values for t_max, R_1 and R_2.

Initialize weights: $w_k = c_l$ for $k = 0,1,2,...,R_1$ $(C_1 > 0)$

$w_k = c_2$ for $k = R_{i+1},...,R_2 (C_2 > 0)$.

Step 2: Present the external signal, S.

$X = S$

Save activation in x_old array for $i = 1,2,3...,x$, for use in the net iteration.

$x\_old_i = x_i$.

Step 3: While $t < t\_max$, do steps 4 to 8.

Step 4: Calculate the net input ($i = 1,2,...,x$).

$$x_i = c_l \sum_{k=-R_1}^{R_1} x\_old_{i+k} + c_2 \sum_{k=-R_2}^{-R_{1-1}} x\_old_{i+k} + c_{21} \sum_{k=-R_{i+1}}^{R_2} x\_old_{i+k}$$

Step 5: Apply activation function.

$X_i = \min(x\_max, \max(0, x_i))$ ($i = 1,2,...,n$)

Step 6: Increment counter, t as $t = t + 1$.

Step 7: Save current activations for use in the next iteration.

$x\_old_i = x_i$ $(i = 1,2,...,n)$

Step 8: Test for stopping condition.

If $t < t\_max$, then continue else stop.

The positive and negative reinforcement have the effect of increasing the activation of units with large initial activations and reducing the activation of units respectively with small initial activations.

Example 4.2 A Mexican Hat network consists of seven input units. The net is initially activated by the input signals [0.0 0.4 0.7 1.0 0.7 0.4 0.0]. The activation function of the neuron is

$$f(x) = \begin{cases} 0 & \text{if } x < 0 \\ x & \text{if } 0 \le x \le 2 \end{cases}$$

The maximum number of iterations are three.

Solution

Step 0: Initialize parameters

$R_1 = 1$

$R_2 = 2$

$C_1 = 0.7$

$C_2 = -0.3$

Step 1: $(t=0)$

The external signal is [0.0 0.4 0.7 1.0 0.7 0.4 0.0], so

$x=[0.0\ 0.4\ 0.7\ 1.0\ 0.7\ 0.4\ 0.0]$

Save in x_old.

$x\_old=[0.0\ 0.4\ 0.7\ 1.0\ 0.7\ 0.4\ 0.0]$

Step 2: The update formulas in step3 are listed as follows:

$x_1=0.7x\_old_1+0.7x\_old_2-0.3x\_old_3$

$x_2=0.7x\_old_1+0.7x\_old_2+0.7x\_old_3-0.3x\_old_4$

$x_3=-0.3x\_old_1+0.7x\_old_2+0.7x\_old_3+0.7x\_old_4-0.3x\_old_5$

$x_4=-0.3x\_old_2+0.7x\_old_3+0.7x\_old_4+0.7x\_old_5-0.3x\_old_6$

$x_5=-0.3x\_old_3+0.7x\_old_4+0.7x\_old_5+0.7x\_old_6-0.3x\_old_7$

$x_6=-0.3x\_old_4+0.7x\_old_5+0.7x\_old_6+0.7x\_old_2$

$x_7=-0.3x\_old_5+0.7x\_old_6+0.7x\_old_7$

Step 3: $(t=1)$

$x_1=0.7(0.0)+0.7(0.4)-(0.3)(0.7)=0.07$

$x_2=0.7(0.0)+0.7(0.4)+0.7(0.7)-(0.3)(1.0)=0.47$

$x_3=-0.3(0.0)+0.7(0.4)+0.7(0.7)+(0.7)(1.0)-(0.3)(0.7)=1.26$

$x_4=-0.3(0.4)+0.7(0.7)+0.7(1.0)+(0.7)(0.7)-(0.3)(0.4)=1.44$

$x_5=-0.3(0.7)+0.7(1.0)+0.7(0.7)+(0.7)(0.4)-(0.3)(0.0)=1.26$

$x_6=-0.3(1.0)+0.7(0.7)+0.7(0.4)+(0.7)(0.0)=0.47$

$x_7=-0.3(0.7)+0.7(0.4)+0.7(0.0)=0.07$

Step 4: $x=[0.07\ 0.47\ 1.26\ 1.44\ 1.26\ 0.47\ 0.07]$

Step 3: $(t=2)$

$x_1=0.7(0.07)+0.7(0.47)-(0.3)(1.26)=0.0$

$x_2=0.7(0.07)+0.7(0.47)+0.7(1.26)-(0.3)(1.44)=0.828$

$x_3=-0.3(0.07)+0.7(0.47)+0.7(1.26)+(0.7)(1.44)-(0.3)(1.26)=1.82$

$x_4=-0.3(0.47)+0.7(1.26)+0.7(1.44)+(0.7)(1.26)-(0.3)(0.47)=2.49$

$x_5=-0.3(1.26)+0.7(1.44)+0.7(1.26)+(0.7)(0.47)-(0.3)(0.07)=1.82$

$x_6=-0.3(1.44)+0.7(1.26)+0.7(0.47)+(0.7)(0.07)=0.828$

$x_7=-0.3(1.26)+0.7(0.47)+0.7(0.07)=0.0$

Step 4: $x=[0.0\ 0.828\ 1.82\ 2.49\ 1.82\ 0.828\ 0.0]$

Step 5: The pattern is shown for activations $t=0,1$ and 2.

4.2.4 Hamming Net

Hamming net is a maximum likelihood classifier net. This network is used to determine the vector which is most similar to an input vector (an n-tuple) among several exemplar vectors. The measure of similarity is obtained from the formula $n - D$, where n is the number of components in the vector.

Hamming distance, D = Number of components in which the vectors differ.

For bipolar vectors x and y,

$$x.y = a - D$$

where a is the number of components in which the vectors agree.

$$a + d = x$$
$$x.y = a - D = 2a - n$$
$$2a = x.y + n$$

When the weights are set to be one-half of the exemplar vector and bias to be $n/2$, the net will find the unit with the closest exemplar simply by finding the unit with the largest net input. Maxnet is used for this purpose. The architecture of Hamming net is given below.

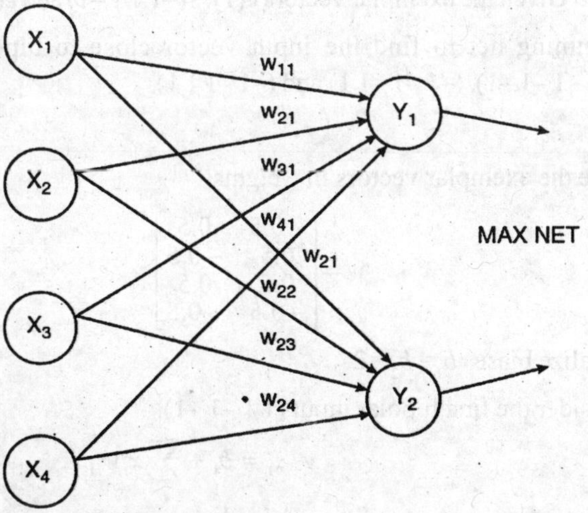

Figure 4.3 *Architecture of Hamming Net*

Application

Bipolar exemplar vectors: $e(1), e(2),..., e(m)$.

Net input y_{inj} to y_j gives the number of components in which the input vector and exemplar vector agree.

Terminology

N = number of input nodes

M = number of output nodes

$E(j) = j$th exemplar vector.

$= (e_1(j),...,e_i(j),...,e_n(j))$

Algorithm

Step 1: Initialize the weights.

$$w_{ij} = \frac{e_i(j)}{2}, (i = 1,..., n; \ j = 1,..., m)$$

Initialize bias values.

$$b_j = \frac{n}{2}, \ (j = 1,..., m)$$

Step 2: For each vector, x do steps 2 to 4.

Step 3: Compute net input to each output unit, y_j.

$$y_{inj} = b_j + \sum_i x_i w_{ij}$$

Step 4: Maxnet iterations are used to find the best match exemplar.

$$y_j(0) = y_{inj} \ (j = 1,..., m)$$

Example 4.3 Given the exemplar vectors $e(1) = (-1\ 1\ 1\ -1)$ and $e(2) = (1\ -1\ 1\ -1)$,

Use Hamming net to find the input vector close to bipolar input patterns $(1\ 1\ -1\ -1)$, $(1\ -1\ -1\ -1)$, $(-1\ -1\ -1\ 1)$ and $(-1\ -1\ 1\ 1)$.

Solution

Step 1: Store the exemplar vectors in weights.

$$w = \begin{bmatrix} -0.5 & 0.5 \\ 0.5 & -0.5 \\ 0.5 & 0.5 \\ -0.5 & -0.5 \end{bmatrix}$$

Initialize biases $b_1 = b_2 = 2$.

Step 2: Consider the first bipolar input $(1\ 1\ -1\ -1)$.

Step 3:

$$y_{-in1} = b_1 + \sum_i x_i w_{i1}$$

$$= 2 + 0 = 2$$

$$y_{-in2} = b_2 + \sum_i x_i w_{i2}$$

$$= 2 + 0 = 2$$

The above values represent Hamming similarity.

Step 4: $y_1(0) = y_2(0) = 2$

Hence the first input vector best matches with the exemplar vectors.

Step 5: Consider the second bipolar input $(1\ -1\ -1\ -1)$.

Step 6:

$$y_{-in1} = b_1 + \sum_i x_i w_{i1}$$
$$= 2 - 1 = 1$$
$$y_{-in2} = b_2 + \sum_i x_i w_{i2}$$
$$= 2 + 1 = 3$$

Step 7: $y_1(0) = 1$; $y_2(0) = 3$.

Since $y_2(0) > y_1(0)$, the second input vector best matches with the exemplar vectors.

Step 8: Consider the third bipolar input (–1 –1 –1 1).

Step 9:

$$y_{-in1} = b_1 + \sum_i x_i w_{i1}$$
$$= 2 - 1 = -1$$
$$y_{-in2} = b_2 + \sum_i x_i w_{i2}$$
$$= 2 - 1 = 1$$

The above values represent Hamming similarity.

Step 10: $y_1(0) = y_2(0) = 1$.

Hence the third input vector best matches with the exemplar vectors.

Step 11: Consider the fourth bipolar input (–1 –1 1 1).

Step 12:

$$y_{-in1} = b_1 + \sum_i x_i w_{i1}$$
$$= 2 + 0 = 2$$
$$y_{-in2} = b_2 + \sum_i x_i w_{i2}$$
$$= 2 + 0 = 2$$

The above values represent Hamming similarity.

Step 13: $y_1(0) = y_2(0) = 2$

Hence the fourth input vector best matches with the exemplar vectors.

4.3 KOHONEN SELF-ORGANIZING MAPS

Kohonen self-organizing maps, otherwise called a topology preserving maps, assume a topological structure among the cluster unit

Kohonen network aims at using the Kohonen learning to adjust the weights and finally result in a pattern classifier. There are *m* cluster units, arranged in a row of one or two dimensional array. The input signals are arranged as *n*-tuples. All inputs are given to all the neurons. The weights of the cluster unit serves as an exemplar of the input pattern associated with the cluster unit.

Kohonen network also follows the "winner-takes-all" policy. The network cluster unit, whose weight vector matches more closely with the input pattern, is considered the winning neuron. The weights of the winning unit and its neighboring units are updated.

The winning is decided based on the Euclidean distance which is given by,

$$\text{Euclidean Distance } D = \sqrt{\sum (x_i - w_{ij})^2}$$

The weight adjustment is performed as $\Delta w_{ij} = \alpha(x_i - w_{ij})y_j$

4.3.1 Architecture

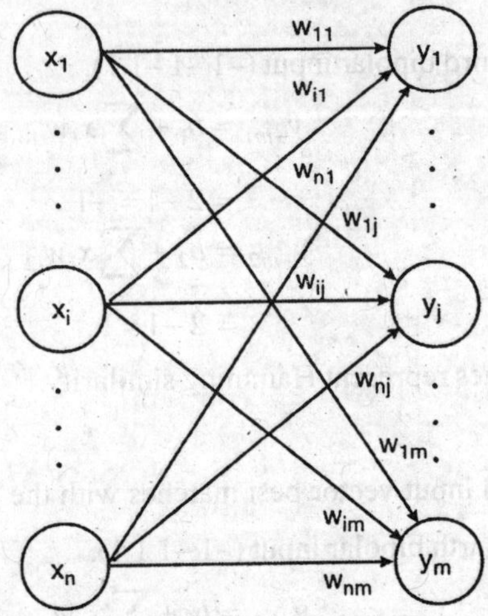

Figure 4.4 *Kohonen Self-organizing Map*

Architectures of Kohonen network as a linear array and a square grid are shown below.

a. Linear array of *n*-tuples:

* (* [* # *] *) *   Centre: #

b. Square Grid

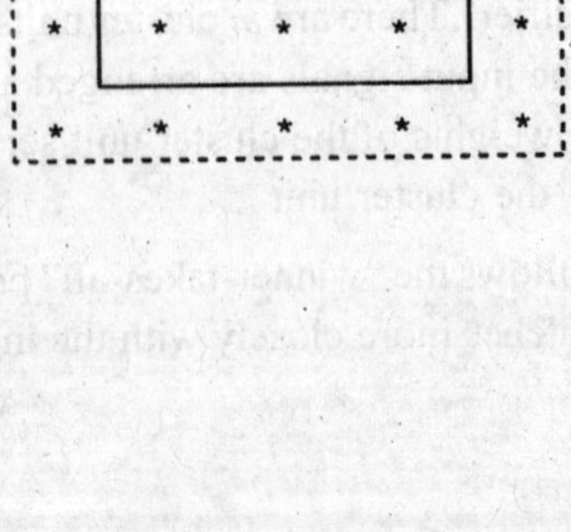

Figure 4.5 *Square Grid*

4.3.2 Algorithm

Step 1: Initialize weights w_{ij}.

Set learning rate and neighborhood parameters.

Step 2: While stopping condition is false, do steps 3 to 8.

Step 3: For each input vector, x do steps 4 to 6.

Step 4: For each j, compute $D(j)$ as:

$$D(j) = \sum (w_{ij} - x_i)^2$$

Step 5: Find the index, J such that $D(J)$ is minimum.

Step 6: For all j

$$w_{i,J}(\text{new}) = w_{i,J}(\text{old}) + \alpha[x_i - w_{i,J}(\text{old})]$$

Step 7: Update learning rate.

Step 8: Reduce radius of topological neighborhood at specified times.

Step 9: Test for stopping condition.

Learning rate α is a gradually decreasing function of time. A geometric decrease would also produce similar results.

During the clustering process, the radius around a cluster unit is decreased.

4.3.3 Formation

Formation of Kohonen map includes two phases: Initial formation of the correct order and final convergence. The second phase takes more time than the first and a lower learning rate also. In general, more iterations are preferred. Weights are initialized with random values.

4.3.4 Application

Kohonen network can be employed in a variety of applications. One recent development of this network is in computer generated music. Also, the more familiar traveling salesman problem could be solved using this network.

In this section the applications that employ self organizing networks are discussed.

4.3.5 Neural Phonetic Typewriter

The ability to recognize and understand human speech has been endowed by the scientists in a machine. The neural phonetic typewriter demonstrates the potential for neural networks to build speaker independent speech recognition into computer. The merging of neural network technology with traditional signal processing and artificial intelligence has led to solve problems. This device transcribes speech into text from unlimited vocabulary in real time with 92 to 97 percent accuracy. The typewriter has significant effect in which training for an individual speaker requires dictation of hundred words and requires ten minutes of time.

For this device, a two dimensional array of nodes is trained using inputs. The input vectors are produced from a series of preprocessing steps performed on the audible sound. This preprocessing includes use of noise canceling microphone, 12 bit analog to digital conversion and 256 point fast fourier transformations. Using Kohonen's clustering algorithm, nodes in two dimensional arrays were allowed to organize themselves in response to input vectors. The resulting map was calibrated by using spectra of phonemes after training. Phonemes were not used explicitly to train network, but it is mostly responded to a single phoneme. A word spoken is sampled, analyzed and given to network as sequence of input vectors. The nodes in network responded and path is traced in map to sequence of input patterns. This analysis can be carried out quickly and efficiently using various techniques including neural network associative memories.

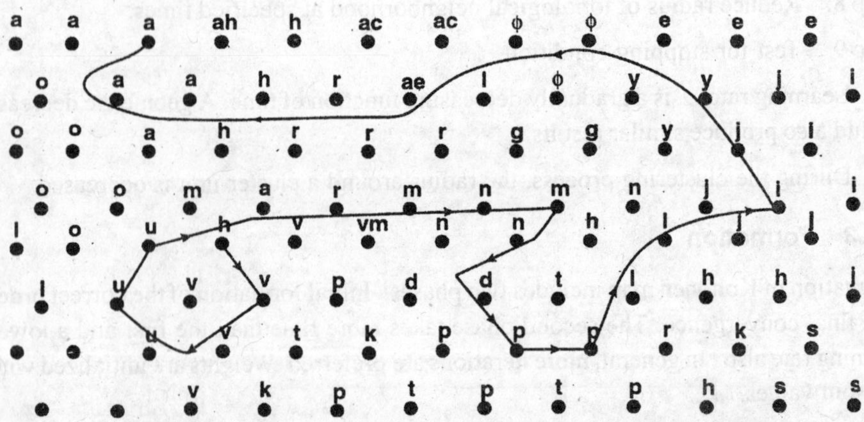

Figure 4.6 (a) *An Ordered Map for Finish Phonemes and Trajectory for Finish Word*

Example 4.4 Consider a Kohonen net with two cluster units and five input units. The weight vectors for the cluster units are $W_1 = [1\ 0.8\ 0.6\ 0.4\ 0.2]$ and $W_2 = [1\ 0.5\ 1\ 0.5\ 1]$. Use the square of the Euclidean distance to find the winning cluster unit for the input pattern $X = [0.5\ 1\ 0.5\ 0.0\ 0.5]$. Find the new weights for the winning unit. Assume learning rate as 0.2.

Solution The architecture of the Kohonen net with five input units and two cluster units along with the weights are shown in the Fig. 4.6(b)

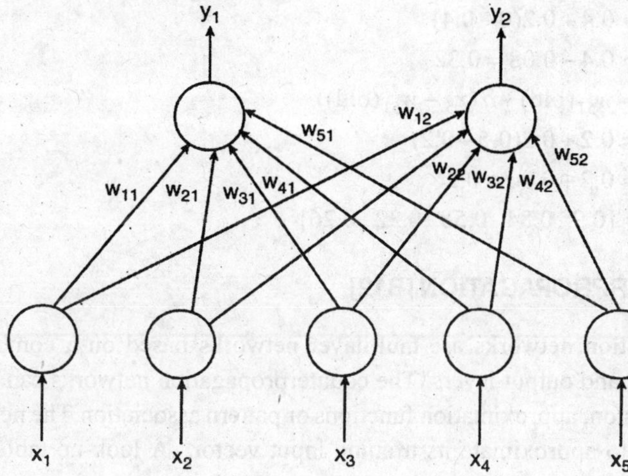

Fig. 4.6 (b)

$W_1 = [1.0\ 0.8\ 0.6\ 0.4\ 0.2]$

$W_2 = [1.0\ 0.5\ 1.0\ 0.5\ 1.0]$

$X = [0.5\ 1.0\ 0.5\ 0.0\ 0.5]$

$$D(j) = \sum_j (w_{ij} - x_i)^2$$

$$D(1) = (1-0.5)^2 + (0.8-1)^2 + (0.6-0.5)^2 + (0.4-0)^2 + (0.2-0.5)^2$$
$$= 0.55$$

$$D(2) = (1-0.5)^2 + (0.5-1)^2 + (1.0-0.5)^2 + (0.5-0)^2 + (1.0-0.5)^2$$
$$= 1.25$$

Since unit 1 has small Euclidean distance, the input vector is closest to cluster node 1 (winner node). The weights on the winning node are updated.

$$w_{ij}(\text{new}) = w_{ij}(\text{old}) + \alpha(x_1 - w_{ij}(\text{old}))$$

This gives the weight W_1 as:

$$w_{11}(\text{new}) = w_{11}(\text{old}) + \alpha(x_1 - w_{11}(\text{old}))$$
$$= 1.0 + 0.2(0.5 - 1.0)$$
$$= 1.0 - 0.1 = 0.9$$
$$w_{21}(\text{new}) = w_{21}(\text{old}) + \alpha(x_2 - w_{21}(\text{old}))$$
$$= 0.8 + 0.2(1.0 - 0.8)$$
$$= 0.8 + 0.04 = 0.84$$
$$w_{31}(\text{new}) = w_{31}(\text{old}) + \alpha(x_3 - w_{31}(\text{old}))$$
$$= 0.6 + 0.2(0.5 - 0.6)$$
$$= 0.6 - 0.02 = 0.58$$

$$
\begin{aligned}
w_{41}(\text{new}) &= w_{41}(\text{old}) + \alpha(x_4 - w_{41}(\text{old})) \\
&= 0.4 + 0.2(0 - 0.4) \\
&= 0.4 - 0.08 = 0.32 \\
w_{51}(\text{new}) &= w_{51}(\text{old}) + \alpha(x_5 - w_{51}(\text{old})) \\
&= 0.2 + 0.2(0.5 - 0.2) \\
&= 0.2 + 0.06 = 0.26 \\
w_1(\text{new}) &= [0.9 \;\; 0.84 \;\; 0.58 \;\; 0.32 \;\; 0.26]
\end{aligned}
$$

4.4 COUNTERPROPAGATION [B12]

Counterpropagation networks are multilayer networks based on a combination of input, clustering and output layers. The counterpropagation networks can be applied in data compression, approximation functions or pattern association. The network uses a look-up table to approximate its training input vector. A look-up table has more training data points in a compressed and manageable form.

The network training includes two stages:

1. Input vectors are clustered. Clusters are formed using dot product metric or Euclidean norm metric.
2. Weights from cluster units to output units are made to produce the desired response.

Types of counterpropagation nets are:

i. Full counterpropagation
ii. Forward only counterpropagation

4.4.1 Full Counterpropagation

The major aim of a full counterpropagation net is to provide an efficient means of representing a large number of vector pairs, **X** : **Y** by adaptively constructing a look-up table. It produces an approximation **X** : **Y** based on input of a **X**-vector alone or input of a **Y**-vector alone or input of an **X** : **Y** pair, possibly with some distorted or missing elements in either or both the vectors.

During the first phase of training of a full counterpropagation network, the training pairs **X** : **Y** are used to form the clusters.

Full counterpropagation also uses the "winner-takes-all" policy, which corresponds to using the dot product metric. Hence, the vectors should be normalized. One way to normalize is to add an extra component. Another means is to use the Euclidean norm.

Architecture

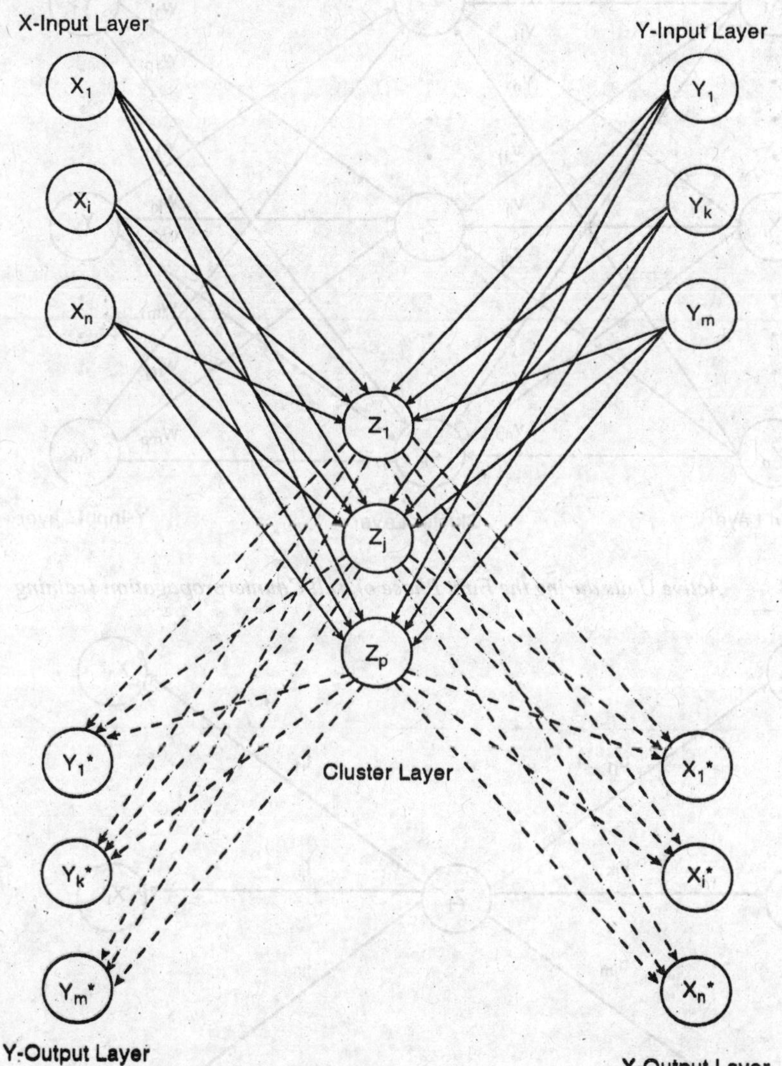

Figure 4.7 *Full Counterpropagation Net*

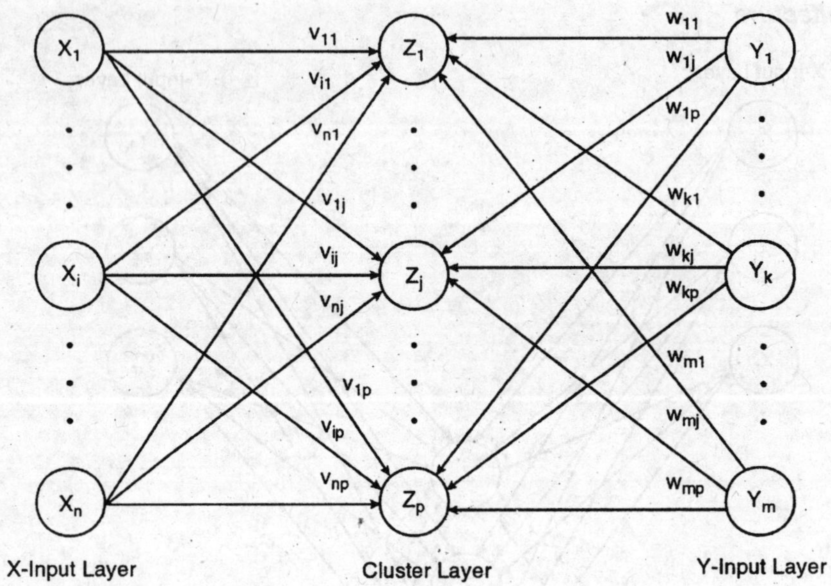

Figure 4.8 *Active Units during the First Phase of Full Counterpropagation Training*

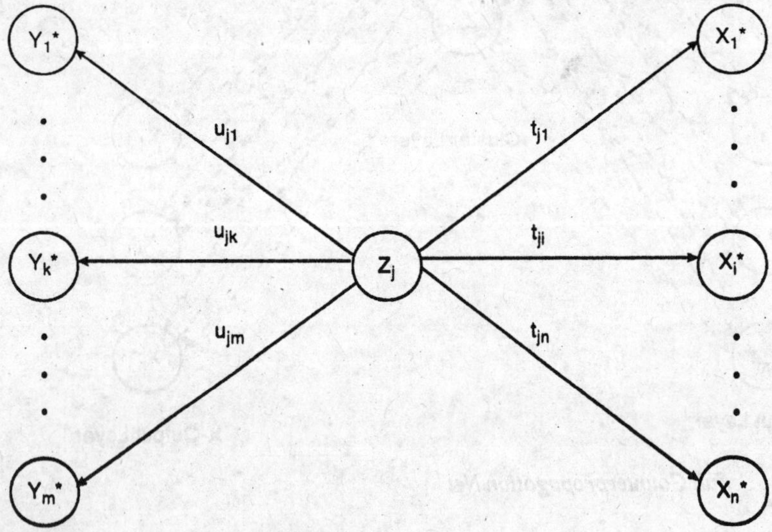

Figure 4.9 *Second Phase Training of the Net*

Algorithm

First phase: In the first phase, the **X** input units, cluster units and **Y** input units are active. Winner takes all.

Learning rule for weight updation:

$$v_{iJ}(\text{new}) = (1-\alpha)v_{iJ}(\text{old}) + \alpha x_i; i = 1,...,n$$

$$w_{ki}(\text{new}) = (1-\beta)w_{kJ}(\text{old}) + \beta y_k; k = 1,...,m$$

This is also known as Kohonen learning which consists of competition among the units and the weight updates for the winning unit.

Second phase: Only unit I remain active in the cluster layer. Weights are updated so that y^* is an approximation to y and x^* is an approximation to x.

Weight updates are made as:

$$u_{Jk}(\text{new}) = (1-a)u_{Jk}(\text{old}) + ay_k; \; k = 1,...,m$$

$$t_{Ji}(\text{new}) = (1-b)t_{Ji}(\text{old}) + bx_i; \; i = 1,...,n$$

This is Grossberg learning.

Terminology

X: Input training vector; $X = (x_1,...x_i,...x_n)$

Y: Target output corresponding to input X; $Y = (y_1,...y_i,...y_m)$

Z_j: Activation of cluster unit, Z_j

X^*: Computed approximation to x vector

Y^*: Computed approximation to y vector

V_{ij}: Weight from x layer unit, x_i to the cluster layer unit, z_j

W_{kj}: Weight from the y layer unit, y_k to the cluster unit z_j

u_{jk}: Weight from the cluster layer unit z_j to the y layer unit y_k^*

t_{jk}: Weight from the cluster layer unit z_j to the x layer unit x_k^*

α, β: Kohonen learning rates

a,b: Grossberg learning rates

Training algorithm

Step 1: Initialize weights and learning rates.

Step 2: While stopping condition to phase 1 training is false, do steps 3 to 8.

Step 3: For each training input pair **X** : **Y**, do steps 4 to 6.

Step 4: Set **X** input layer activations to vector, **X**.

Set **Y** input layer activations to vector, **Y**.

Step 5: Find winning cluster unit, z call its index, J

Step 6: Update weights for unit, z_J:

$$y_{iJ}(\text{new}) = (1-\alpha)v_{iJ}(\text{old}) + \alpha x_i; \; i = 1,...,n$$

$$w_{kJ}(\text{new}) = (1-\beta)w_{kJ}(\text{old}) + \beta y_k; \; k = 1,...,m$$

Step 7: . Reduce learning rates α, β.

Step 8: Test for stopping condition for phase 1 training.

Step 9: While stopping condition for phase 2 is false, do steps 10 to 16.

Step10: For each input training pair (*x*:*y*), do steps 11 to 14.

Step 11: Set *x* input layer activations to vector, **X**.

Set *y* input layer activations to vector, **Y**.

Step 12: Find winning cluster unit, call its index, *J*.

Step 13: Update weights for unit z_J:

$$v_{iJ}(\text{new}) = (1-\alpha)v_{iJ}(\text{old}) + \alpha x_i; \quad i = 1,\ldots,n$$

$$w_{kJ}(\text{new}) = (1-\beta)w_{kJ}(\text{old}) + \beta y_k; \quad k = 1,\ldots,m$$

Step 14: Update weights from Z_J to output layers.

$$u_{Jk}(\text{new}) = (1-a)u_{Jk}(\text{old}) + a y_k; \quad k = 1,\ldots,m$$

$$t_{Ji}(\text{new}) = (1-b)t_{Ji}(\text{old}) + b x_i; \quad i = 1,\ldots,n$$

Step 15: Reduce learning rates.

Step 16: Test for stopping condition for phase 2 training.

The following equations are used to find the metric distance.

$$\text{Dot product matrix}: Z_{inJ} = \sum_i x_i v_{iJ} + \sum_k y_k w_{kJ}$$

$$\text{Euclidean distance}: DJ = \sum_i (x_i - v_{iJ})^2 + \sum_k (y_k - w_{kJ})^2$$

Application

Step 1: Initialize weights.

Step 2: For each input pair *x*:*y*, do steps 3 to 5.

Step 3: Set *X* input layer activations to vector, **X**.

Set *Y* input layer activations to vector, **Y**.

Step 4: Find cluster unit Z_J that is closest to input pair.

Step 5: Compute $x_i^* = t_{Ji}$

$Y_k^* = u_{Jk}$

Example 4.5 A full counterpropagation net to complement the function $y = 1/x$. For the function, $y = 1/x$, we have 10 cluster units in the interval [0.1, 10].

The network has one input unit and one output unit.

Cluster Unit	V	W
Z_1	0.11	9.0
Z_2	0.14	7.0
Z_3	0.20	5.0
Z_4	0.30	3.3
Z_5	0.6	1.6
Z_6	1.6	0.6
Z_7	3.3	0.30
Z_8	5.0	0.20
Z_9	7.0	0.14
Z_{10}	9.0	0.11

Step 0: Initialize weights.

Step 1: For the input $x = 0.12, y = 0.0$, do steps 2 to 4.

Step 2: Set X input layer activations to vector, **X**.

Set Y input layer activations to vector, **Y**.

Step 3: Find the index J of the winning cluster unit.

$$D_1 = (0.12-0.11)^2 + (0.00-9.00)^2 = 81$$
$$D_2 = (0.12-0.14)^2 + (0.00-7.00)^2 = 49$$
$$D_3 = (0.12-0.20)^2 + (0.00-5.00)^2 = 25$$
$$D_4 = (0.12-0.30)^2 + (0.00-3.30)^2 = 11$$
$$D_5 = (0.12-0.60)^2 + (0.00-1.60)^2 = 2.8$$
$$D_6 = (0.12-1.60)^2 + (0.00-0.60)^2 = 2.6$$
$$D_7 = (0.12-3.30)^2 + (0.00-0.30)^2 = 10.2$$
$$D_8 = (0.12-5.00)^2 + (0.00-0.20)^2 = 23.9$$
$$D_9 = (0.12-7.00)^2 + (0.00-0.14)^2 = 47.4$$
$$D_{10} = (0.12-9.00)^2 + (0.00-0.11)^2 = 78.9$$

The winning cluster unit is 6.

Step 4: Compute approximations to x and y:

$$x^* = t_j = 1.6$$
$$y^* = u_j = 0.6$$

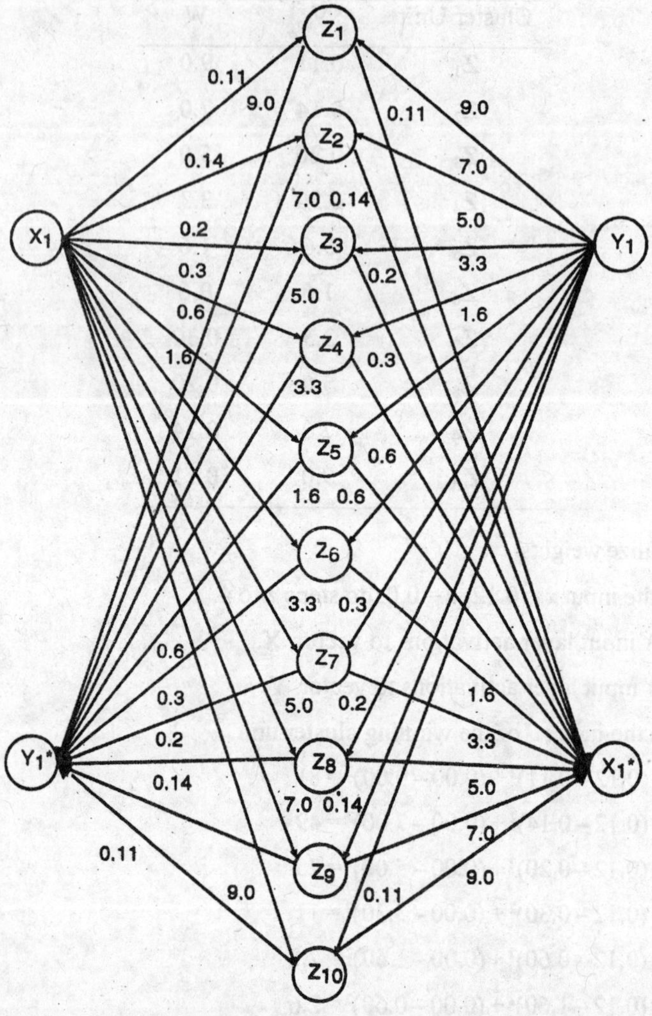

Figure 4.10 *Full Counterpropagation Network for Function y = 1/x*

If we base our search for the winning cluster unit or distance from the x input to the corresponding weight for each cluster unit, we find the following in steps 3 and 4.

Step 3: Find the index J of the winning cluster unit

$D_1 = (0.12 - 0.11)^2 = 0.0001$

$D_2 = (0.12 - 0.14)^2 = 0.0004$

$D_3 = (0.12 - 0.20)^2 = 0.064$

$D_4 = (0.12 - 0.30)^2 = 0.032$

$D_5 = (0.12 - 0.60)^2 = 0.23$

$D_6 = (0.12 - 1.60)^2 = 2.2$

$$D_7 = (0.12 - 3.30)^2 = 10.1$$
$$D_8 = (0.12 - 5.00)^2 = 23.8$$
$$D_9 = (0.12 - 7.00)^2 = 47.3$$
$$D_{10} = (0.12 - 9.00)^2 = 81$$

Thus based on the input from x only, the closest cluster unit is $J = 1$.

Step 4: Compute approximations to x and y:

$$x^* = t_j = 0.11$$
$$y^* = u_j = 9.00$$

4.4.2 Forward Only Counterpropagation

Forward only counterpropagation is a simplified version of full counterpropagation net where the mapping from x to y is well-defined while that from y to x is not. Thus, this network uses only the first stage of training of full counterpropagation nets. But this net uses the Euclidean distance between the input vector and the weight vector for the Kohonen unit. However, either of the dot product metric or the Euclidean distance can be used.

Architecture The architecture is similar to that of the backpropagation net, but the forward only counterpropagation net has interconnections among the units in the cluster layer which are not shown in Fig. 4.11. In general, after completion, only one unit will be active and that unit will send signals to the output layer.

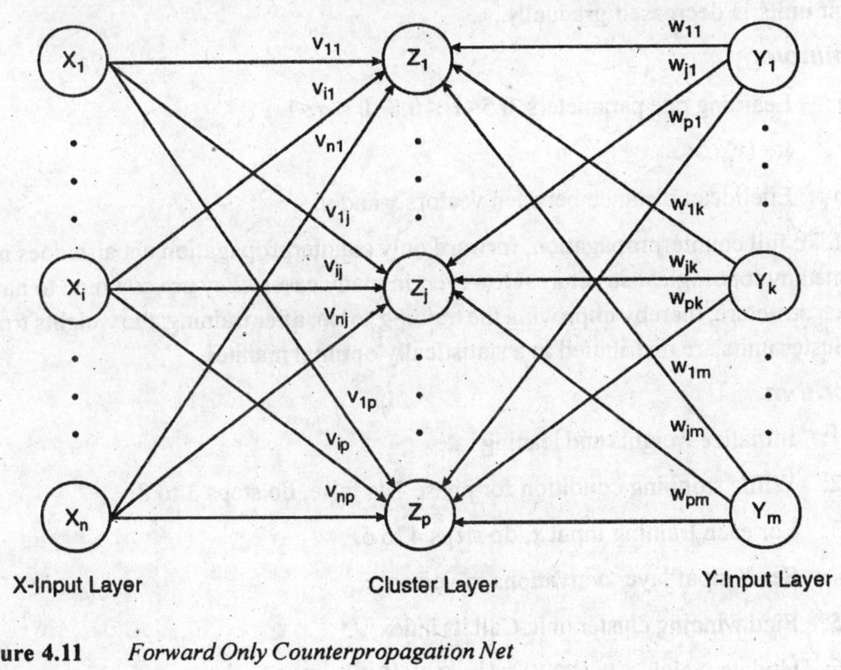

Figure 4.11 *Forward Only Counterpropagation Net*

Algorithm Initially, an input vector is presented to the input units. Learning takes place through several iterations. After each training set has been presented, the learning rate is reduced. After training the weights from the input layer to the cluster layer, the weights from the cluster layer to the output layer are trained.

Once, the input is presented to the input layer, the output is presented to the output layer. The winning cluster unit sends a signal of 1 to the output layer. Each output unit has a computed input signal w_{jk} and target y_k. Based on the difference in these values, the weights between these winning cluster unit and the output layers are updated.

Learning rule for weights from input to cluster units.

$$\begin{aligned} v_{ij}(\text{new}) &= v_{ij} + \alpha(x_i - v_{ij}) \\ &= (1-\alpha)v_{ij}(\text{old}) + \alpha x_i \end{aligned}$$

Learning rule for weights from the cluster to output units.

$$\begin{aligned} w_{jk}(\text{new}) &= w_{jk} + \alpha(y_k - w_{jk}) \\ &= (1-a)w_{jk}(\text{old}) + a y_k \end{aligned}$$

Activation of the cluster unit.

$$Z_j = \begin{cases} 1 & \text{if } j = J \\ 0 & \text{otherwise} \end{cases}$$

Hence, the learning rule for weights from the cluster units to the output units continues to be a low value, while the learning rate for training weights from cluster to output units is decreased gradually.

Terminology

α, a: Learning rate parameters: $0.5 < a < 0.8 : 0 < a < 1$

x: $x = (x_1, \ldots x_i, \ldots, x_n)$

$\|x - v\|$: Euclidean distance between vectors x and v.

Like full counterpropagation, forward only counterpropagation net also does not assume any topological structure. However, in many cases, they are assumed to have a linear structure, thereby improving the training. Also, after training, the weights from the cluster units are distributed in a statistically optimal manner.

Algorithm

Step 1: Initialize weights and leaning rate.

Step 2: While stopping condition for phase 1 is false, do steps 3 to 8.

Step 3: For each training input x, do steps 4 to 6.

Step 4: Set X input layer activations to vector, x.

Step 5: Find winning cluster unit. Call its index, J.

Step 6: Update weights $v_{ij}(\text{new}) = (1-\alpha)v_{ij}(\text{old}) + \alpha x_i$; $i = 1, \ldots, n$

Step 7: Reduce the learning rate, α.

Step 8: Test for stopping condition for phase 1 training.

Step 9: While stopping condition for phase 2 training is false, do steps 10 to 16 (a is small).

Step 10: For each input training pair $x{:}y$, do steps 11to 14.

Step 11: Set X input layer activations to vector, x.

Set Y output layer activations to vector, y.

Step 12: Update weights (a is small):

$$v_{iJ}(\text{new}) = (1-\alpha)v_{iJ}(\text{old}) + \alpha x_i; \quad i = 1,\ldots,n$$

Step 13: Update weights from units, Z_J to the output units:

$$w_{Jk}(\text{new}) = (1-a)w_{Jk}(\text{old}) + ay_k; \quad k = 1,\ldots m$$

Step 14: Reduce learning rate a.

Step 15: Test for stopping condition for phase 2 training.

For steps 5 and 11, in case of a tie, the unit with the smallest index is considered.

Application A CPN can be effectively used to classify images into various categories. The problem identified is to determine the angle of rotation of the principal axis of an object in two dimensions directly from the raw video image of the object. The object considered is a model of space shuttle that can be rotated 360 degrees about a singlc axis of rotation.

The architecture of a space craft orientation system is shown in Fig. 4.12.

The video camera and the frame digitizer capture a 256 × 256 pixel image of a model. This image is reduced to a 16 × 16 pixels and is then thresholded to produce a binary image. The resulting 256 component vector is used as an input to neural network, which responds by giving the sine and cosine of the rotation model. The output values are translated as movement commands to mechanical robot assembly. The movement command instructs the robot to reach out and pick an object. The angle is used to rotate the robot's wrist to proper orientation to aid for proper movement.

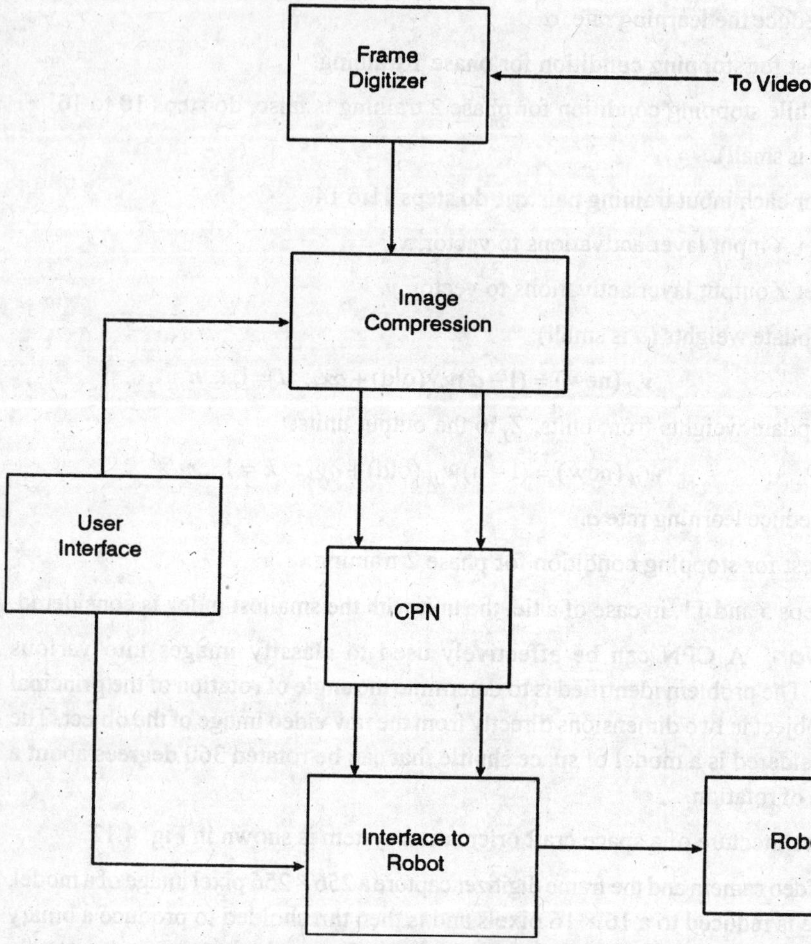

Figure 4.12 *Architecture of Space Craft Orientation System*

The system uses a Counter Propagation Network with 258 input units, 12 hidden units and 2 output units. The hidden neurons are trained to categorize the input vectors into different classes. There are 12 neurons in that layer and 12 different vectors are used to train the network. These 12 vectors represent the images of the shuttle in 30 degree movements (0 : 30 : 360). Since these 12 input vectors contribute to 12 categories the training of non competitive layer consists of setting each unit's weight equal to one of the input vectors. The output unit learns to associate the correct sine and cosine values with each of the classes represented on the middle layer.

Since there are only 12 units in hidden layer, this network will classify the input only into 12 categories. This problem can be alienated by adding more units in the middle layer allowing for many finer classifications of input samples. Another approach is to allow the output units to perform an interpolation of inputs that do not match with the training patterns to within a specified tolerance.

The output values will be given by the equation:

$$y_k = \sum_j w_{kj} z_j$$

When the ith hidden unit is the winner then $y_k = w_{ki}$, since $z_j = 1$ for $j = 1$ and $z_j = 0$ otherwise. Further the output of the winning units is proportional to how close the input pattern is i.e. $z_j \propto \cos\theta_j$.

If we restrict the total output from the middle layer as unity then the output is given by

$$y_k = w_{ki} z_i + w_{kj} z_j$$

where ith and jth units on the middle layer are winners and $z_i + z_j = 1$.

The network output will be the linear interpolation of the outputs that would be obtained from the two patterns that matches with the winning neurons.

Using this approach the network will be able to classify the input samples correctly. The network is not prone to noise or contradictory data and hence it is robust.

Example 4.6 Forward only counterpropagation net for the function $y = 1/x$.

In this example, we consider the performance of a forward only counterpropagation net to form a look-up table for the function, $y = 1/x$ on the interval [0.1, 10.0]. Suppose we have 10 cluster units (in cluster layer), there is one X input layer unit and one Y output layer unit. Suppose further we have a large number of training points (the x values for our function) uniformly distributed between 0.1 and 10.0 and presented in a random order. If we use a linear structure on the cluster units, the weights (form the input unit to the 10 cluster units) will be approximately 0.5, 1.5, 2.5, 3.5 ... 9.5 after the first phase of training.

After second phase of training, the weights to the Y output units will be approximately 5.5, 0.75, 0.4 ... 0.1. Thus the approximations to the function values will be much more accurate for large values of x than for small values. Fig. 4.13 illustrates the weights associated with each cluster unit.

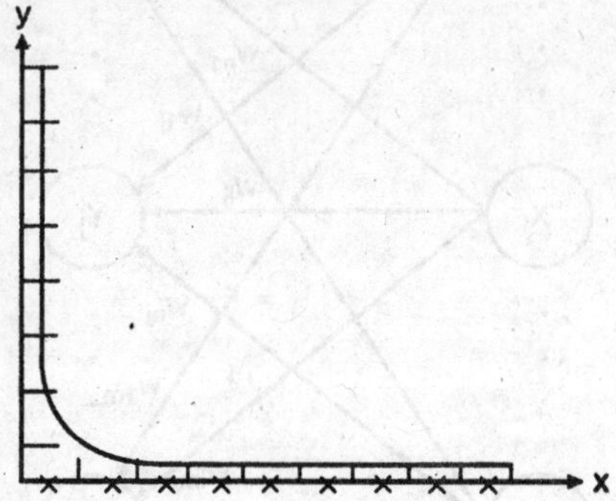

Figure 4.13 *Result for y = 1/x*

Comparing the results with the example of full counterpropagation we see that even if the net is intended only for approximating the mapping from x to y, the full counterpropagation net may distribute the cluster units in a manner that produces more accurate approximations over the entire range of input values.

4.5 LEARNING VECTOR QUANTIZATION

4.5.1 Vector Quantization

One of the common applications of competitive learning is adaptive vector quantization for data compression (e.g. speech and image data). In this approach, a given set of X data points is grouped into n groups (templates) so that later one may use an enclosed version of the corresponding template of any input vector to represent the vector as opposed to using the vector itself. Vector quantization is a technique whereby the input space is divided into a number of distinct regions and for each region a code book vector is defined.

4.5.2 Learning Vector Quantization

Kohonen designed supervised versions of vector quantization called Learning Vector Quantization (LVQ) for adaptive pattern classification. Here, class information is used to fine-tune the code book vector so as to improve the quality of the classifier decision regions. It is assumed that a set of training pattern with known classifications is provided along with an initial distribution of reference vectors.

4.5.3 Architecture

The architecture of an LVQ net is similar to that of a Kohonen's self-organizing map without a topological structure. In addition, each output unit is assigned to a known class.

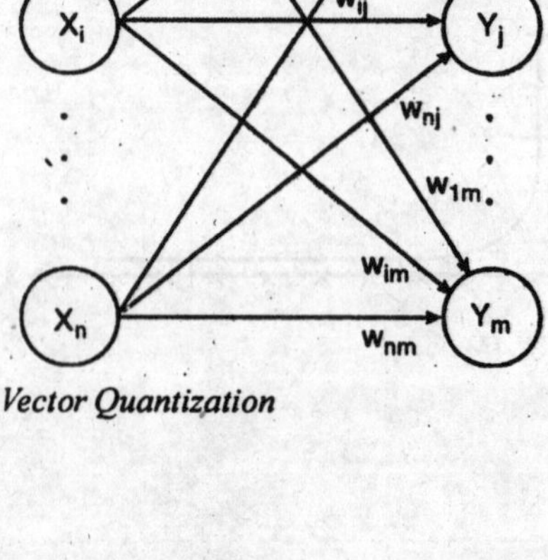

Figure 4.14 *Learning Vector Quantization*

Terminology

X : Training vector $(x_1, x_2, x_3 \ldots, x_n)$

D : Target class for the input training vector

C_j : Class represented by the jth output unit

W_j : Weight vector for the jth output unit

w_{ij} : Weight connected from the ith input neuron to the jth cluster unit

m : Number of cluster units

Algorithm

Step 1: Assign first m input vectors as reference input vectors.

Step 2: While stopping condition is false do steps 3 to 7.

Step 3: For each training input vector X do steps 4 and 5.

Step 4: Find the winner so that $\|X - W_J\|$ is minimum.

Step 5: Update W_J [if the winner represents the current class]:

$$\text{If } D = C_j \text{ then}$$
$$W_J(\text{new}) = W_J(\text{old}) + a\,[X - W_J(\text{old})].$$
$$\text{If } D \neq C_j \text{ then}$$
$$W_J(\text{new}) = W_J(\text{old}) - a\,[X - W_J(\text{old})].$$

Step 6: Reduce learning rate, α as

$$\alpha(\text{new}) = \frac{\alpha(\text{old})}{1 + \alpha(\text{old})}$$

Step 7: Test stopping condition.

The condition may be for a fixed number of iterations as the learning rate reaches sufficiently a low value.

Example 4.7 In the following example, two reference vectors are used. The input vectors represent two classes 1 and 2.

Vector	Class
(1,1,0,0)	1
(0,0,0,1)	2
(0,0,1,1)	2
(1,0,0,0)	1
(0,1,1,0)	2

The first two vectors will be used to initialize the two reference vectors. Thus, the first output will represent class 1, the second class 2. This leaves vectors (0,0,1,1), (1,0,0,0) and (0,1,1,0) as training vectors. Only one iteration is shown.

Step 0: Initialize weights:

$$W_1 = (1,1,0,0)$$
$$W_2 = (0,0,0,1)$$

Initialize learning rate: $\alpha = 0.1$

Step 1: Begin computation.

Step 2: For input vector $x = (0,0,1,1)$ with $T = 2$, do steps 3 to 4.

Step 3: $J = 2$, since x is closer to W_2 than W_1.

Step 4: Since $T = 1$ and $C_2 = 2$, update W_2 as follows:

$$W_2 = (0,0,0,1) + 0.1[(0,0,1,1) - (0,0,0,1)]$$
$$= (0,0,0.1,1)$$

Step 2: For input vector $x = (1,0,0,0)$ with $T = 1$, do steps 3 to 4.

Step 3: $J = 1$

Step 4: Since $T = 1$ and $C_1 = 1$, update W_1.

$$W_1 = (1,0.9,0,0) - 0.1[(0,1,1,0) - (1,0.9,0,0)]$$
$$= (1.1,0.89,-0.1,0)$$

Step 2: For input vector $x = (0,1,1,0)$ with $T = 2$, do steps 3 to 4.

Step 3: $J = 1$

Step 4: Since $T = 2$ and $C_1 = 1$, update W_1.

$$W_1 = (1,0.9,0,0) + 0.1[(0,1,1,0) - (1,0.9,0,0)]$$
$$= (1.1,0.89,-0.1,0)$$

Step 5: This completed one epoch of training. Reduce learning rate.

Step 6: Test stopping condition.

SHORT QUESTIONS AND ANSWERS

1. What are fixed weight competitive nets? Give examples.

   A sample clustering net that uses fixed exemplars is known as fixed weight competitive nets e.g. Maxnet, Mexican hat, Hamming net.

2. Sketch the architecture of Maxnet.

   The architecture of Maxnet is shown in Fig. 4.15.

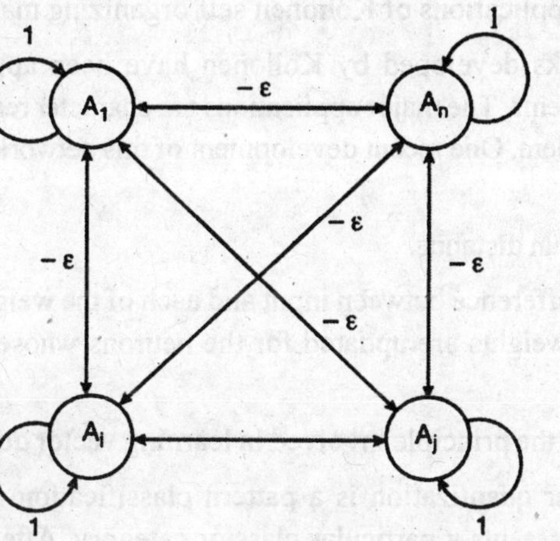

Figure 4.15 *Maxnet*

3. **What are ordered maps?**

Nets that learn to respond at different parts to differences in input are called ordered maps.

4. **Draw the architecture of Mexican hat and give its activation function.**

The architecture of Mexican hat is shown in Fig. 4.16.

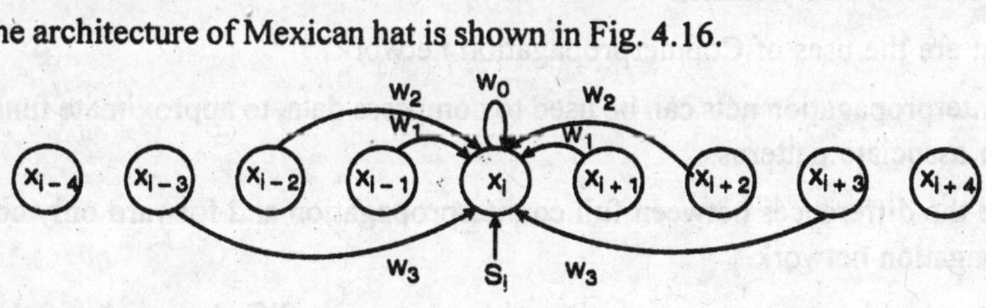

Figure 4.16 *Mexican Hat Network*

The activation of unit X_i at time t is given by:

$$x_i(t) = f\left[s_i(t) + \sum_k w_k x_i + k(t-1) \right]$$

where the terms in the summation are the weighted signals from other units at the previous time-step.

5. **What is winner-takes-all or competitive learning or clustering principle?**

Many neural nets use the idea of competition among neurons to enhance the contrast in activations of the neuron. In winner-takes-all principle, only one neuron with the largest activation is allowed to remain on.

6. **What are 'Topology Preserving' maps?**

The self organizing neural networks are also called as topology preserving maps. They assume a topological structure among the cluster units.

7. **What are the applications of Kohonen self organizing maps?**

   Neural networks developed by Kohonen have been applied to an interesting variety of problems. The major applications are character recognition and travelling sales man problem. One recent development of this network is computer generated music.

8. **Define Euclidean distance.**

   The absolute difference between input and each of the weights is called Euclidean distance. The weights are updated for the neurons whose Euclidean distance is minimum.

9. **Briefly explain the principle involved in learning vector quantization.**

   Learning vector quantization is a pattern classification method in which each output unit represents a particular class or category. After training, an LVQ net classifies an input vector by assigning it to the same class as the output unit that has its weight vector closest to the input vector.

10. **What do you mean by inhibitory cluster?**

    In competitive learning, once a unit wins the competition it inhibits others in its neighborhood from firing. A group of cells for which such inhibition occurs is called an inhibitory cluster.

11. **What are the uses of Counterpropagation network?**

    Counterpropagation nets can be used to compress data, to approximate functions or to associate patterns.

12. **State the differences between full counterpropagation and forward only counter propagation network.**

    Forward only counterpropagation nets are a simplified version of the full counterpropagation nets. Forward only counterpropagation differs from full counterpropagation in using only the x vectors to form the clusters on the Kohonen units during the first stage of training.

13. **Define Hamming distance.**

    The distance between two binary patterns in terms of the number of elements in which they differ is called Hamming distance. (After the US engineer R.W. Hamming, who in the 1950s used this measure to develop error correcting codes).

14. **Define firing rule.**

    The rule states "Take a collection of training patterns for a node, some of which cause it to fire and others which prevent it from doing so. Then the patterns not in the collection cause the node to fire if, on comparison, they have more input elements in common with the 'nearest' pattern in the one taught set than with the nearest in the zero taught set. If there is a tie, then the pattern remains in the undefined state."

15. **State the rules of competitive learning.**

For competitive learning, the units in a given layer are broken into a set of non-overlapping clusters.

- **A unit learns if and only if it wins the competition with other units in its cluster.**
- **The fixed total amount of weight for unit is designated as:** $\sum_i w_{ji} = 1.$

16. **Sketch the architecture of full counterpropagation network.**

The architecture of the full counterpropagation network is known in Fig. 4.17.

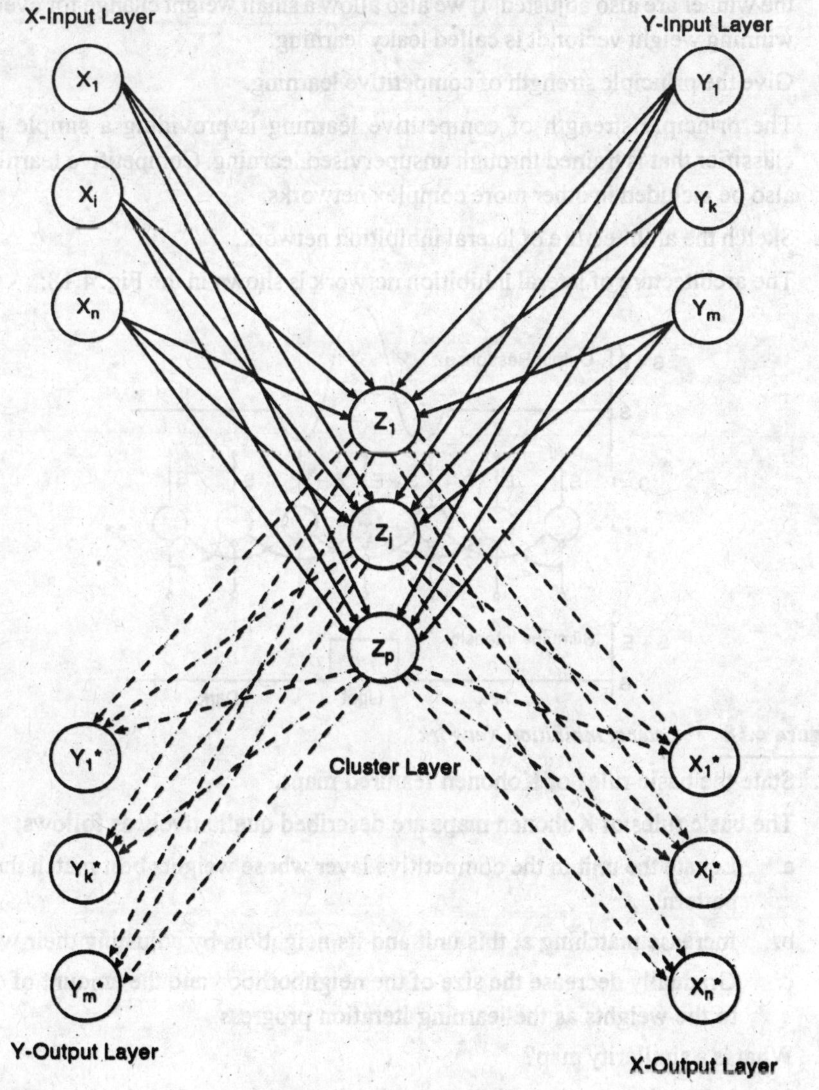

Figure 4.17 *Architecture of Full Counterpropagation Network*

17. Define lateral inhibition.

The Kohonen network uses intra-layer connections to moderate the competition. The output of each node acts as an inhibitory input to the other nodes but is actually excitatory in its neighborhood. Thus, even though there is only one winner node, more than one nodes are allowed to change their weights. This complex scheme for moderating competition within a layer is known as lateral inhibition.

18. Define leaky learning.

In the Kohonen network, the weights associated with the neighboring neurons of the winner are also adjusted. If we also allow a small weight change for every non-winning weight vector, it is called leaky learning.

19. Give the principle strength of competitive learning.

The principle strength of competitive learning is providing a simple pattern classifier that is trained through unsupervised learning. Competitive learning can also be included in other more complex networks.

20. Sketch the architecture of lateral inhibition network.

The architecture of lateral inhibition network is shown in the Fig. 4.18:

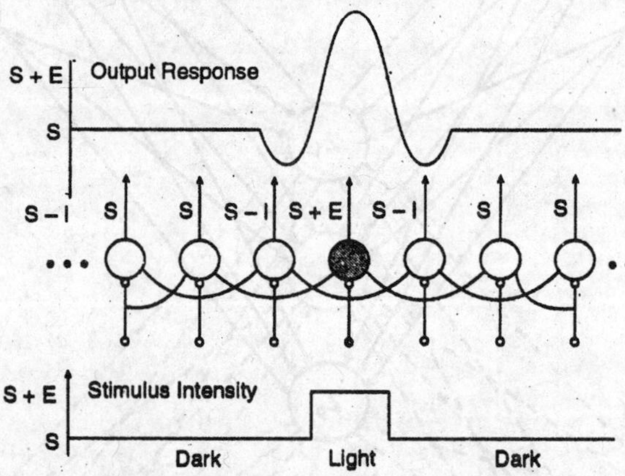

Figure 4.18 *Lateral Inhibition Network*

21. State the basic rules of Kohonen featured maps.

The basic rules of Kohonen maps are described qualitatively as follows:

a. Locate the unit in the competitive layer whose weights best match the input pattern.

b. Increase matching at this unit and its neighbors by adjusting their weights.

c. Gradually decrease the size of the neighborhood and the amount of change to the weights as the learning iteration progress.

22. What is a similarity map?

In the trained network, each competitive layer unit responds best to a particular pattern input. Because the same phenomenon can vary considerably in its acoustic characteristics, different units in the competitive layer will win the competition when slightly different forms of the same phenomenon are presented. In addition, the same unit will sometimes win the competition for more than one phenomenon. It is possible to map this phenomenon across the competitive layer of the trained network resulting in a similarity map in which the distance between two units is approximately proportional to the dissimilarity of sounds to which the different units respond.

23. What do you mean by normalization?

    Normalization means that the length of the vector is 1.

    $\|X\| = 1.0$ where $\|X\| = \sqrt{\sum_i x_i^2} = 1$

24. State the applications of counterpropagation.

    Some of the applications of counterpropagation are: image compression, data compression and vector quantization.

25. How do you compute normalized vector?

    The equation to compute normalized vector is $\frac{E'}{\|E'\|}$, where E' is the data vector and E is the normalized vector. The resulting vector, E has length 1, and is used as input to the network.

REVIEW QUESTIONS

1. What is a self organizing map?
2. What is a Maxnet?
3. What is the activation function used for a Maxnet?
4. Define competition.
5. What are positive and negative reinforcement regions?
6. Briefly explain a Hamming net.
7. Explain the salient features of Kohonen Self Organizing Map.
8. Draw the architecture of a full counterpropagation net.
9. What is a forward only counterpropagation network?
10. What is the purpose of Learning Vector Quantization?
11. Explain self organizing Map and its training algorithm.
12. Explain the structure and working principle of counterpropagation networks.
13. What are the merits of Kohonen Self-organizing Map?
14. Explain the various techniques used to initialize weight vectors during the training of a Kohonen layer.
15. What is the main function of a Learning Vector Quantization network?

CHAPTER

5

Backpropagation Network

5.1 HISTORICAL BACKGROUND

The limitation of the single layer neural network was a major factor for the "quiet years" of the 1970's in the history of backpropagation. The discovery and widespread dissemination of an effective general method of training a multilayer neural network played a major role in the re-emergence of neural networks as a tool for solving a wide variety of problems.

A method of propagating the error back to the hidden units had been discovered by Werbos in 1974, but had not gained wide publicity. This method was discovered independently by David Parker (1985) and by Le Cun (1986) again. It is similar to an earlier algorithm in optimal control theory developed by Bryston & Ho (1969). Parker's work was later refined by psychologists David Rumelhart of the University of California at San Diego and James McClelland of Carnegie Mellon University in the Parallel Distributed Processing Group and they publicized it.

5.2 INTRODUCTION

The backpropagation network can be used to solve problems in many areas. One such application is the NET talk which learnt to read English aloud. As is the case with most neural networks, the aim is to train the net to achieve a balance between the net's ability to respond (memorization) and the ability to give reasonable responses to the input that is similar, but not identical to the one used in training (generalization).

The training of a backpropagation net involves 3 stages: the feedforward of the input training pattern, the calculation and backpropagation of the associated error and the weight adjustments. After the net has been trained, its application involves only the feedforward phase.

A multilayer net can learn only input patterns to an arbitrary accuracy. More than one hidden layer can also be used though one is sufficient. The weight adjustment is based on the generalized delta rule. A weight in a neural network is a segment of the information about the input signal that has to be stored.

5.3 ARCHITECTURE

A backpropagation neural network is a multilayer, feedforward neural network with an input layer, an output layer and a hidden layer. The neurons in the hidden and output layers have biases (similar to weights) which are connections from units whose output is always 1.

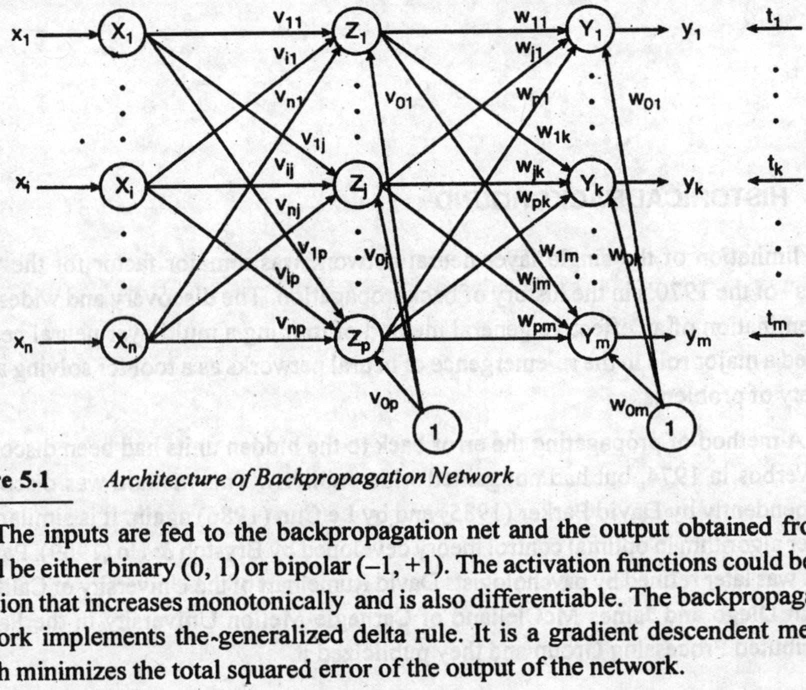

Figure 5.1 *Architecture of Backpropagation Network*

The inputs are fed to the backpropagation net and the output obtained from it could be either binary (0, 1) or bipolar (–1, +1). The activation functions could be any function that increases monotonically and is also differentiable. The backpropagation network implements the generalized delta rule. It is a gradient descendent method which minimizes the total squared error of the output of the network.

5.4 ALGORITHM

Backpropagation training takes place in three stages.

i. Feedforward of the input training pattern
ii. Backpropagation of the associated error and
iii. Weight adjustment.

During feedforward, each input neuron (X_i) receives an input signal and broadcasts it to each hidden neuron, which in turn computes the activation and passes it on to each output unit, which again computes the activation to obtain the net output.

During training, the net output is compared with the target value and the appropriate error is calculated. From the error, the error factor δ_k is obtained which is used to distribute the error back to the hidden layer. The weights are updated accordingly. In a similar manner, the error factor δ_j is calculated for units Z_j. After the error factors are obtained, the weights are updated simultaneously.

5.4.1 Terminology

x: Input training vector

$x = (x_1, x_2, ..., x_i, ..., x_n)$.

t: Output target vector

$t = (t_1, t_2, ..., t_j, ..., t_m)$.

δ_k: Portion of error correction weight adjustment for w_{jk} that is due to an error at the output unit Y_k, which is backpropagated to the hidden units that feed it into the unit Y_k.

δ_j: Portion of error correction weight adjustment for v_{ij} that is due to the backpropagation of error to the hidden unit, Z_j.

a: Learning rate.

X_i: ith input unit.

v_{oj}: Bias on jth hidden unit.

Z_j: jth hidden unit.

Net input to Z_j, $z_{inj} = v_{oj} + \sum_i x_i v_{ij}$

and $z_j = f(z_{inj})$.

w_{ok}: Bias on kth output unit.

Y_k: kth output unit.

Net input to Y_k, $z_{ink} = w_{ok} + \sum_i z_j w_{jk}$

and $y_k = f(y_{ink})$.

5.4.2 Activation Function

Characteristics possessed by an activation function are

i. Continuity
ii. Differentiability
iii. Non-decreasing monotony

Usually the activation function is expected to saturate i.e., approach finite maximum and minimum values asymptotically. The activation functions commonly used for backpropagation nets are :

i. Binary sigmoidal which has a range [0, 1] and
ii. Bipolar sigmoidal which has a range [−1, +1].

5.4.3 Derivation of Learning Rule for Backpropagation Procedure

The derivation is made for an arbitrary activation function $f(x)$.

The output of the kth output neuron, y_k is:

$$y_k = f(y_{ink})$$

where y_{ink} is the net input to the kth output neuron which is written as:

$$y_{ink} = \sum_j z_j w_{jk}$$

The error function to be minimized is:

$$E = 0.5 \sum_k (t_k - y_k)^2 \tag{5.1}$$

$$\frac{\partial E}{\partial w_{jk}} = -(t_k - y_k)\frac{\partial y_k}{\partial w_{jk}}$$

$$= -(t_k - y_k)\frac{\partial f(y_{ink})}{\partial y_{ink}}.\frac{\partial y_k}{\partial w_{jk}}$$

$$= -(t_k - y_k) f'(y_{ink}) z_j \tag{5.2}$$

Let $$\delta_k = (t_k - y_k) f'(y_{ink}) \tag{5.3}$$

For weights connected from input to hidden units:

$$\frac{\partial E}{\partial v_{ij}} = -\sum (t_k - y_k)\frac{\partial y_k}{\partial v_{ij}}$$

$$= -\sum_k (t_k - y_k)\frac{\partial f(y_{ink})}{\partial y_{ink}}.\frac{\partial y_{ink}}{\partial v_{ij}}$$

$$= -\sum_k (t_k - y_k) f'(y_{ink})\frac{\partial (y_{ink})}{\partial z_j}.\frac{\partial z_j}{\partial v_{ij}}$$

$$= -\sum_k \delta_k w_{jk}\frac{\partial f(z_{inj})}{\partial z_{inj}}.\frac{\partial z_{inj}}{\partial v_{ij}}$$

$$= -\sum_k \delta_k w_{jk} f'(z_{inj}).x_i \tag{5.4}$$

Let $$\delta_j = \sum_k \delta_k w_{jk} f'(z_{inj}) \tag{5.5}$$

The change in weights of the output units are given by

$$\Delta w_{jk} = -\alpha \frac{\partial E}{\partial w_{jk}}$$

$$= \alpha \delta_k z_j \tag{5.6}$$

Similarly, the changes in weights for the hidden units are

$$\Delta v_{ij} = -\alpha \frac{\partial E}{\partial v_{ij}}$$
$$= -\alpha \delta_j x_i$$

5.4.4 Training Algorithm

Step 1: Initialize the weights.

Step 2: While stopping condition is false, execute steps 3 to 10.

Step 3: For each training pair x:t, do steps 4 to 9.

Step 4: Each input unit X_i, $i = 1, 2, ..., n$ receives the input signal, x_i and broadcasts it to the next layer.

Step 5: For each hidden layer neuron denoted as Z_j, $j = 1,2, ...,p$.

$$z_{inj} = v_{oj} + \sum_i x_i v_{ij}$$
$$z_j = f(z_{inj})$$

Broadcast z_j to the next layer.

Step 6: For each output neuron Y_k, $k = 1,2,...,m$

$$y_{ink} = w_{ok} + \sum_j z_j w_{jk}$$
$$y_k = f(y_{ink})$$

Step 7: Compute δ_k for each output neuron, Y_k.

$$\delta_k = (t_k - y_k) f'(y_{ink})$$
$$\Delta w_{jk} = \alpha \delta_k z_j$$
$$\Delta w_{ok} = \alpha \delta_k \quad \text{since } z_0 = 1$$

Step 8: For each hidden neuron,

$$\delta_{inj} = \sum_{k=1}^{m} \delta_k w_{jk} \quad j = 1,2,..., p$$
$$\delta_j = \delta_{inj} f'(z_{inj})$$
$$\Delta v_{ij} = \alpha \delta_j x_i$$
$$\Delta v_{oj} = \alpha \delta_j$$

Step 9: Update weights.

$$w_{jk}(\text{new}) = w_{jk}(\text{old}) + \Delta w_{jk}$$
$$v_{ij}(\text{new}) = v_{ij}(\text{old}) + \Delta v_{ij}$$

Step 10: Test for stopping condition.

5.5 CHOICE OF CHOOSING THE VARIOUS PARAMETERS FOR A NETWORK TRAINED BY BACKPROPAGATION [B10, B19, B38, B42]

There are various parameters to be chosen while training a network using the backpropagation algorithm.

5.5.1 Choice of Initial Weights and Bias Random Initialization

This is a means of initializing the weights at random. The choice of initial weights will influence whether the net reaches a global (or only a local) minimum of the error and if so, how fast it converges. Also, the weight updation depends on the derivative of the activation functions of both the upper and lower units. Hence, it is important to choose the initial weights, so that neither the activation function nor its derivative is zero. Also the weights should neither be too large nor too small.

Weights can be initialized within the range (–1, +1) or (– 0.5, + 0.5).

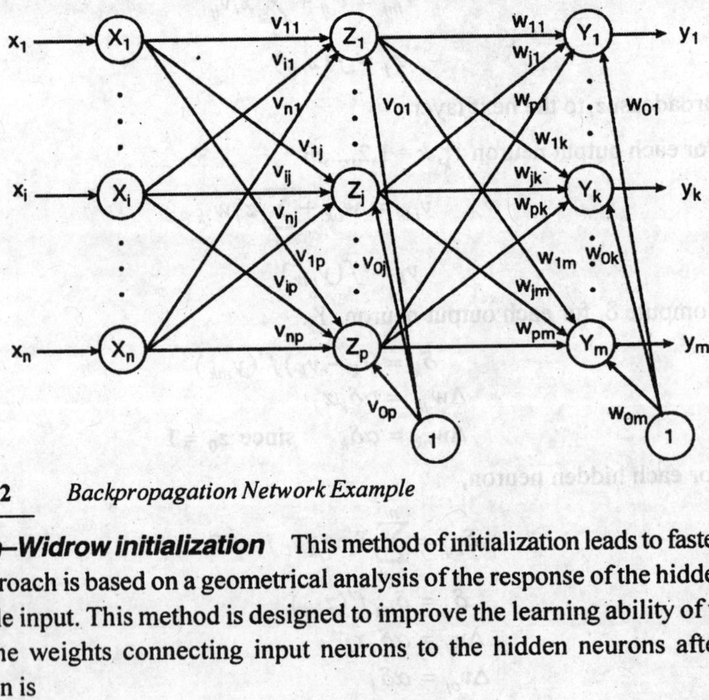

Figure 5.2 *Backpropagation Network Example*

Nyugen–Widrow initialization This method of initialization leads to faster learning. This approach is based on a geometrical analysis of the response of the hidden neurons to a single input. This method is designed to improve the learning ability of the hidden units. The weights connecting input neurons to the hidden neurons after random allocation is

$$V_{ij}(\text{new}) = \beta \frac{V_{ij}(\text{old})}{\left\|\overline{V}_j(\text{old})\right\|} \tag{5.9}$$

where $\overline{V}_j$ is the average weight calculated for all values of i.

Also the scale factor, $\beta = 0.7(p)^{1/n}$ is introduced

where n is the number of input neurons and p is the number of hidden neurons.

5.5.2 Frequency of Weight Updates

There are two approaches for learning viz. per-pattern and per-epoch learning

In per-pattern method, learning occurs after every sample pattern is fed while in per-epoch, learning occurs after every epoch. (An epoch is one cycle through the entire set of training vectors.) The weight changes are accumulated and finally a single change occurs at the end of each epoch in per-epoch training.

$$\wedge w = \sum_{p=1}^{p} \Delta w_p \tag{5.10}$$

The training time can be reduced by exploiting parallelism in per-epoch training, where "p" different processors calculate the weight changes for each pattern independently, followed by a phase in which all errors are paralleled in this manner.

5.5.3 Choice of Learning Rate

Weight changes in backpropagation are proportional to the negative gradient of the error. This guideline determines the relative changes that must occur in different weights when a training sample(s) is presented. But, it does not fix the exact magnitudes of the desired weight changes. These magnitude changes are dependent on the learning rate.

A large learning rate leads to rapid learning but the weights may oscillate, while lower learning rates lead to slower learning.

Methods suggested for adopting learning rate are as follows.

i. A simple heuristic way suggests starting with a large learning rate and steadily decreasing it. Changes to the weight vector must be small in order to reduce oscillations or any divergence (when the net has converged to an optimum). It is expected that larger changes in error would occur earlier at the initial stages while it decreases slowly in later stages.

ii. Another heuristic suggestion is to increase the learning rate in order to improve performance and to decrease the learning rate in order to worsen the performance.

iii. Another means is to double the learning rate until the error value worsens.

5.5.4 Alternative Weight Update Procedure: Momentum Factor

In backpropagation with momentum, the weight change is in a direction that is a combination of the current gradient descent.

This approach is beneficial when some training data are very different from the majority of the data. A learning rate is also chosen appropriately.

The weight update formula used here is:

$$w_{jk}(t+1) = w_{jk} + K\delta_j z_j + \mu[w_{jk} - w_{jk}(t-1)] \text{ or}$$
$$\Delta w_{jk}(t+1) = K\delta_k z_j + \mu\Delta w_{jk}(t) \text{ and}$$
$$v_{ij}(t+1) = v_{ij}(t) + KL_j x_i + \mu[v_{ij}(t) - v_{ij}(t-1)] \text{ or}$$
$$\Delta v_{ij}(t+1) = K\delta_j z_i + \mu[\Delta v_{ij}(t)]$$

where $0 < \mu < 1$.

The momentum factor is added to obtain a faster convergence.

Salient features of using a momentum factor:

i. Reasonable weight adjustments could be made as long as the corrections are in the same direction for several patterns.
ii. Smaller learning rate checks the larger response to the error from the training patterns.
iii. Reduces the possibility of the net to find weights in a local minimum.
iv. With the introduction of the momentum factor, the net proceeds in the direction of the current gradient and the previous direction of the weight corrections.

Limitations of using a momentum factor:

i. Learning rate places the upper limit on the amount by which the weight can be changed.
ii. Momentum factor can cause weight changes to be in a direction that would increase the error.

5.5.5 Number of Hidden Layers and Nodes

For a neural net with more than one hidden layer, the calculations performed for a single layer is repeated for all the layers and are finally summed up. But the number of hidden units required for an application needs to be determined separately. Kolmogorov existence theorem helps to determine the number of hidden layers.

Kolmogorov existence theorem Any continuous function of n variables can be computed by using only linear summations and nonlinear but continuously increasing functions of only one variable.

The theorem states effectively that a three layer perceptron with $n(2n + 1)$ nodes using continuously increasing nonlinearities can compute any continuous function of n variables. A three layer perceptron could then be used to create any continuous likelihood function required in a classifier.

5.5.6 Number of Training Pairs

The number of training pairs required for good training depends on several factors. A rule of thumb obtained from related statistical problems is to have atleast 5 to 10 times as many training samples as the number of weights to be trained. The rule of thumb is summarized as follows:

The question to be answered here is, "Under what circumstances can I be assured of a net, which is trained to classify correctly the testing patterns drawn from the same sample space?". Specifically, if the net is trained to classify the fraction $1-(e/2)$ of the training patterns correctly, where, can I be sure that it will classify $1-e$ of the testing patterns correctly?

The answer is that if there are enough training patterns, the net will be able to generalize as desired. Enough training patterns is given by the condition

$$W/P = e$$

where P is the number of training patterns and W is the number of weights to be trained.

This is the necessary condition. The necessary condition is also given as:

$$P > \frac{|w|}{1-a} \tag{5.11}$$

where a is the expected accuracy for the test set.

The sufficient condition is given as.

$$P \geq \frac{|w|}{1-a} \log \frac{n}{1-a} \tag{5.12}$$

where n is the number of nodes.

5.5.7 Generalizability

For a large network, it is possible that repeated training iterations improve the learning of the net, but the resulting network may perform poorly for test data. This phenomenon is called overtraining.

One solution as suggested by Hecht–Nielsen (1990) is to monitor the error on the test set and terminate the training when the error increases. Training may also be halted even when the network performance on the training set continues to improve.

To eliminate random fluctuations, the performance of the network over the test is monitored over several iterations. Weight changes are computed solely on the basis of network's performance on the training data. With this stopping criterion, final weights depend on the test data in an indirect manner. Since the weights are not obtained from the current test data, it is expected that the net will continue to perform well on future test data.

A net with large number of nodes is capable of memorizing the training set at the expense of generalization. Hence, smaller nets are preferred over larger ones.

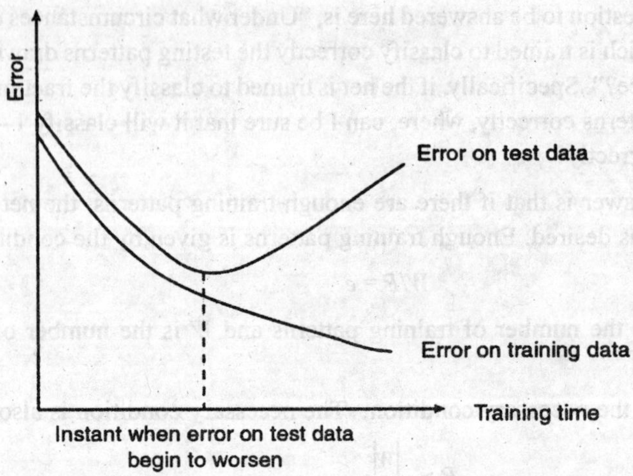

Figure 5.3 *Change in Error with Training Time, on Training Set and Test Set*

Another useful means to improve generalization is to introduce noise in the training set.

5.5.8 Adaptive Learning Rates

Weight changes in the standard backpropagation algorithm occurs in the direction of the most rapid decrease of the error surface for the current weights. In general, this does not move the weights directly towards the optimal weight vector. A variety of methods have been suggested to modify the direction of weight adjustment.

One way to improve the training speed is to change the learning rate. Another method is based on the determination of the maximum safe set "p" size at each stage of training. This method provides protection against overshoot of minimum error that can occur in other forms of backpropagation.

The most extensive work deals with the "risk-taking" algorithms. An extension of this type of algorithm is the delta-bar-delta approach.

Delta-bar-delta The general approach is to allow each weight to have its own learning rate and allow the learning rate to vary as training takes place. In addition to these assumptions, two heuristic approaches are used to determine changes in learning rate for each weight. If the weight change is in the same direction, the learning rate for that weight increases otherwise it decreases.

The delta-bar-delta rule consists of a weight update and a learning rate update rule. The weight update rule is:

$$\begin{aligned} w_{jk}(t+1) &= w_{jk}(t) - \alpha j_k(t+1)\frac{\partial E}{\partial w_{jk}} \\ &= w_{jk}(t) + \alpha j_k(t+1)\delta_k z_j \end{aligned} \tag{5.13}$$

where $w_{jk}(t)$ is the arbitrary weight at time t

$\delta_{jk}(t)$ is the learning rate for that weight at time t

E is the squared error for the pattern presented at time t

Here, the direction of weight change is no longer in the direction of the negative gradient.

For each output unit, "delta" is $\Delta_{jk} = \dfrac{\partial E}{\partial w_{ij}} = -\delta_k z_j$

and "delta-bar" is $\Delta_{jk}(t) = (1-\beta)\Delta_{jk}(t) + \beta\Delta_{jk}(t-1)$ (5.14)

For each hidden unit, $\Delta_{ij} = \dfrac{\partial E}{\partial_{vij}} = -\delta_{jxi}$

$$\Delta_{jk}(t) = (1-\beta)\Delta_{jk}(t) + \beta\Delta_{jk}(t-1); 0 < \beta < 1 \tag{5.15}$$

If $\Delta_{jk}(t-1)$ and $\Delta_{ij}(t)$ and are of the same sign, then the learning rate is increased otherwise it is decreased. The new learning rate is given by,

$$\alpha_{jk}(t+1) = \begin{cases} \beta_{jk}(t) + k; & \text{if } \Delta_{jk}(t-1)\Delta_{jk}(t) > 0 \\ (1-\alpha)\alpha_{jk}(t); & \text{if } \Delta_{jk}(t) < 0 \\ \alpha_{jk}(t); & \text{otherwise} \end{cases}$$

The parameters k and β must be specified by the user.

5.6 STRICTLY LOCAL BACKPROPAGATION [B7, B16]

Backpropagation has been lacking biological plausibility regarding the sharing of information among processors. The strictly local backpropagation overcomes these drawbacks. A strictly local backpropagation net has 3 types of units: cortical units, synaptic units and thalamic units.

A cortical unit sums its inputs and sends the result as a signal to the next unit above it.

5.6.1 Architecture

The function of a synaptic unit is to receive a single input signal from the cortical unit, apply an activation function, multiply the result by a weight and pass the result to a single thalamic unit above. The identity function is used as the activation function. The weight for each output synaptic unit is 1. The thalamic unit compares the computed output with the target and sends an appropriate error signal (if any) to each output synaptic unit. The error signal multiplied by its weight, and the derivative of the activation function are sent to the cortical unit.

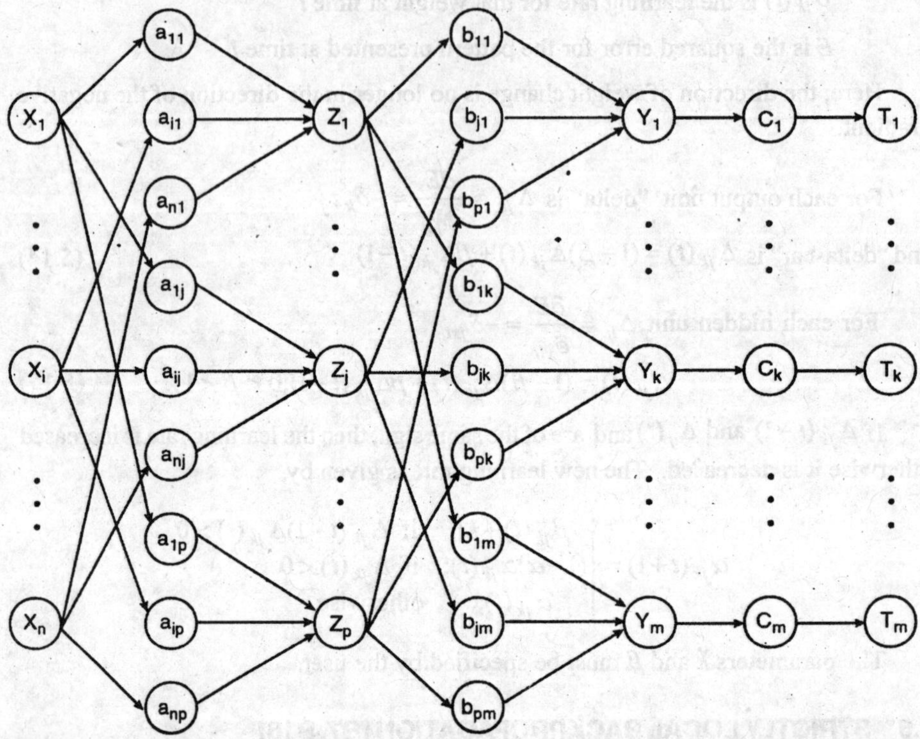

Figure 5.4 *Strictly Local Backpropagation Network*

Finally, the hidden cortical unit sums its inputs and passes it on to the input synaptic unit, which then computes the weight update term. Other variations can also be brought into this net and it could also be expanded to overcome various other biological implausibilities.

5.6.2 Algorithm

The strictly local backpropagation algorithm involves three stages:

i. Feedforward
ii. Backpropagation of error
iii. Weight update

Feedforward stage

i. The input cortical unit receives the input signal and passes it to the input synaptic unit.
ii. The input synaptic unit multiplies the signal with the weight and passes it on to the hidden cortical unit.

iii. The signal is summed up and sent to the hidden synaptic unit.

iv. The activation function is applied to the signal and is then multiplied by the weight.

v. The signals are then summed up.

vi. In the output synaptic unit, th ıctivation function is applied and the output is passed on to the thalamic unit.

Backpropagation of error

vii. Calculate the error.

viii. The derivative of the activation function is multiplied with the error.

ix. The output cortical unit sends the input δ_k to the units below it.

x. In the hidden synaptic unit, weight correction is calculated and is then multiplied by the weight and the derivative of the activation function.

xi. The hidden cortical unit sums up the inputs from the units above.

xii. The weight correction (updation) is calculated in the input synaptic unit.

xiii. The weights are finally updated.

xiv. Training is terminated.

Example 5.1 For the neural network shown in Fig. 5.5, with the initial data (weights), determine the new weights after applying the sample (0, 0) once. Assume learning rate as 0.3 and the activation function for the hidden and output neurons as $\frac{1}{1+e^{-x}}$.

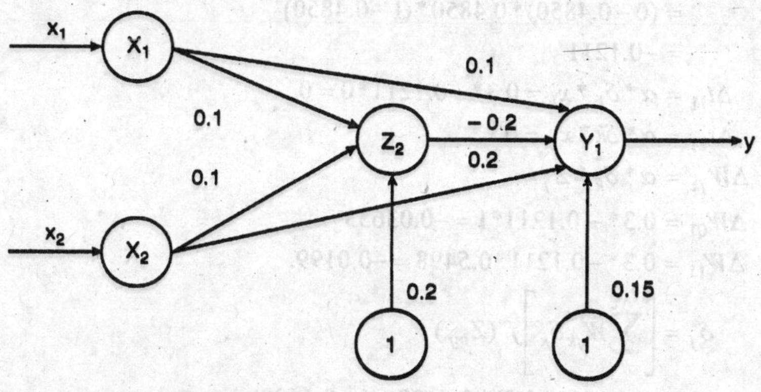

Figure 5.5 *Network for Example 5.1*

Solution

Given :

$V_{11} = V_{21} = 0.1$

$t_{11} = 0.1$

$t_{21} = 0.2$

$W_{11} = -0.2$

$W_{01} = 0.15$

$V_{01} = 0.2$

Learning rate, $\alpha = 0.3$

Activation function, $f(x) = \dfrac{1}{1+e^{-x}}$

First Epoch:

For the first sample (0, 0) the target is 0.

Learning rate, $\alpha = 0.3$

$$\begin{aligned}
Z_{in1} &= (0.1 * x_1) + (0.1 * x_2) + (1 * 0.2) \\
&= (0.1 * 0) + (0.1 * 0) + (1 * 0.2) \\
&= 0.2 \\
Z_1 &= \frac{1}{1+e^{-z_{in1}}} = \frac{1}{1+e^{-0.2}} = 0.5498 \\
y_{in1} &= -0.2 * 0.4502 + 0.1 * 0 + 0.1 * 0 + 0.15 \\
&= 0.05996 \\
y_1 &= \frac{1}{1+e^{0.05996}} = 0.4850 \\
\delta_k &= (t - y_1) * y_1 * (1 - y_1) \\
&= (0 - 0.4850) * 0.4850 * (1 - 0.4850) \\
&= -0.1211 \\
\Delta t_{11} &= \alpha * \delta_k * x_1 = 0.3 * -0.1211 * 0 = 0 \\
\Delta t_{21} &= \alpha * \delta k * x_2 = 0 \\
\Delta W_{jk} &= \alpha * \delta_k * Z_j \\
\Delta W_{01} &= 0.3 * -0.1211 * 1 = -0.03633 \\
\Delta W_{11} &= 0.3 * -0.1211 * 0.5498 = -0.0199. \\
\delta_j &= \left[\sum_k W_{jk} \delta_k\right] f'(Z_{inj}) \\
\delta_1 &= (-0.1211 * 0.2) * 0.5498 * (1 - 0.5498) \\
&= -0.00599 \\
\Delta V_{ij} &= \alpha * \delta_j * x_j \\
\Delta V_{11} &= 0.3 * 0.00599 * 0 = 0 \\
\Delta V_{21} &= 0 \\
\Delta V_{01} &= 0.3 * 0.00599 = 0.00001798 \\
V_{ij}(\text{new}) &= V_{ij}(\text{old}) + \alpha * \delta_j * x_j \\
V_{11}(\text{new}) &= 0.1 + 0 = 0.1 \\
V_{21}(\text{new}) &= 0.1
\end{aligned}$$

$$V_{01}(\text{new}) = 0.2 + m0.0001798 = 0.2001798$$
$$W_{jk}(\text{new}) = W_{jk}(\text{old}) + \alpha * \delta_k * Z_j$$
$$W_{11}(\text{new}) = -0.2 - 0.01997 = -0.21997$$
$$W_{01}(\text{new}) = 0.5 - 0.03637 = 0.1133$$
$$t_{11}(\text{new}) = 0.1; t_{12}(\text{new}) = 0.2$$

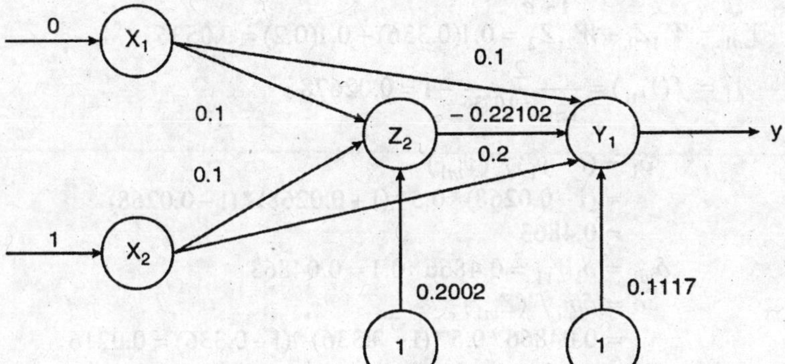

Figure 5.6 *Network After One Sample Pass*

Example 5.2 Find the new weights when the net shown below is presented the input pattern (1 1 1) and the target output is 1. Use a learning rate of 0.1 and bipolar sigmoidal activation function. The bias is set to 1.

Solution

Activation function: $f(x) = \dfrac{2}{1+e^{-x}} - 1$ and $f'(x) = 0.5(1 + f(x))\,(1 - f(x))$.

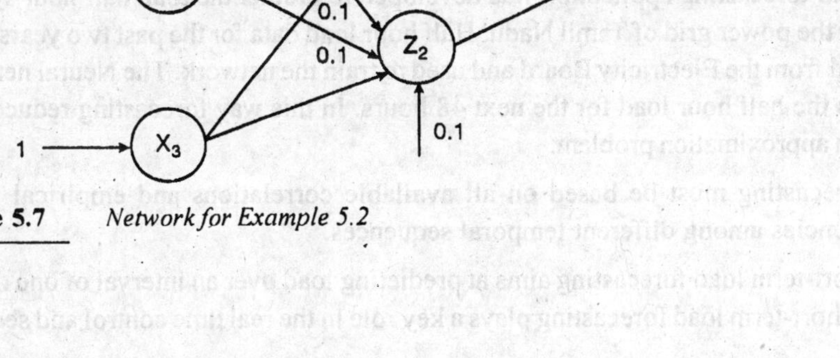

Figure 5.7 *Network for Example 5.2*

$$Z_{in1} = V_{01} + \sum_{i=1}^{3} x_i V_{1i} = 0.1+0.2+0.2+0.2 = 0.7$$

$$Z_1 = f(Z_{in1}) = \frac{2}{1+e^{-0.7}} - 1 = 0.336$$

$$Z_{in2} = 0.1+0.1+0.1+0.1 = 0.4$$

$$Z_2 = f(Z_{in2}) = \frac{2}{1+e^{-0.4}} - 1 = 0.1974$$

$$Y_{in1} = W_{11}Z_1 + W_{21}Z_2 = 0.1(0.336)+0.1(0.2) = 0.0536$$

$$Y_1 = f(Y_{in1}) = \frac{2}{1+e^{-0.0536}} - 1 = 0.02678$$

$$\begin{aligned}
\delta_1 &= (t-y_1)f'(y_{in1}) \\
&= (1-0.0268)*0.5*(1+0.0268)*(1-0.0268) \\
&= 0.4863 \\
\delta_{in1} &= \delta_1 W_{11} = 0.4866*0.1 = 0.04863 \\
\delta &= \delta in_1 f'(Z_{in1}) \\
&= 0.04866*0.5*(1+0.336)*(1-0.336) = 0.0216 \\
\Delta V_{11} &= \alpha*\delta*x1 = 0.1*0.0216*1 = 0.00216 \\
\Delta V_{21} &= \alpha*\delta*x2 = 0.1*0.0216*1 = 0.00216 \\
\Delta V_{31} &= \alpha*\delta*x3 = 0.1*0.0216*1 = 0.00216 \\
\Delta V_{01} &= \alpha*\delta = 0.1*0.0216 = 0.00216 \\
V_{11}(\text{new}) &= V_{11}(\text{old}) + \Delta V_{11} = 0.2+0.00216 = 0.20216 \\
V_{21}(\text{new}) &= V_{21}(\text{old}) + \Delta V_{21} = 0.2+0.00216 = 0.20216 \\
V_{31}(\text{new}) &= V_{31}(\text{old}) + \Delta V_{01} = 0.1+0.00216 = 0.10216
\end{aligned}$$

Thus the new weights are $V_{11} = V_{21} = 0.20216$, $V_3 = 0.10216$

and $V_{01} = 0.10216$.

5.7 APPLICATIONS OF BACKPROPAGATION ALGORITHM

5.7.1 Short-term Load Forecasting

Load forecasting is an essential tool for operation and planning of power systems. It is required for unit commitment, energy transfer scheduling and load dispatch. A short term load forecasting application was developed to predict the total half hour system load for the power grid of Tamil Nadu. Half hour load data for the past two years were obtained from the Electricity Board and used to train the network. The Neural network predicts the half hour load for the next 48 hours. In this way forecasting reduces the function approximation problem.

Forecasting must be based on all available correlations and empirical inter-dependencies among different temporal sequences.

Short-term load forecasting aims at predicting load over an interval of one day or week. Short-term load forecasting plays a key role in the real time control and security functions of an energy management system. Short term power system load is mainly dependent on nonlinear combinations of variables that can be classified according to their dependence on weather, social and seasonal factors. Temperature and humidity are the most dependent weather factors. Social variables that affect the system load include daily human activities such as work, school and environment. Variations in load requirement results from seasonal changes and demographic factors.

Load is forecast using back propagation algorithm. Input data processing is introduced in order to improve forecast accuracy.

The schemes used in developing the Artificial Neural Networks:

(a) Selection of an appropriate Artificial Neural Networks
(b) Selection of nonlinear transformation of direct inputs as additional Artificial Neural Network input variables
(c) The training process which eliminated the need for online update of neural network parameters.

Training The input pattern consists of 59 variables for the previous day, denoted by I and forecast day denoted by $I+1$. For the Ith day we have 48 half hourly loads P_i, maximum, minimum and average loads for the Ith day, load factor, maximum temperature, humidity for four timings of the day.

The output pattern consists of 48 half hourly forecasted loads for day $(I+1)$th day.

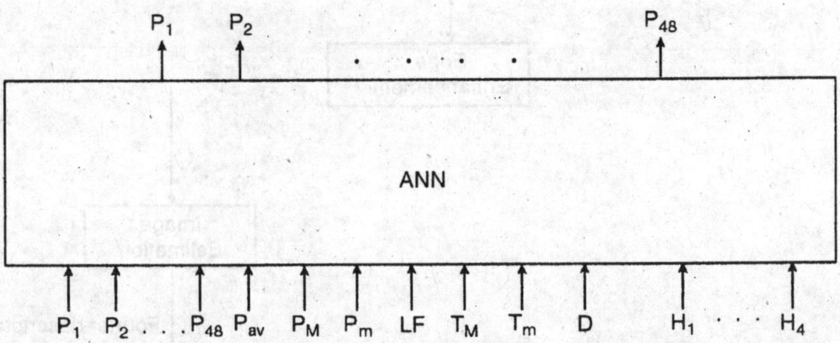

P_i	-	half-hour load (MW)	LF	-	Load Factor
P_{av}	-	Average load (MW)	T_M	-	Maximum temperature
P_M	-	Maximum Load (MW)	T_m	-	Minimum temperature
P_m	-	Minimum Load (MW)	D	-	Type of day
H_i	-	Humidity			

Figure 5.8

The data of two years was used for training the network.. The above network was trained using the data samples of one year while the other year's data was used for testing. The input to the network were normalized in the range of (0,1).

The above neural network was trained to do the forecasting accurately. Preprocessing of input data was introduced to improve the accuracy of forecast.

5.7.2 Image Processing

The role of input is vital to recognise objects. It forms a part of computer vision. The objects have to be acquired, digitized and further processed to provide useful information.

Image acquisition is done using image sensors like point sensors, linear sensors and two dimensional sensors. The analog information on the intensity of image is passed through digitizers and suitable utilities for preprocessing.

The process of edge enhancement permits the elimination of irrelevant information in the digitized images, thus facilitating the recognition of objects. In edge enhancement, image processing is done by edge detection where it separates the object from its background and extracts the contour of the object.

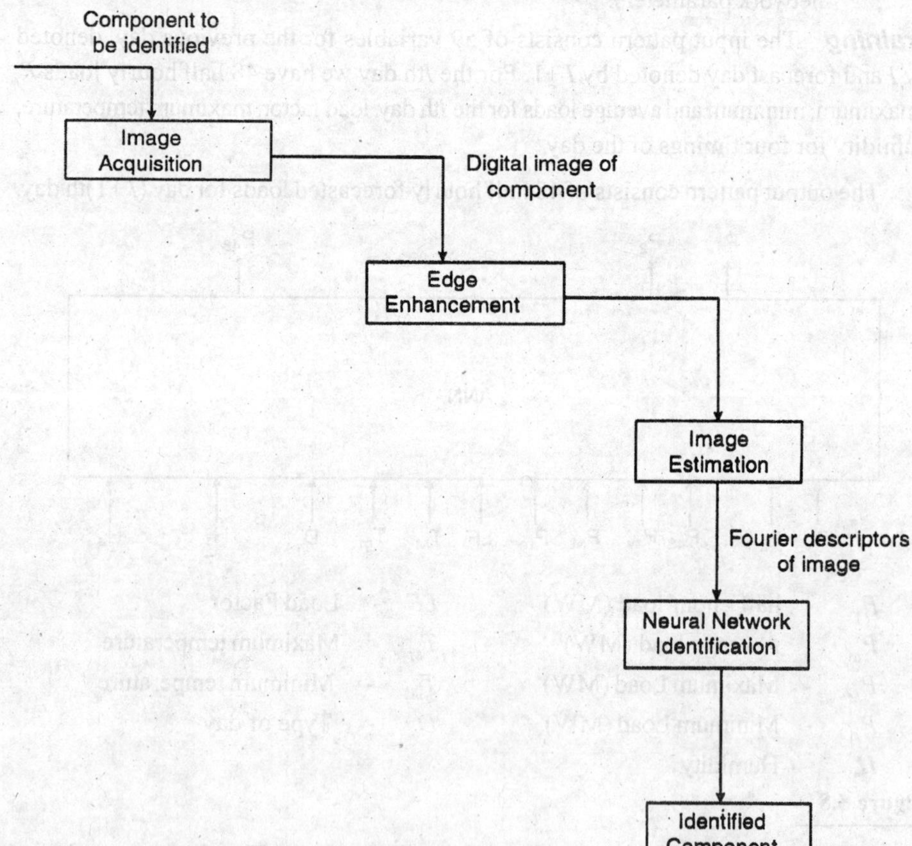

Figure 5.9 *Schematic Sketch for Image Processing*

5.7.3 Online Motor Fault Detection

The internal faults in motor especially turn to turn faults can be determined by using neural networks. The motor characteristics viz. current and speed varies as turn to turn faults occur. A turn to turn fault is simulated and the motor performance characteristics under fault condition are analyzed. The artificial neural network is trained by using back propagation algorithm with the load test readings. The current and speed are measured and given as inputs to trained neural network through analog to digital converter card.

The possibility of incipient faults is inherent in the machines due to stress involved in the conversion of electrical energy to mechanical energy and vice versa. Early fault detection allows preventive maintenance to be scheduled for the machines that might not ordinarily be due to service. Electric motor can fail both mechanically and electrically. Electrical failures are about failure of the electrical insulation system since the copper conductors do not lose their ability to carry current.

The electrical insulation may be of primary insulation, phase to phase insulation and turn to turn insulation. Deterioration of turn to turn insulation is a major cause of motor failures. The reasons for deterioration may be differential thermal stress, differential coefficient of expansion, or magnetic force due to winding currents.

The various fault detection methods aid in achieving continuous online fault detection of motors. The various methods include radio frequency monitoring, particle analysis method, meggar test and surge comparison testing.

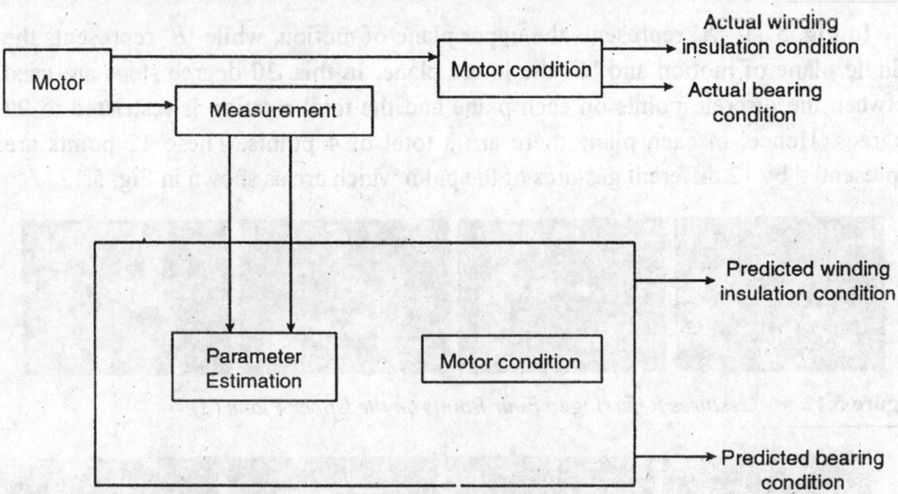

Figure 5.10 *Schematic Sketch for Online Motor Fault Detection*

Thus this scheme serves as a useful means of online fault detection. In real time applications where a faulty motor has to be replaced, the application serves a useful purpose.

5.7.4 Gesture Recognition

Gesture recognition has for long been considered as one of the most futuristic options of Artificial Intelligence and user interface.

Gestures can be defined as the use of motions of the limbs or the body as a means of expression or the movement of the body or limb that expresses or emphasizes an idea, sentiment or attitude.

A simple code language is used to move to various positions. The whole scope of the movement of the arm is as shown in Fig. 5.11.

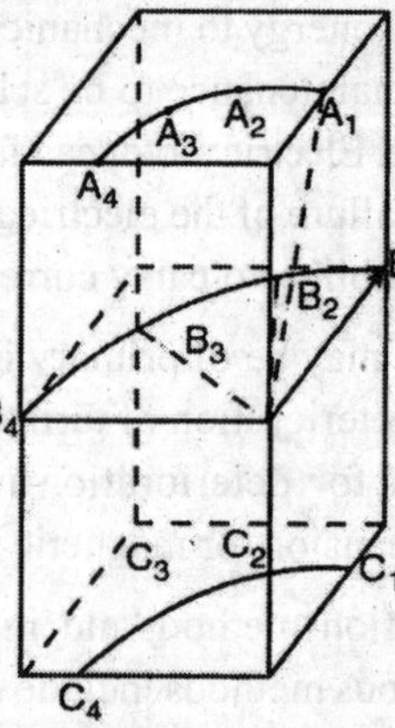

Figure 5.11 *Scope of Movement of the Arm*

In Fig. 5.11, '*A*' represents the upper plane of motion, while '*B*' represents the middle plane of motion and '*C*' the lower plane. In this, 30 degree steps are used between the discrete points on each plane and the total rotation is restricted to 90 degrees. Hence, in each plane there are a total of 4 points. These 12 points are represented by 12 different gestures of the palm which are as shown in Fig. 5.12.

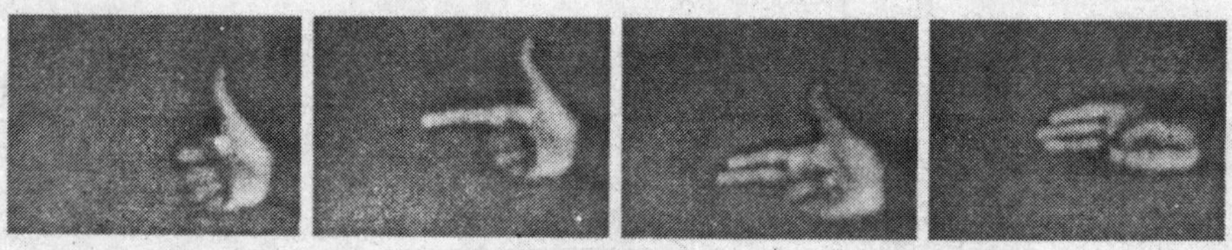

Figure 5.12 a *Gestures Referring to Four Points on the Upper Plane (A)*

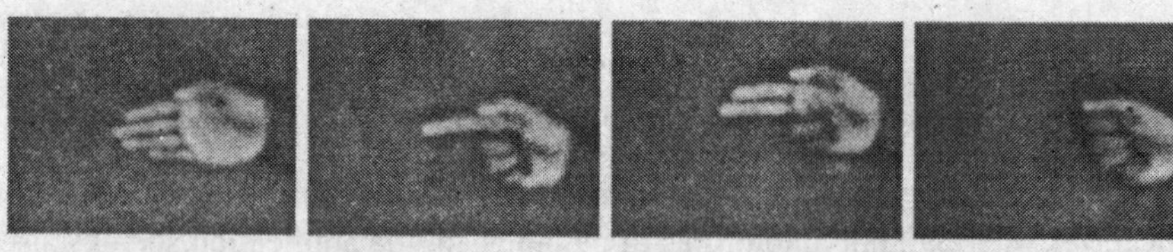

Figure 5.12 b *Gestures Referring to Four Points on the Middle Plane (B)*

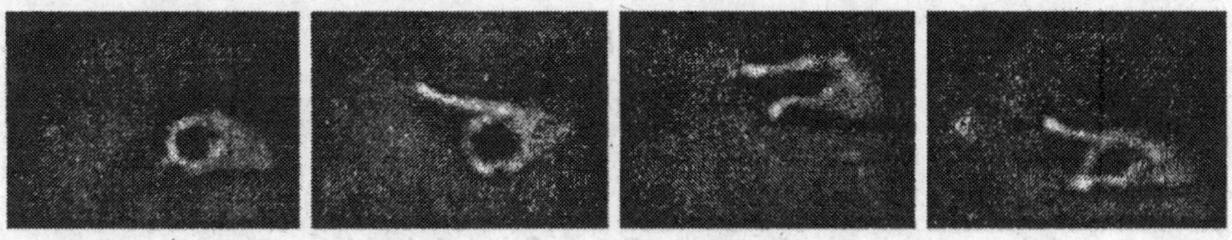

Figure 5.12 c *Gestures Referring to Four Points on the Lower Plane (C)*

12 sets of similar gestures at various locations, using the same experimental set-up, constant illumination parameters and in the same working area are taken and used for training.

The constant illumination parameters for the images representing 12 gestures are given in Table 1.

Table 1 Illumination Parameters

Background : Black	
Contrast	120
Saturation	130
Brightness	120
Exposure	189
Gain	70
White balance	255

In the case of true RGB images, the intensities of the red, green, blue components are separated and the mean, median and standard deviation for the whole image are calculated. Along with this, the mean, median and standard deviation for the luminosity of the image are found. Each gesture is represented by a total of 12 parameters.

Back Propogation network has always been a widely used method in the case of supervised training schemes. Such methods work well with clustering type of problems. In this case, the various gestures are classified into 12 different clusters, representing 12 different points on the 3-D working plane. This problem requires 12 input neurons and 12 output neurons in the case of RGB images. The hidden neurons are fixed through trial and error method for efficient training. Along with the conventional BP network, a simple scheme is suggested for improving the training of the network.

In conventional methods, the learning rate of the neurons is fixed at a particular value. Here, a new adaptive learning rate scheme is used wherein the learning rate of each and every neuron is different and fixed by a scheme considering the weights connected to that neuron and the output of the same.

$$L_h[j] = \frac{\sum W[i][j]}{\sum [W[i][j]]^2} H[j] \tag{5.16}$$

$$L_o[k] = \frac{\sum V[j][k]}{\sum [V[j][k]]^2} C[k] \tag{5.17}$$

where

$L_h[j]$ represents the Learning Rate of the jth hidden neuron.

$L_o[k]$ represents the Learning Rate of the kth output neuron.

$W[i][j]$ represents the weight connected from ith input neuron to jth hidden neuron.

$V[j][k]$ represents the weight connected from jth hidden neuron to kth output neuron.

$H[j]$ represents output of the jth hidden neuron.

$C[k]$ represents output of the kth output neuron.

In this scheme, the learning rate is updated only when the cumulative error of the present epoch is less than the cumulative error of the previous epoch, otherwise the learning rates of the previous epoch are retained.

Using this scheme, the network is trained and the results are compared with conventional method and tabulated in Table 2. The Cumulative Error Vs Epoch graph is shown in Fig. 5.13.

Table 2 Comparison of Proposed Scheme with Conventional BP

Input Neurons : 12	Hidden Neurons : 12	Output Neuron : 12
Momentum Factor = 0.7	Activation function : Binary Sigmoidal	
Parameters	Conventional BP **(Learning Rate = 0.1)**	Proposed BP
Mean Epoch	15746.833008	4485.919922
Max Epoch	18061.000000	4923.000000
Min Epoch	14161.000000	4019.000000
SD	980.503906	204.222519

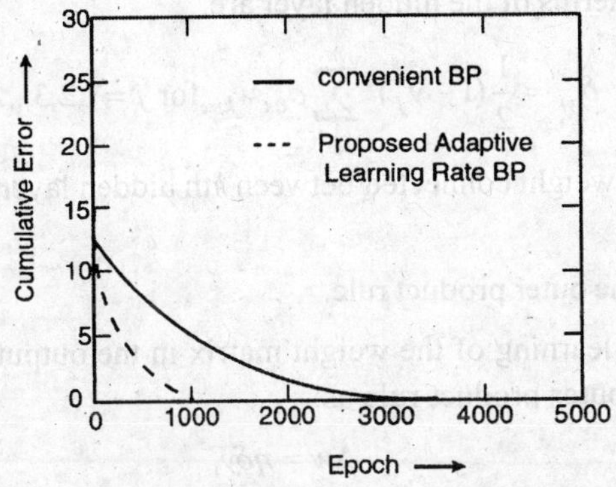

Figure 5.13 *Cumulative Error Versus Epoch*

SHORT QUESTIONS AND ANSWERS

1. **Justify the term 'backpropagation algorithm'.**

   In a backpropagation network, the input samples are fed to the system (network), the error is propagated back to the input layer from the output layer and then the weights are updated. Since the error is propagated back to the input layer, before weight updation, the algorithm is referred to as 'backpropagation algorithm'.

   What are the steps involved in backpropagation algorithm?

   Backpropagation algorithm involves the following steps in the training process:

   1. **The learning begins with the feedforward phase.**
   2. **Error signal are determined.**
   3. **The error gradients are calculated.**
   4. **Finally, the weights are updated.**

3. **Briefly explain the stopping condition for the learning process.**

   During the training process of a backpropagation network, the cumulative cycle error of input to output mapping is computed as a sum of all continuous output errors in the entire training set. The final error value for the entire training cycle is calculated after each completed pass through the training set. The learning process stops when the final error value is less than tolerance value.

4. **Give the error signal term for a two layer network.**

   The error signal term of the output layer are:

$$\delta_{ok} = \frac{1}{2}(t_k - y_k)(1 - y^2{}_k) \text{ for } k = 1,2,3,\dots, m$$

where t_k is the target sample

$yk = f(y_{ink})$ where y_{ink} is the sum of weighted inputs to kth output neuron.

The error signal terms of the hidden layer are:

$$\delta_{yj} = \frac{1}{2}(1-y_j)^2 \sum_{k=1}^{m} \delta_{ok} w_{kj} \quad \text{for } j = 1,2,3,\ldots, p$$

where w_{kj} is the weight connected between kth hidden layer neuron and jth layer neuron.

5. Explain briefly the outer product rule.

   The incremental learning of the weight matrix in the output and hidden layer is obtained by the outer product rule as:

$$\Delta w = \eta \delta y_t$$

   where δ is the error signal vector of a layer,

   y_t is the input signal vector to that layer.

6. What is meant by cumulative error computation?

   For the purpose of assessing the quality and success of training, the cumulative error must be computed for the entire batch of training patterns. The cumulative error is computed over the error backpropagation training cycle and is expressed as a quadratic error.

$$E = \frac{1}{2} \sum_{p=1}^{p} \sum_{k=1}^{k} (t_{pk} - y_{pk})^2$$

7. What is meant by root mean square normalized error?

   Cumulative error computation is not suitable for comparison of networks with different number of training patterns P, and having a different number of output neurons. For networks with same number of outputs k, the root mean square normalized error, E_{rms}, is computed as shown below.

$$E_{rms} = \frac{1}{pk} \sqrt{\sum_{p=1}^{p} \sum_{k=1}^{k} (t_{pk} - y_{pk})^2}$$

8. Define the term 'decision error'.

   The 'decision error' reflects the accuracy of neural network classifiers. The decision error is defined as:

$$E_d = \frac{N_{err}}{pk}$$

   where N_{err} is the total number of bit errors resulting at k threshold outputs over the complete training cycle and P is the number of training samples.

9. What is meant by threshold logic unit?

   The activation block of a neuron can be represented by a discrete neuron functional block diagram consisting of a summing node and the limiting thresholding function which is known as threshold logic unit (TLU).

10. Give the reasons for failure in approximation applications of a backpropagation neural network.

The reasons for failure in approximation applications can be attributed to:

a. Incomplete learning,
b. Inadequate (too high or too low) number of hidden neurons,.
c. Lack of a deterministic relationship between the input and target output values used for training.

11. What are the possibilities for the prevention of failure in approximation application of a backpropagation network?

The possible solutions for the prevention of failure in approximation applications are:

a. If the functions to approximate are not bounded and cannot be properly scaled, the use of the linear mapping by the second layer may offer a solution.
b. The ordinary 'sigmoidal' activation function can be replaced by the simple identity activation function of the output neurons.

12. What is meant by credit assignment?

The essence of the error backpropagation algorithm is the evaluation of the contribution of each particular weight to the output error. This is often referred to as a problem of credit assignment. Since the objective function of a neural network contains continuously differentiable functions of weights, the evaluation of credit assignment can be easily accomplished numerically.

13. What are the difficulties encountered while training a backpropagation network?

The implementation of backpropagation algorithm may encounter different difficulties such as:

a. Error minimization procedure may produce only a local minima.
b. Time taken by the network to learn is variable.

14. What is meant by local minima?

While training a network by backpropagation algorithm it is possible that the training phase is stopped at local minima, with the assumption that it is the actual minima, when in reality it is not. This may result in improperly trained network and the output will not be satisfactory.

15. When is the training of a network stopped?

While the network is trained by backpropagation algorithm, for each iteration the error value is calculated. The computed mean square error is compared with the previous epoch values. The training is stopped when the error value begins to rise, after it had been decreasing steadily as the net begins to memorize and lose its generalization property.

16. 'Local minima are not a major problem in backpropagation training'-Explain.

    The stochastic nature of the backpropagation algorithm holds the key for local minima and it is not a major problem in the training procedure. The square error surfaces produced for various input patterns are random. The larger the neural network, the better the training outcome.

17. What are the factors that improve the convergence of the training?

    a. Statistical nature of inputs and outputs.

    b. Superposition of noise with the zero mean value that can increase the efficiency of training process when the inputs are purely deterministic.

18. 'Choice of initial weights play a major role in training procedures'-Elucidate.

    The weights of the network to be trained are typically initialized with small random values. The initialization strongly affects the ultimate solution because:

    (i) Equal weights initialization for unequal weights solution may not train the net properly.

    (ii) Error may stabilize and continuing the training beyond a certain low error plateau results in undesirable shift of weights.

19. What is meant by incremental learning and gradient descent on minimization?

    The backpropagation learning error based on a single pattern error reduction requires a small adjustment of weights which follows each presentation of the training pattern. This scheme is called incremental updating. The backpropagation learning also implements the gradient-like descent minimization of the overall error function computed over the complete cycle of 'p' presentations provided the learning is constant, and η is sufficiently small.

20. Give the advantages of incremental updating technique.

    a. The algorithm implements a true gradient descent downhill of the error surface.

    b. During the computer simulation, the weight adjustments determined by the algorithm need not be stored and gradually compounded.

21. What is the drawback of incremental learning?

    The network trained by incremental learning may be skewed towards the most recent patterns in the cycle. To counteract this specific pattern, either a small learning constant η should be used or cumulative weight changes must be imposed.

22. What is the effect of weight adjustment in proportion to the derivative of activation function?

    Since the weights are adjusted in proportion to the value of derivative of activation function, f' (net), weights that are connected to units responding in their mid range are mostly changed. The weights of uncommitted neurons with certain responses are thus affected more strongly than those of neurons that are already heavily turned on or turned off.

23. What is the main drawback of gradient-based optimization schemes?

The effectiveness and convergence of error backpropagation algorithm depends significantly on learning constant. However, the optimum value of the learning constant depends on the problem being solved and there is no single learning constant value suitable for different training cases—a common problem with all gradient-based optimization schemes. The error surfaces frequently possess properties that make the procedures slow to converge.

24. What is the purpose of momentum method?

The purpose of the momentum method is to accelerate the convergence of error propagation algorithm. This method supplements the current weight adjustment with a fraction of the most recent weight adjustment.

25. Why is gradient descent method chosen to minimize error, E?

One way to minimize E is based on the gradient descent method. Since the output of the kth output layer node, y_k depends on the network weights, E is also a function of the network weights. According to gradient descent, the direction of weight change of w, should be in the same direction of $-\frac{\partial E}{\partial w}$.

26. Define 'cross-talk' when referred to training a network.

The inability to obtain appropriate weights is partly due to a phenomenon called 'cross-talk' which is defined as follows: "Learning is unsuccessful because different training samples require conflicting changes made to the same weight." If there is a separate output node for each class, each weight on the outer layer can focus on learning a specific task, rather than on performing multiple duties.

27. "Initial weights are generally chosen to be small" - Why?

Training is generally commenced with randomly chosen initial weight values, typically small in magnitude (–1.0 to 1.0 or – 0.5 to 0.5), since larger weight magnitudes may drive the output of layer 1 nodes to saturation, requiring large amounts of training time to emerge from the saturated state; this phenomenon results from the behaviour of sigmoid functions.

28. What are the various possible methods of initialization of weight?

   i. Random initialization,
   ii. Nyugen – Widrow initialization

29. What are the two methods of weight updation?

The two methods of weight update or learning are:

   i. Per-pattern learning
   ii. Per-epoch learning

30. **Give details about a few techniques for proper choice of learning rate.**

    The following are some of the methods suggested for adapting the learning rate as computation proceeds:

    a. A simple heuristic is to begin with a large value for η in the early iterations and steadily decrease it.

    b. Another heuristic is to increase η at every iteration that improves performance by some significant amount and to decrease η at every iteration that worsens performance by some significant amount.

    c. One method is to adjust the value of the learning rate, based on the principle of steadily doubling the learning rate, until the error value worsens.

       $i = 0$; $w_{new} = -E'(w)t$;
       while $E(w_{new}) < E(w)$ do
       $i = i + 1$; $w = w_{new}$;
       $w_{new} = w - E'(w)2^i t$
       end while.

       We then choose $\eta = 2^{i-1}t$ as the largest learning rate.

    d. Based on the second derivative of the error measure which provides information regarding the rate with which the first directive changes.

31. **Define the property of 'over-training'.**

    It is possible that repeated training iterations in a large network improve the performance of the network on training data (eg. by "memorizing" training samples), but the resulting network may perform poorly on test data. This phenomenon is called over-training.

32. **Give a method to monitor the performance of the network.**

    Hetch-Nielson proposed that the weights should be adjusted only on the basis of the training set, but the error should be monitored on the test set. Training continues as long as the error on the test set continues to decrease and is terminated if the error on the test set increases.

33. **How is it possible to prevent random fluctuations?**

    To prevent random fluctuations, performance over the test set is monitored over several iterations. This method does not suggest using the test data for training. Weight changes are computed solely on the basis of the network's performance on training data.

34. **Why are smaller nets preferred over larger nets?**

    A network with large number of nodes (and therefore edges) is capable of memorizing the training set but may not generalize well. For this reason, networks of smaller sizes are preferred over larger networks. Thus, over-training can be avoided by using networks with a small number of parameters (hidden nodes and weights).

35. What is Lippmann's approach for hidden layers and nodes?

Lippmann pointed out that for classifying tasks solved using a feedforward neural network with d input nodes, the hidden layer nodes often function as hyper planes that effectively partition d-dimensional space into various regions. Each node in the next layer represents a cluster of points that belong to the same class.

36. How many samples are needed for good training?

As a rule of thumb, it is advisable to have atleast five to ten times as many training samples as the weights to be trained. Baum and Hawsker suggested the following method, on the basis of the desired accuracy on the test set.

$$P > \frac{|w|}{(1-a)}$$

where

P = (desired) number of patterns,

$|w|$ = number of weights to be trained and

a = expected accuracy on the test set.

A sufficient condition that answer performance is:

$$P \geq \frac{|w|}{(1-a)} \log \frac{n}{1-a}$$

where n is the number of nodes.

REVIEW QUESTIONS

1. How is weight adjustment done in backpropagation network?
2. Draw the architecture of a backpropagation network.
3. What are the activation functions commonly used in backpropagation network?
4. Mention the methods by which initial weights can be determined for a backpropagation algorithm.
5. What is Nyugen – Widrow rule?
6. What are the methods involved in determining the learning rate in a backpropagation algorithm.
7. Define momentum factor.
8. What are the salient features of using momentum factor?
9. What are the limitations of using momentum factor?
10. State Kolmogrov existence theorem.
11. Explain delta-bar-delta approach.
12. Draw the architecture of a strictly local backpropagation network.

13. What are the stages involved in the training of a strictly local backpropagation algorithm?
14. What are non sigmoidal activation functions?
15. Differentiate between standard backpropagation and strictly local back propagation algorithm.
16. Is it true that "winner takes all" paradigm can have many inputs but only one output?

CHAPTER

6

Adaptive Resonance Theory

6.1 INTRODUCTION

Adaptive Resonance Theory (ART) network was developed by Gail Carpenter and Steven Grossberg in 1987. This network serves the purpose of cluster discovery (cluster discovery network). The ART network learns clusters in unsupervised mode. In addition, the network can accommodate new clusters without affecting the storage or recall capabilities of clusters already learnt. The network produces clusters by itself if such clusters are identified in the input data, and stores the clustering information about patterns or features without prior information about the possible number and type of clusters. Essentially the network "follows the leader" after it generates the first cluster with the first input pattern received. It then creates the second cluster if the distance of the second cluster exceeds a certain threshold, otherwise the pattern is clustered with the first cluster. As is often in the case of clustering nets, the weight on the cluster unit may be considered to be an example for the patterns placed on the cluster.

ART nets are designed to allow the user to control the degree of similarity of patterns placed on the same cluster. However, since the input patterns may differ in the level of detail, the relative similarity of an input pattern to the weight vector for a cluster unit is used rather than the absolute difference between the vectors.

As the net is trained, each training pattern may be presented several times. A pattern may be placed on one cluster unit, the first time it is presented, and then placed on a different cluster unit when it is presented later (due to weight changes while learning other patterns). A stable net will not return a pattern to a previous cluster. In other words, a pattern oscillating among different cluster units at different stages of training indicates an unstable net.

Some nets achieve stability by gradually reducing the learning rate as the same set of training patterns is presented many times. However, this does not allow the net to learn readily a new pattern that is presented for the first time. The ability of a net to respond to (learn) a new pattern equally well at any stage of training is called plasticity. ART nets are designed to be both stable and plastic.

The basic architecture of ART nets has the following salient features:

- An input processing field called the F_1 layer. This F_1 layer consists of two parts namely input portion layer and (b) interface portion layer.
- A cluster unit called the F_2 layer. The F_2 layer is a competitive layer. The cluster unit with the largest net input becomes the candidate to learn the input patterns.
- A reset mechanism to control the degree of similarity of patterns placed on the same cluster.

Two distinct models are based on ART namely ART1 and ART2 networks. ART1 self organizes recognition categories for arbitrary sequence of binary input patterns and ART2 does the same for either binary or analog inputs.

6.2 ART1 NETWORK

ART1 attempts to create an autonomous learning system (ART1 fulfills most of the conditions of an autonomous learning system but falls short of ideal). It can categorize input patterns automatically and will recall well known patterns immediately. The network searches as for the unknown pattern and if it is not found, learns the new pattern. By adjusting a single parameter, the network can recognize its pattern categorization into coarser or finer distinctions. In many ways, the network fulfills the requirement of an autonomous learning system, which requires the network to learn from mistakes and observations.

6.2.1 Structure of ART1

ART1 is a good example of self-organizing network. It is similar to forward only counter propagation network. It uses some extra-circuitry (Fig. 6.1) to perform competitive learning and vigilance. When the network is in operation it behaves as a "follow my leader" classifier. It receives input patterns and produces classification codes for these patterns. There are no distinct phases of learning and operating, it does both these functions at the same time.

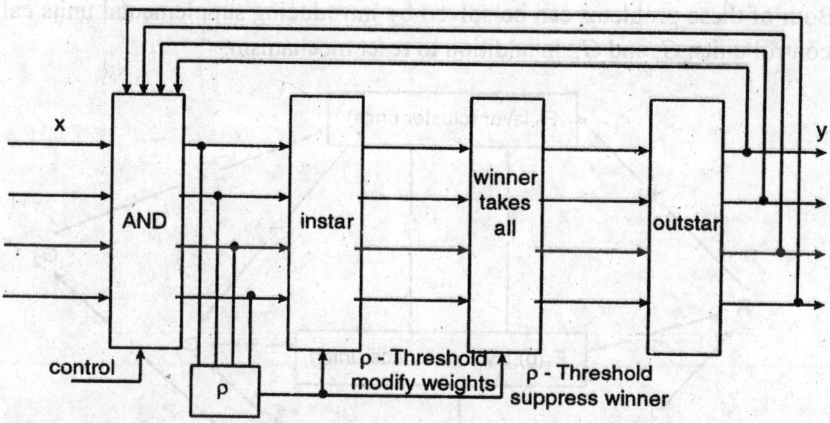

Figure 6.1 *Grossberg's ART1 Network*

6.2.2 Architecture of ART1

ART1 network consists of computational units and supplemental units.

Computational units The computational units are F_1 units, F_2 units and a reset mechanism. (Fig. 6.2)

Supplemental units The supplemental units (Fig. 6.3) are important from a theoretical point of view. They provide a mechanism by which the computations performed by the algorithm can be accomplished by using neural networks principles. The computational algorithm of ART1 represents a more involved neural process than can be represented in terms of just F_1 units, F_2 units and a reset mechanism. The difficulty is that these units are required to respond differently at different stages of the process and unlike a biological neuron it does not have a method for deciding what to do and when.

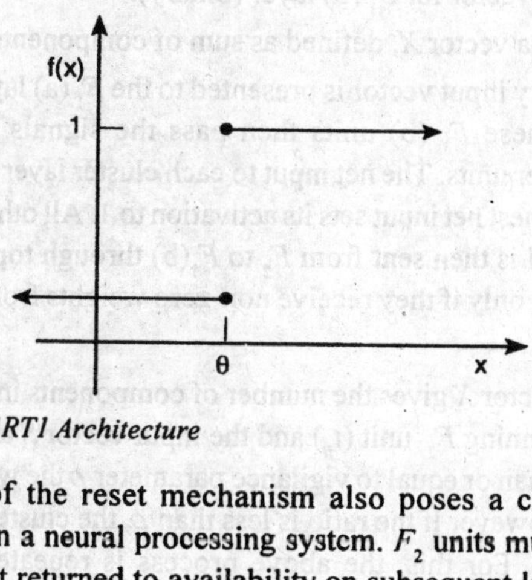

Figure 6.2 *Basic ART1 Architecture*

The operation of the reset mechanism also poses a challenge in terms of implementation within a neural processing system. F_2 units must be inhibited under certain conditions, but returned to availability on subsequent learning trials.

Both of these problems can be solved by introducing supplemental units called gain control units, G_1 and G_2 in addition to reset mechanism.

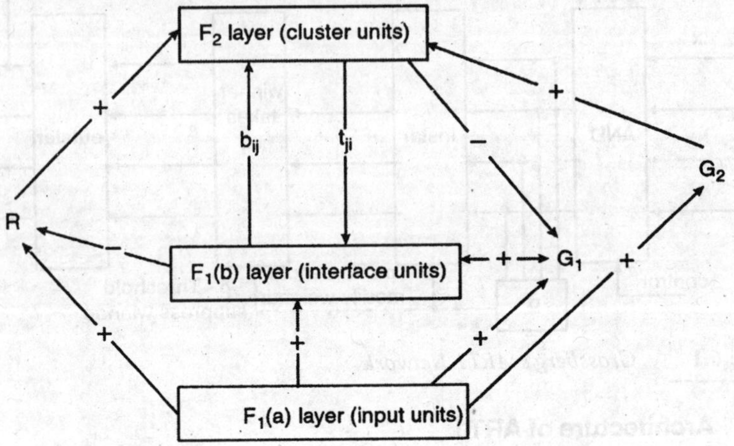

Figure 6.3 *Supplemental Units*

6.2.3 Algorithm

Nomenclature

Let n - number of components in the input vector.

m - maximum number of clusters that can be formed.

b_{ij} - bottom-up weights (from F_1 (b) unit X_i to F_2 unit Y_j).

t_{ji} - top-down weights (from F_2 unit Y_j to F_1 (b) unit X_i).

ρ - vigilance parameter.

S - binary input vector (n-tuple).

X - activation vector for F_1 (b) layer (binary).

$\|X\|$ - norm of a vector X, defined as sum of components x_i.

Description A binary input vector is presented to the F_1 (a) layer from where the X units receive them. These F_1 (b) units then pass the signals through connection weights (b_{ij}) to the cluster units. The net input to each cluster layer neuron is calculated. The neuron with the highest net input sets its activation to 1. All other neuron activations are set to zero. A signal is then sent from F_2 to F_1(b) through top-down weights (tji). The X units remain 'on' only if they receive non-zero weights from both the F_1 (a) and F_2 units.

The norm of the vector X gives the number of components in which the top-down weight vector of the winning F_2 unit (t_{ji}) and the input vector S are both 1. If the ratio of $\|X\|$ to $\|S\|$ is greater than or equal to vigilance parameter ρ the weights of the winning cluster are adjusted. However if the ratio is less than ρ, the cluster unit is rejected and another unit is chosen. For this, the above process is repeated after all neurons' activations are reset to zero, except the winning neuron of the previous trial which is inhibited.

The whole process continues until either a match is found or all neurons are inhibited. If the latter is the case, it is better to reduce the value of ρ or increase the number of cluster units. Another way of attending to this case is by simply designating the input stimulus as "outlier" which cannot be clustered. At the end of each presentation all cluster units are returned to inactive states.

Training algorithm

Step 1: Initialize parameters.

$$L > 1$$
$$0 < \rho \le 1$$

Initialize weights.

$$0 < b_{ij} < \frac{L}{L-1+n}$$
$$t_{ji}(0) = 1$$

Step 2: When stopping condition is false, execute steps 3 to 14.

Step 3: For each training input, do steps 4 to 13.

Step 4: Set activation of all F_2 units to zero.

Set activation of F_1 (a) units to input vector S.

Step 5: Compute the norm of S.

$$\|S\| = \sum_i S_i$$

Step 6: Send input signal from F_1 (a) to F_1 (b) layer.

$$x_i = s_i$$

Step 7: For each F_2 node that is not inhibited,

$$\text{if } y_1 \ne -1 \text{ then } y_j = \sum_i b_{ij} x_i$$

Step 8: When reset is true, execute steps 9 to 12.

Step 9: Find J such that $y_J \ge y_j$ for all nodes j.

if $y_j = -1$, then all nodes are inhibited and this pattern cannot be clustered.

Step 10: Recompute activations, x of F_1 (b)

$$x_i = S_i t_{ji}$$

Step 11: Compute the norm of vector, X

$$\|X\| = \sum_i x_i$$

Step 12: Test for reset

$$\text{If } \frac{\|X\|}{\|S\|} = \rho \text{ then } y_j = -1 \text{ and execute step 7.}$$

Step 13: Update weights for node J.

$$b_{iJ}(\text{new}) = \frac{Lx_i}{L - 1 + \|x\|}$$

$$t_{ji}(\text{new}) = x_i$$

Step 14: Test for stopping condition.

6.3 ART2 NETWORK

ART2 network is similar to ART1 but performs tasks on continuous-valued signals. The differences between ART2 and ART1 reflect the modifications needed to accommodate patterns with continuous valued components. The F_1 field in ART2 includes a combination of normalization and noise suppression, in addition to the comparison of the bottom-up and top-down signals needed for reset mechanism. ART2 network works on two types of continuous-valued signals, namely "noisy binary" signals and "truly continuous" signals. In the former, the information is conveyed as "on" or "virtually off". In the case of the latter, information is conveyed as a range of values.

6.3.1 Architecture

The F_1 layer consists of six types of units (the w,x,u,v,p and q units). There are n units in each of these types. A supplemental unit between the W and X units receives signals from all the W units, computes the norm of the vector, W and sends this signal to each of these X units. Each of these also receives an excitatory signal from the corresponding W unit.

The activation of the winning F_2 unit is d, where $0 < d < 1$. The action of F_2 layer is unchanged from ART1.

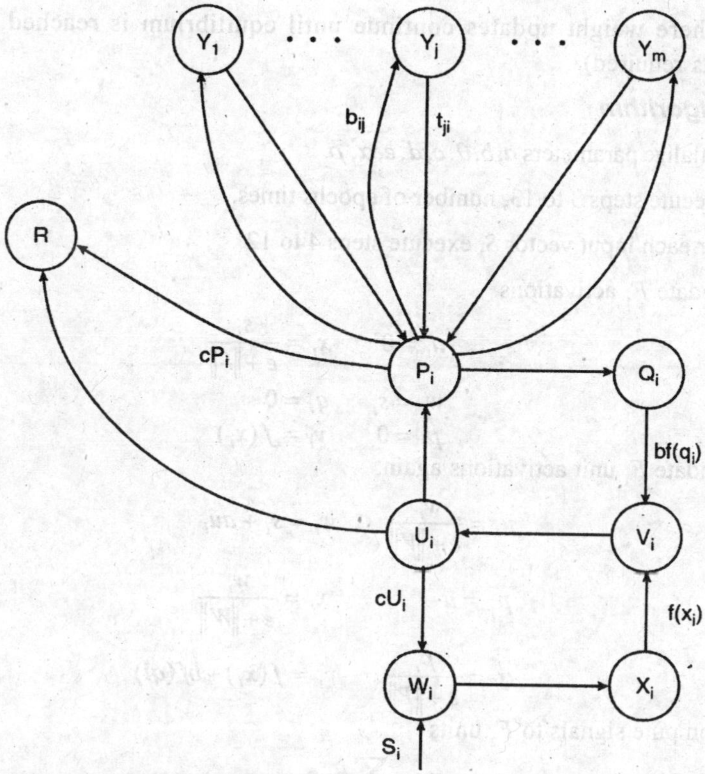

Figure 6.4 *Basic ART2 Architecture*

6.3.2 Algorithm

Description A learning trial consists of one presentation of an input pattern. The input signal $s = (s_1, s_2, \ldots, s_i, \ldots, s_n)$ continues to be sent while all the actions described below are performed. All the activations are initially set to zero.

The computation cycle within the F_1 layer originates with the computation of the activation unit U_i. Next, a signal is sent from each unit U_i to its associated units, W_i and P_i. The activations of W_i and P_i units are then computed. Unit W_i sums the signal it receives from U_i and the input signal s_i. P_i totals the signals received from U_i and top-down signals. The activations of Q_i and X_i are normalized versions of W_i and P_i. An activation function is applied to each of these units before these signals are sent to V_i.

After all activations in the F_1 layer reach equilibrium, the P units send their signals to F_2 layer where a winner take all competition chooses the candidate cluster unit to attain the input pattern. The reset mechanism receives signals from U_i and P_i units of F_1 layer. The algorithm here is similar to the ART1 network. But the weight updation could be done in two ways. The two learning modes of ART2 are slow learning–where only one iteration of the weight update equations occurs on each learning trial (large number of presentations with little computation in each trial is required) and fast learning–where weight updates continue until equilibrium is reached (fewer presentations required).

Training algorithm

Step 1: Initialize parameters $a, b, \theta, c, d, e, \alpha, \rho$.

Step 2: Execute steps 3 to 13, number of epochs times.

Step 3: For each input vector S, execute steps 4 to 12.

Step 4: Update F_1 activations.

$$u_i = 0 \qquad x_i = \frac{s_i}{e + \|S\|}$$

$$w_i = s_i \qquad q_i = 0$$

$$p_i = 0 \qquad v_i = f(x_i)$$

Update F_1 unit activations again.

$$u_i = \frac{v_i}{e + \|V\|} \qquad w_i = s_i + au_i$$

$$p_i = u_i \qquad x_i = \frac{w_i}{e + \|W\|}$$

$$q_i = \frac{p_i}{e + \|P\|} \qquad v_i = f(x_i) + bf(qi)$$

Step 5: Compute signals to F_2 units

$$y_j = \sum_i b_{ij} p_i$$

Step 6: When reset is true, execute steps 7 to 8.

Step 7: Find F_2 unit, Y_j with largest signal.

Step 8: Check for reset.

$$u_i = \frac{v_i}{e + \|V\|}$$

$$p_i = u_i + dt_{ji}$$

$$r_i = \frac{u_i + cp_i}{e + \|U\| + c\|p\|}$$

If $\|R\| < p - e$, then

$y_j = -1$(inhibit J)

Reset is true; Repeat step 5.

If $\|R\| \geq p - e$, then

$$w_i = s_i + au_i$$

$$x_i = \frac{w_i}{e + \|W\|}$$

$$q_i = \frac{p_i}{e + \|P\|}$$

$$v_i = f(x_i) + bf(q_i)$$

Step 9: Execute steps 10 - 11, number of learning iterations times.

Step 10: Update weights for winning unit, J.

Step 11: Update F_1 activations.

$$u_i = \frac{v_i}{e + \|V\|}$$

$$w_i = s_i + au_i$$

$$p_i = u_i + dt_{ji}$$

$$x_i = \frac{w_i}{e + \|W\|}$$

$$q_i = \frac{p_i}{e + \|P\|}$$

$$v_i = f(x_i) + bf(q_i)$$

Step 12: Test for stopping condition.

Step 13: Test for number of epochs.

Example 6.1 Consider an ART1 neural net with four F_1 units and three F_2 units. After some training, the weights are as follows:

Bottom-up weights b_{ij}

$$\begin{pmatrix} 0.67 & 0.0 & 0.2 \\ 0.0 & 0.0 & 0.2 \\ 0.0 & 0.0 & 0.2 \\ 0.0 & 0.67 & 0.2 \end{pmatrix}$$

Top-down weights t_{ji}

$$\begin{pmatrix} 1 & 0 & 0 & 0 \\ 0 & 0 & 0 & 1 \\ 1 & 1 & 1 & 1 \end{pmatrix}$$

Determine the new weight matrices after the vector (0,0,1,1) is presented if

a. ρ is 0.3 b. ρ is 0.7

Solution

a. ρ is 0.3

Step 0: Initialize parameters.

$$n = 4, m = 3, L = 2, \rho = 0.3.$$

$$b_{ij} = \begin{pmatrix} 0.67 & 0.0 & 0.2 \\ 0.0 & 0.0 & 0.2 \\ 0.0 & 0.0 & 0.2 \\ 0.0 & 0.67 & 0.2 \end{pmatrix}$$

$$t_{ji} = \begin{pmatrix} 1 & 0 & 0 & 0 \\ 0 & 0 & 0 & 1 \\ 1 & 1 & 1 & 1 \end{pmatrix}$$

Step 1: Begin computation.

Step 2: For input vectors (0,0,1,1), execute steps 3 to 12.

Step 3a: Set activations of all F_2 units to zero.

Step 3b: Set activations of all $F_1(a)$ units to input vector.

$$S=(0,0,1,1)$$

Step 4: Compute norm of S:

$$\|S\|=2$$

Step 5: Compute activations for each node in the F_1 layer:

$$X=(0,0,1,1)$$

Step 6: Compute net input to each node in the F_2 layer.

$$Y_1 = 0.67 * 0 + 0 * 0 + 0 * 1 + 0 * 1 = 0.0$$

$$Y_2 = 0 * 0 + 0 * 0 + 0 * 1 + 0.67 * 1 = 0.67$$

$$Y_3 = 0.2 * 0 + 0.2 * 0 + 0.2 * 1 + 0.2 * 1 = 0.4$$

Step 7: When reset is true, execute steps 8 to 11.

Step 8: Since unit Y_2 has the largest net input $J = 2$.

Step 9: Recompute the activation of F_1 layer.

$$x_i = s_i * t_{2i};$$
$$\text{Currently } t_2 = (0,0,0,1)$$
$$\text{Therefore } x = (0,0,0,1)$$

Step 10: Compute the norm of x:

$$\|X\|=1$$

Step 11: Test for reset.

$$\frac{\|X\|}{\|S\|} = \frac{1}{2} = 0.5 > 0.3$$

Therefore, reset is false. Proceed to step 12.

Step 12: Update b_2: however there is no change in the bottom-up weight matrix.

$$b_{ij} = \begin{pmatrix} 0.67 & 0.0 & 0.2 \\ 0.0 & 0.0 & 0.2 \\ 0.0 & 0.0 & 0.2 \\ 0.0 & 0.67 & 0.2 \end{pmatrix}$$

Similarly, the top-down weight matrix remains the same.

$$t_{ji} = \begin{pmatrix} 1 & 0 & 0 & 0 \\ 0 & 0 & 0 & 1 \\ 1 & 1 & 1 & 1 \end{pmatrix}$$

Step 13: Test for stopping condition.

b. ρ is 0.7

Step 0: Initialize parameters.

$n = 4,\ m = 3,\ L = 2,\ \rho = 0.3$

$$b_{ij} = \begin{pmatrix} 0.67 & 0.0 & 0.0 \\ 0.0 & 0.0 & 0.2 \\ 0.0 & 0.0 & 0.2 \\ 0.0 & 0.67 & 0.2 \end{pmatrix}$$

$$t_{ji} = \begin{pmatrix} 1 & 0 & 0 & 0 \\ 0 & 0 & 0 & 0 \\ 1 & 1 & 1 & 1 \end{pmatrix}$$

Step 1: Begin computation.

Step 2: For input vectors (0,0,1,1), do steps 3 to 12.

Step 3a: Set activations of all F_2 units to zero.

Step 3b: Set activations of all F_1(a) units to input vector.

$$S = (0,0,1,1)$$

Step 4: Compute norm of S:

$$\|S\| = 2$$

Step 5: Compute activations for each node in the F_1 layer:

$$X = (0,0,1,1)$$

Step 6: Compute net input to each node in the F_2 layer.

$$Y_1 = 0.67 * 0 + 0 * 0 + 0 * 1 + 0 * 1 = 0.0$$

$$Y_2 = 0 * 0 + 0 * 0 + 0 * 1 + 0.67 * 1 = 0.67$$

$$Y_3 = 0.2 * 0 + 0.2 * 0 + 0.2 * 1 + 0.2 * 1 = 0.4$$

Step 7: When reset is true, execute steps 8 to 11.

Step 8: Since unit Y_2 has the largest net input $J = 2$.

Step 9: Recompute the activation of F_1 layer.

$$x_i = s_i * t_{2i};$$
$$\text{Currently } t_2 = (0,0,0,1)$$
$$\text{Therefore } x = (0,0,0,1)$$

Step 10: Compute the norm of x:

$$\|X\| = 1$$

Step 11: Test for reset.

$$\frac{\|X\|}{\|S\|} = \frac{1}{2} = 0.5 < 0.7$$

Therefore, reset is true, so inhibit Y_2:

$$Y_2 = -1.0$$

Proceed to step 7.

Step 7: When reset is true, execute steps 8 to 11.

Step 8: Now the values for F_2 layer are:

$$Y_1 = 0.0$$
$$Y_2 = -1.0$$
$$Y_3 = 0.4$$

So, unit Y_3 has the largest net input and $J = 3$.

Step 9: Recompute the activation of F_1 layer.

$$x_i = s_i * t_{2i};$$
$$\text{Currently } t_2 = (1,1,1,1)$$
$$\text{Therefore } x = (0,0,1,1)$$

Step 10: Compute the norm of x.

$$\|X\| = 2$$

Step 11: Test for reset

$$\frac{\|X\|}{\|S\|} = \frac{2}{2} = 1.0 \geq 0.7$$

Therefore, reset is false. Proceed with step 12.

Step 12: Update b_3. Bottom-up weight matrix becomes:

$$b_{ij} = \begin{pmatrix} 0.67 & 0.0 & 0.0 \\ 0.0 & 0.0 & 0.0 \\ 0.0 & 0.0 & 0.67 \\ 0.0 & 0.67 & 0.67 \end{pmatrix}$$

Update t_3. The top - down weight matrices becomes.

$$t_{ji} = \begin{pmatrix} 1 & 0 & 0 & 0 \\ 0 & 0 & 0 & 1 \\ 0 & 0 & 1 & 1 \end{pmatrix}$$

Step 13: Test for stopping condition.

Example 6.2 Consider an ART1 neural net with four F_1 units and three F_2 units. Determine the new weight matrices after the vectors (1,1,1,1), (1,1,1,0), (1,0,1,1) and (0,1,1,1) are presented. Consider a vigilance parameter of 0.4.

Solution

Step 0: Initialize parameters.

$n = 4,\ m = 3,\ L = 2,\ \rho = 0.4$

Initialize weights.

$b_{ij}(0) = 0.2 \qquad t_{ji}(0) = 1$

Step 1: Start the computation.

Step 2: For the first input vector (1,1,1,1), execute steps 3 to 12.

Step 3a: Set activations of all F_2 units to zero.

Step 3b: Set activations of all F_1(a) units to input vector.

$$S = (1,1,1,1)$$

Step 4: Compute norm of S:

$$\|S\| = 4$$

Step 5: Compute activations for each node in the F_1 layer:

$$X = (1,1,1,1)$$

Step 6: Compute net input to each node in the F_2 layer.

$$Y_1 = 0.2 * 1 + 0.2 * 1 + 0.2 * 1 + 0.2 * 1 = 0.8$$

$$Y_2 = 0.2 * 1 + 0.2 * 1 + 0.2 * 1 + 0.2 * 1 = 0.8$$

$$Y_3 = 0.2 * 1 + 0.2 * 1 + 0.2 * 1 + 0.2 * 1 = 0.8$$

Step 7: While reset is true, execute steps 8 to 11.

Step 8: Since unit Y_1 has the largest net input $J = 1$.

Step 9: Recompute the activation of F_1 layer.

$$x_i = s_i * t_{ji};$$

Currently $t_1 = (1,1,1,1)$

Therefore $x = (0,0,0,1)$

Step 10: Compute the norm of x:

$$\|X\| = 4$$

Step 11: Test for reset.

$$\frac{\|X\|}{\|S\|} = \frac{4}{4} = 1.0 > 0.4$$

Therefore, reset is false. Proceed to step 12.

Step 12: Update b_1. The bottom-up weight matrix becomes:

$$b_{ij}(\text{new}) = \frac{2x}{7 + \|x\|}$$

$$b_{ij} = \begin{pmatrix} 0.2 & 0.2 & 0.2 \\ 0.2 & 0.2 & 0.2 \\ 0.2 & 0.2 & 0.2 \\ 0.2 & 0.2 & 0.2 \end{pmatrix}$$

Similarly, the top–down weight matrix becomes.

$$t_{ji}(\text{new}) = x_i$$

$$t_{ji} = \begin{pmatrix} 1 & 0 & 0 & 0 \\ 0 & 0 & 0 & 1 \\ 1 & 1 & 1 & 1 \end{pmatrix}$$

Step 2: For the second input vector (1,1,1,0), execute steps 3 to 12.

Step 3a: Set activations of all F_2 units to zero.

Step 3b: Set activations of all F_1(a) units to input vector.

$$S=(1,1,1,0)$$

Step 4: Compute norm of S:

$$\|S\| = 3$$

Step 5: Compute activations for each node in the F_1 layer:

$$X=(1,1,1,0)$$

Step 6: Compute net input to each node in the F_2 layer.

$$Y_1 = 0.2 * 1 + 0.2 * 1 + 0.2 * 1 + 0.2 * 1 = 0.6$$

$$Y_2 = 0.2 * 1 + 0.2 * 1 + 0.2 * 1 + 0.2 * 1 = 0.6$$

$$Y_3 = 0.2 * 1 + 0.2 * 1 + 0.2 * 1 + 0.2 * 1 = 0.6$$

Step 7: If reset is true, execute steps 8 to 11.

Step 8: Since unit Y_1 has the largest net input $J = 1$.

Step 9: Recompute the activation of F_1 layer.

$$x_i = s_i * t_{li};$$

Currently t_1 = (1,1,1,0)

Therefore x = (1,0,1,1)

Step 10: Compute the norm of x:

$$\|X\|=3$$

Step 11: Test for reset.

$$\frac{\|X\|}{\|S\|}=\frac{3}{3}=1.0>0.4$$

Therefore, reset is false. Proceed to step 12.

Step 12: Update b_1. The bottom-up weight matrix.

$$b_{ij}=\begin{pmatrix}0.5 & 0.2 & 0.2\\ 0.5 & 0.2 & 0.2\\ 0.5 & 0.2 & 0.2\\ 0.0 & 0.2 & 0.2\end{pmatrix}$$

Similarly, the top-down weight matrix becomes:

$$t_1=\begin{pmatrix}1 & 1 & 1 & 0\\ 1 & 1 & 1 & 1\\ 1 & 1 & 1 & 1\end{pmatrix}$$

Step 2: For the third input vector (1,0,1,1), execute steps 3 to 12.

Step 3a: Set activations of all F_2 units to zero.

Step 3b: Set activations of all F_1(a) units to input vector.

$$S=(1,0,1,1)$$

Step 4: Compute norm of S:

$$\|S\|=3$$

Step 5: Compute activations for each node in the F_1 layer:

$$X=(1,0,1,1)$$

Step 6: Compute net input to each node in the F_2 layer.

$$Y_1=0.5*1+0.5*1+0.5*1+0.0*1=1.0$$

$$Y_2=0.2*1+0.2*0+0.2*1+0.2*1=0.6$$

$$Y_3=0.2*1+0.2*0+0.2*1+0.2*1=0.6$$

Step 7: If reset is true, execute steps 8 to 11.

Step 8: Since unit Y_1 has the largest net input $J=1$.

Step 9: Recompute the activation of F_1 layer.

$$x_i=s_i*t_{Ji};$$

Currently $t_1=(1,1,1,0)$

Therefore $x=(1,0,1,1)$

Step 10: Compute the norm of x:

$$\|X\|-3$$

Step 11: Test for reset.

$$\frac{\|X\|}{\|S\|} = \frac{3}{3} = 1.0 > 0.4$$

Therefore, reset is false. Proceed to step 12.

Step 12: Update b_1. The bottom-up weight matrix.

$$b_{ij} = \begin{pmatrix} 0.5 & 0.2 & 0.2 \\ 0.5 & 0.2 & 0.2 \\ 0.5 & 0.2 & 0.2 \\ 0.0 & 0.2 & 0.2 \end{pmatrix}$$

Similarly, the top – down weight matrix becomes:

$$t_1 = \begin{pmatrix} 1 & 1 & 1 & 0 \\ 1 & 1 & 1 & 1 \\ 1 & 1 & 1 & 1 \end{pmatrix}$$

Step 2: For the fourth input vector (0,1,1,1), execute steps 3 to 12.

Step 3a: Set activations of all F_2 units to zero.

Step 3b: Set activations of all F_1(a) units to input vector.

$$S=(0,1,1,1)$$

Step 4: Compute norm of S:

$$\|S\| = 3$$

Step 5: Compute activations for each node in the F_1 layer:

$$X=(0,1,1,1)$$

Step 6: Compute net input to each node in the F_2 layer.

$$Y_1 = 0.5 * 0 + 0.5 * 1 + 0.5 * 1 + 0.5 * 1 = 0.5$$

$$Y_2 = 0.2 * 0 + 0.2 * 1 + 0.2 * 1 + 0.2 * 1 = 0.6$$

$$Y_3 = 0.2 * 0 + 0.2 * 1 + 0.2 * 1 + 0.2 * 1 = 0.6$$

Step 7: If reset is true, execute steps 8 to 11.

Step 8: Since unit Y_1 has the largest net input $J = 1$.

Step 9: Recompute the activation of F_1 layer.

$$x_i = s_i * t_{li};$$

Currently $t_1 = (1,0,1,1)$

Therefore $x = (0,1,1,1)$

Step 10: Compute the norm of x:

$$\|X\| = 3$$

Step 11: Test for reset.

$$\frac{\|X\|}{\|S\|} = \frac{3}{3} = 1.0 > 0.4$$

Therefore, reset is false. Proceed to step 12.

Step 12: Update b_1. The bottom-up weight matrix.

$$b_{ij} = \begin{pmatrix} 0.0 & 0.2 & 0.2 \\ 0.5 & 0.2 & 0.2 \\ 0.5 & 0.2 & 0.2 \\ 0.5 & 0.2 & 0.2 \end{pmatrix}$$

Similarly, the top – down weight matrix becomes:

$$t_1 = \begin{pmatrix} 0 & 1 & 1 & 1 \\ 1 & 1 & 1 & 1 \\ 1 & 1 & 1 & 1 \end{pmatrix}$$

Step 13: Test for stopping condition.

This completes one epoch of training ART1 after presenting all the four input patterns.

Example 6.3 Consider an ART2 neural net having a noise suppression parameter as 0.7. The net is presented with an input vector s = (0.71, 0.69). There are ten fixed weights in the F_1 layer.

Solution

Step 0: Initialize parameters.

$$S = (0.71, 0.69)$$
$$a = 10$$
$$\theta = 0.7$$

Step 1: If stopping condition is false, execute steps 2 to 10.

Step 2: For each input vector S execute step 3 to 9.

Step 3: Initialize F_1 unit activations:

$$u = (0.0, 0.0)$$
$$w = s + au = (0.71, 0.69)$$
$$p = u = (0.0, 0.0)$$
$$x = \frac{w}{\|w\|} = (0.71, 0.69)$$
$$q = \frac{p}{\|p\|} = (0.0, 0.0)$$
$$v = f(x) + bf(q) = (0.71, 0.69)$$

Step 4: Update F_1 unit activations again.

Step 5: If reset is true, execute steps 6 to 7.

Step 6: Test for reset: $w = s + au = (0.71, 0.69) + 10(0.71, 0.69)$

$$= (7.81, 7.59)$$

$$x = \frac{w}{\|w\|} = (0.71, 0.69)$$

$$q = \frac{p}{\|p\|} = (0.71, 0.69)$$

$$v = f(x) + bf(q)$$

$$= (0.71, 0.69) + 10(0.71, 0.69)$$

$$= (7.81, 7.59)$$

Reset is false. Proceed to step 7.

Step 7: Update the weights using $\alpha = 0.6$.

$$t_{ji}(\text{new}) = 0.54 * u_i + 0.946 * t_{ji}(\text{old})$$

$$= 0.54(0.71, 0.69)$$

$$= (0.38, 0.37)$$

Step 8: Update F_1 unit activations:

$$u = (0.71, 0.69)$$

$$w = (0.71, 0.69) + 10(0.71, 0.69)$$

$$= (7.81, 7.59)$$

$$p = (0.71, 0.69) + 0.9(0.38, 0.37)$$

$$= (1.05, 1.02)$$

$$x = (0.71, 0.69)$$

$$q = (0.71, 0.69)$$

$$v = (7.81, 7.59)$$

Step 9: Update the top-down weights.

$$T = (0.54)u + 0.946t(\text{old})$$

$$= 0.54(0.71, 0.69) + 0.946(0.38, 0.37)$$

$$= (0.74, 0.67)$$

Step 10: Test for stopping condition.

6.4 SPATIAL TEMPORAL NETWORK

Artificial Neural Network (ANN) systems discussed so far in this text are applicable to the recognition of the spatial information patterns (such as BPN, ART, etc.,). For example, the two-dimensional cluster classification by BPN network. Input patterns applied to these networks need not be necessarily time correlated. In these network systems, classification of current input pattern has no effect on the previous or subsequent patterns applied to the network.

In this chapter, we will focus on a new ANN architecture that can directly deal with the spatial as well as the temporal aspects of the input patterns. In these networks, recognition of spatial patterns is time correlated in addition to the spatial information contained within the pattern. These networks are called spatiotemporal pattern (STP), which recognizes the time-correlated sequence of spatial patterns.

STP recognition is important for several applications. Speech recognition, radar analysis and sonar echo classifications are a few examples. In speech recognition, the waveform for a spoken word is converted into a sequence of power spectra. An individual pattern is called a spatial pattern. The sequence of spatial patterns, one at each time interval forms the STP.

6.4.1 Formal Avalanche

The basic development of the STP network is the formal avalanche structure developed by Grossberg [1]. The top two layers of this network structure resembles the counter propagation network (CPN). Multiple outstars are used in both the networks but in slightly different manner. In CPN, the hidden layer is a winner-take all competitive layer. The spatial patterns are presented to the input layer and a winning hidden layer neuron is found. The outstar corresponding to the winner is excited. The outputs of the outstar depends upon the previously learned mapping whereas the avalanche structure demonstrates the learning and recalling of a complex spatiotemporal pattern.

6.4.2 Architecture of Spatio Temporal Networks (STNs)

The architecture, learning and recalling of the network is discussed by using the example of speech recognition as the source for STPs. Fig. 6.5 shows the generation of STPs from spoken words. The transducer converts the sound signals into an electrical signal $s_i(t)$. Then the spectrum analyzer measures the power contained in each of n frequency bins. At any instant, the spectrum analyzer gives the sequence of a vector whose components are the powers of various channels. For example, the power spectrum for the *i*th word at time $t = t_1$ is given by,

$$P_i(t_1) = (P_{il}(t_1), P_{i2}(t_1), \ldots, P_{in}(t_1))^T$$

For each word, the STP consists of sequence of vectors of the form $P_i(t_j)$. The STP for the *i*th word P_i is given by,

$$P_i = \{P_i(t_1), P_i(t_2), \ldots, P_i(t_j)\}$$

The number of vectors in the word P_i must be specified. For accuracy, we must sample the power spectrum at a frequency that is at least double the bandwidth of the original signal.

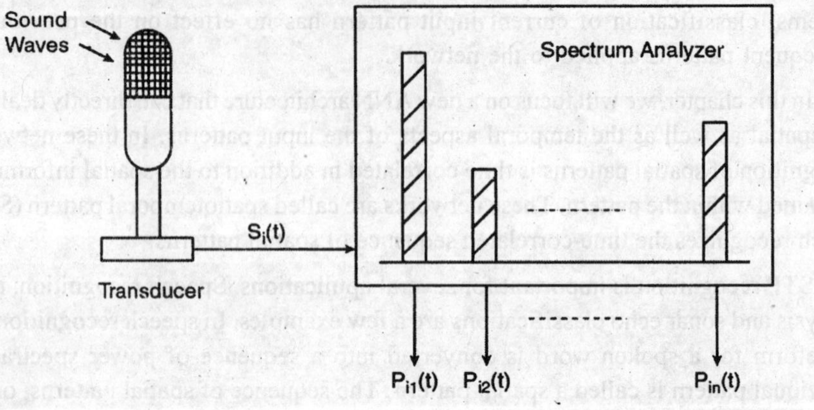

Figure 6.5 *Generation of Power Spectra from Speech Signal*

STN for speech recognition Fig. 6.6 shows the structure of STN to recognize a single word. This structure can be extended to recognize multiple words.

Let the network be tuned for a specific word. First, the spectral analysis is performed while a person utters the word. For more generalization, we might take the mean of the power spectra produced by different speakers. If the average time required to pronounce the word is t and the sampling rate is v per second, then the number of vector components needed to represent the word is given as

$$m = vt$$

Hence the number of channels in the spectrum analyzer is m. The network contains m processing elements. The STP for the word is of the form

$$P_1 = \{P_1(t_1),\ P_1(t_2),\ldots,\ P_1(t_m)\}$$

The weight vectors for each element of the network is assigned as $z_1 = P_1(t_1)$, $z_2 = P_1(t_2),\ldots, z_m = P_1(t_m)$, where $\|P_1(t_j)\| = 1$. Therefore, the dimension of weight matrix of each processing element is also equal to m.

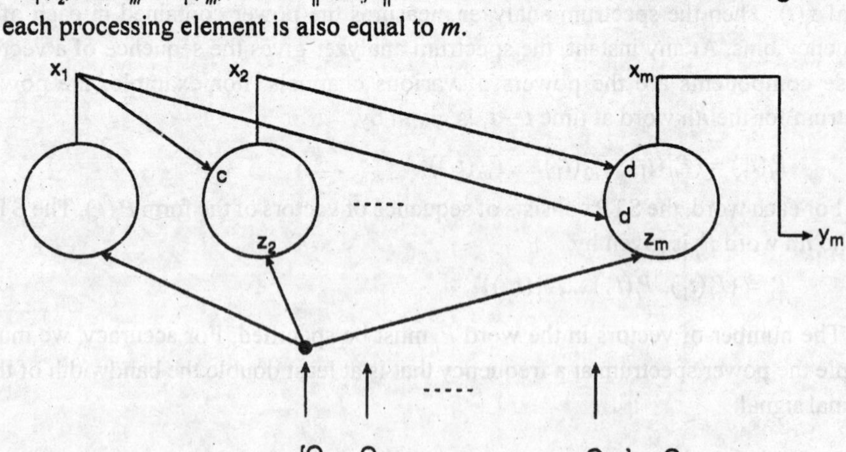

Figure 6.6 *Architecture of Spatio Temporal Network for Single Word Recognition*

Let $Q_1 = \{Q_1(t_1), Q_1(t_2),..., Q_1(t_m)\}$ be the STP obtained from the output of the spectrum analyzer, while a person repeats the word into the transducer. This STP is applied to the network as a test vector to verify its response. Assume that the patterns obtained from the spectrum analyzer is normalized to one. For simplification, we define $Q_{li} = Q_1(t_i)$.

Each Q_{li} vector is applied as inputs to the processing elements and this vector is allowed to remain there for a time equal to the sampling period of the power spectrum. After this time, the next input vector $Q_{1,i+1}$ is applied to the network and the process is repeated till Q_{1m} vector is applied. The net input value and the activation of each element is computed as follows:

Each unit receives a net input value from the dot product of the input pattern and the corresponding weight vector as in other types of neural networks ($Q_{li}.z_i$). Also, each unit receives an additional input signal from outputs of all the preceding units as shown in Fig. 6.6. The weights associated with these inputs are set to a constant $d < 1$. The total input applied to the ith unit is computed as

$$I_1 - Q_{li} z_i + d \sum_{k=1}^{i=1} x_k \tag{6.1}$$

where, x_k is the output of the kth unit. The output of the ith unit is modeled by using the first order differential equation

$$X_i = A(-ax_i + b[I_i - \Gamma]^+) \tag{6.2}$$

where a and b are positive constants. The function $[u]^+$ is defined by

$$[u]^+ = \begin{cases} u & \text{if } u > 0 \\ 0 & \text{if } u \le 0 \end{cases} \tag{6.3}$$

In eqn. (6.3), the value of u is taken as $u = [I_1 - \Gamma]$ and Γ is the threshold value which is taken as a constant. Let us take $s = -ax_i + b[I_i - \Gamma]^+$, the attack function A(s) is defined by the following equation

$$A(s) = \begin{cases} s & \text{if } s > 0 \\ cs & \text{if } s \le 0 \end{cases} \tag{6.4}$$

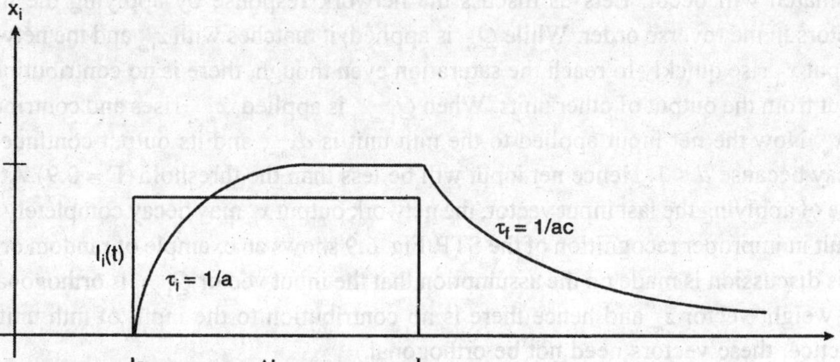

Figure 6.7 *Response of a Processing Element*

The value of c lies between 0 and 1. The rise and fall time of the processing elements differ from each other due to the effect of attack function. Fig. 6.7 shows the response of a processing element whose net input exceeds the threshold value. From the figure, it is observed that the rising edge has a time constant of $1/a$ and the falling edge has a time constant of $1/ac$ which is longer than the rise time.

The network output is the output obtained from the last processing unit x_m and is represented as $y = x_m$. The outputs obtained from the network provides the matches between the test pattern and the pattern previously stored in the network. For successful operation of the network, we shall rely on the dynamic behavior of the output values. Let's consider a test case $Q_1 = P_1$, which means $Q_{1i} = P_1(t_i)$ for all the value of i. The response of the network for this test pattern shall be analyzed by applying the input vectors of the test pattern Q_1. It is assumed that the threshold value is large (say 0.9) such that a close match between the test input vector (Q_{1i}) and its associated weight vector (z_i) is required to produce a non zero output.

When Q_{11} is applied, it matches with weight vector z_1 exactly and the corresponding output x_1 rises quickly. All the other outputs are in the quiescent state. The input vector remains there for a period equal to the sampling time of the power spectrum analyzer and hence x_1 will saturate. Once the time elapses, Q_{11} is removed and Q_{12} is applied. Now x_1 starts to decay and x_2 begins to rise quickly, since the input Q_{12} matches with the weight vector z_2. The falling time of x_1 is greater than its rise time as shown if fig. 6.8. and it will continue to contribute some positive input to the unit 2. Similarly, when Q_{13} is applied x_3 starts to rise and the previous outputs x_1 and x_2 will contribute as positive input to the unit 3. This process continues till the last input vector is applied to the network. By the time the final input vector Q_{1m} is applied, it matches with z_{1m} and the corresponding output x_m reaches saturation which is the network output represented as, $y=x_m$. Fig. 6.8 shows a simple five unit STN for pattern recognition of a word. From the figure it is clear that the activity pattern appears to flow smooth from left to right.

The input vectors have to be applied in the proper sequence, otherwise pattern mismatch will occur. Lets us discuss the network response by applying the input vectors in the reverse order. While Q_{1m} is applied, it matches with z_{1m} and the network output x_m rise quickly to reach the saturation even though, there is no contribution of input from the output of other units. When $Q_{1,m-1}$ is applied, x_{m-1} rises and contributes to x_m. Now the net input applied to the mth unit is dx_{m-1} and its output continues to decay because $d < 1$. Hence net input will be less than the threshold ($\Gamma = 0.9$). At the time of applying the last input vector, the network output x_m may decay completely and result in improper recognition of the STP. Fig. 6.9 shows an example of random order. This discussion is made on the assumption that the input vector $Q_{1,m-1}$ is orthogonal to the weight vector z_m and hence there is no contribution to the input of mth unit. In practice, these vectors need not be orthogonal.

The decay time of the unit output is longer than the rise time and hence the network has the property of being insensitive to the speed at which the STP is presented.

The tolerance of time variation is a desirable characteristic in STN since different speakers speak the same word at different rates.

The STN described so far is used for the recognition of a single word. For the recognition of multiple words, the network is replicated for each word. Fig. 6.10 shows the STN for recognition of *N* distinct words.

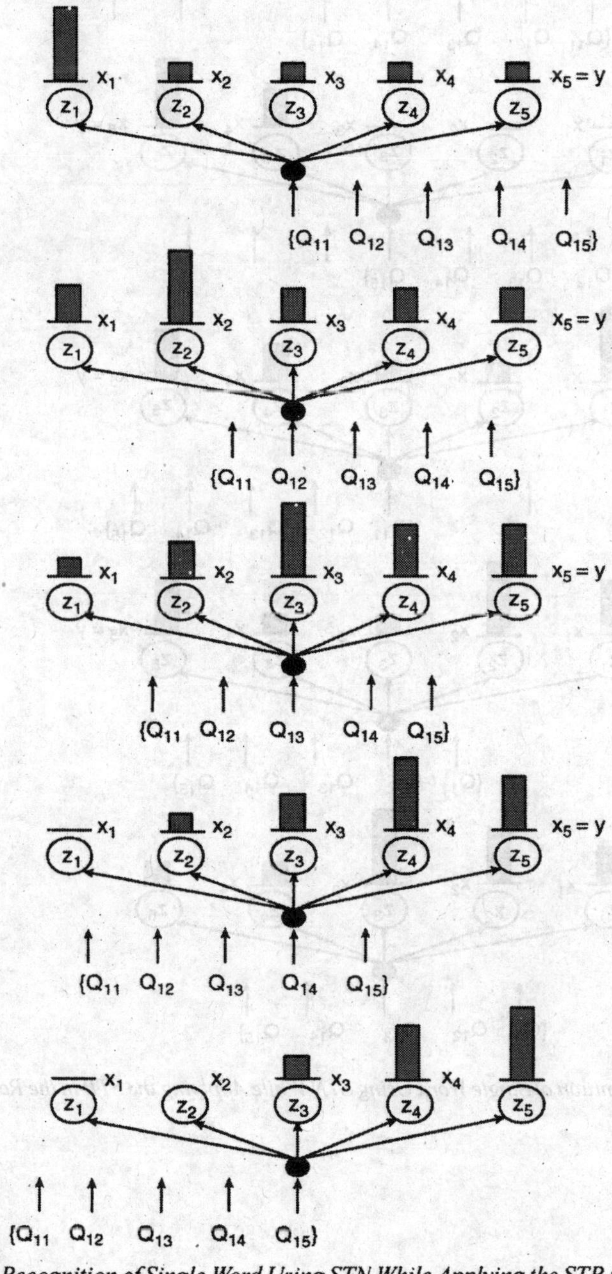

Figure 6.8 *Recognition of Single Word Using STN While Applying the STP in the Proper Order*

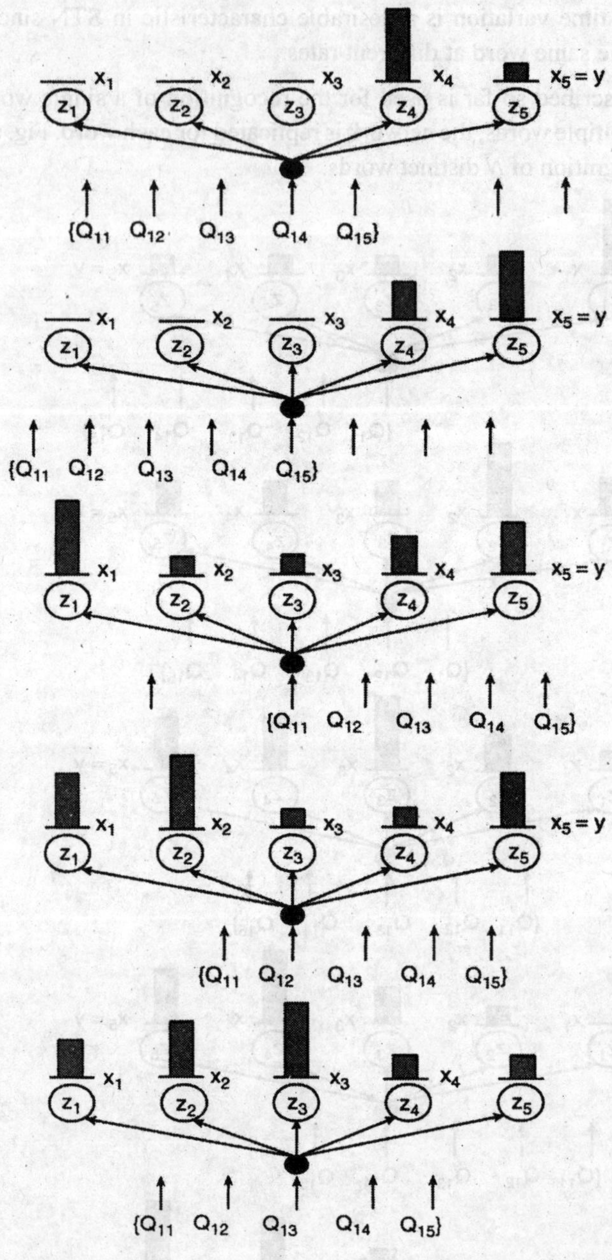

Figure 6.9 *Recognition of Single Word Using STN While Applying the STP in the Random Order*

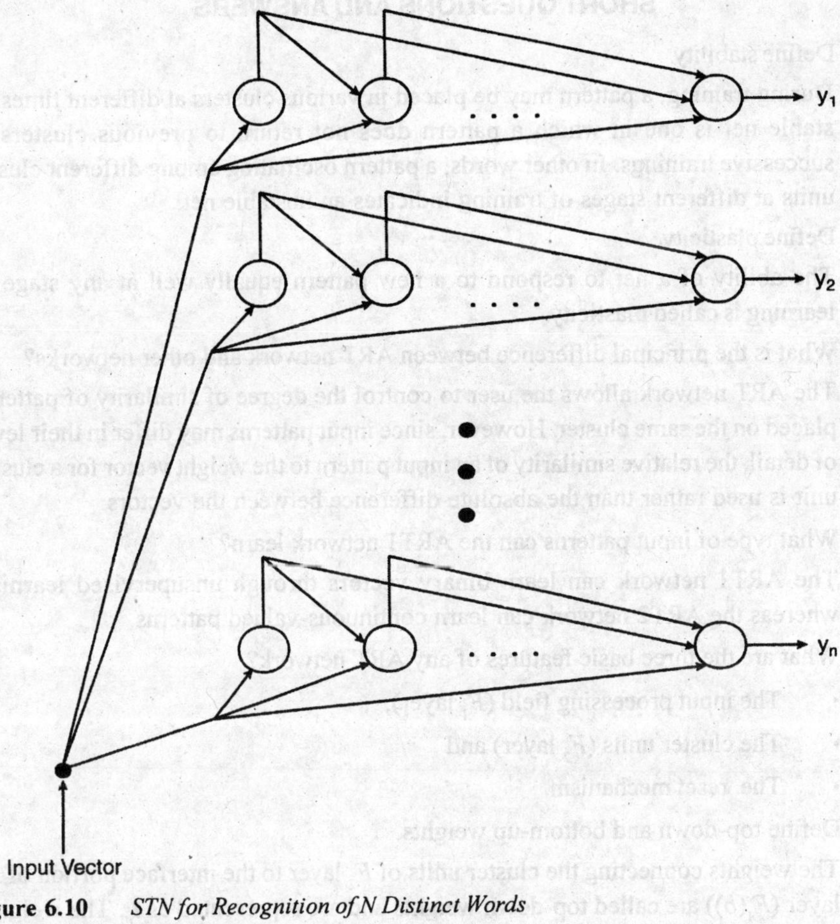

Figure 6.10 *STN for Recognition of N Distinct Words*

6.4.3 Applications of STNs

We have discussed STN by taking the application of speech recognition. It can also be used for radar analysis and sonar-echo classification as described earlier in this chapter. The General Dynamics Corporation built a prototype sonar-echo classification by using the STN architecture [2]. For this classification, the incoming sonar signals were converted to STP using power spectrum analyzer with proper time sequence. The network on training with seven civilian boats was able to identify the vessels correctly from the incoming sonar signals.

REFERENCES

[1] Stephen Grossberg. Learning by neural networks. In Stephen Grossberg, editor, *Studies of Mind and Brain.* D. Reidel Publishing, Boston, MA, pp 65–156, 1982.

[2] Robert L. North. Neurocomputing: Its impact on the future of defense systems. *Defense Computing*, 1(1), January–February 1988.

SHORT QUESTIONS AND ANSWERS

1. Define stability.

   During training, a pattern may be placed in various clusters at different times. A stable net is one in which a pattern does not return to previous clusters in successive trainings. In other words, a pattern oscillating among different cluster units at different stages of training indicates an unstable net.

2. Define plasticity.

   The ability of a net to respond to a new pattern equally well at any stage of learning is called plasticity.

3. What is the principal difference between ART network and other networks?

   The ART network allows the user to control the degree of similarity of patterns placed on the same cluster. However, since input patterns may differ in their level of detail, the relative similarity of an input pattern to the weight vector for a cluster unit is used rather than the absolute difference between the vectors.

4. What type of input patterns can the ART1 network learn?

   The ART1 network can learn binary vectors through unsupervised learning whereas the ART2 network can learn continuous-valued patterns.

5. What are the three basic features of any ART network?

   - The input processing field (F_1 layer),
   - The cluster units (F_2 layer) and
   - The reset mechanism.

6. Define top-down and bottom-up weights.

   The weights connecting the cluster units of F_2 layer to the interface portion of F_1 layer ($F_1(b)$) are called top-down weights and are represented as t_{ji}. The weights connected from the interface portion to the cluster units are called bottom-up weights and are represented by b_{ij}.

7. What is meant by vigilance parameter?

   The degree of similarity required for patterns to be assigned to the same cluster unit is controlled by a user specified parameter called the vigilance parameter.

8. Comment on the states of the cluster units of an ART network during training.

   The F_2 node is in one of the three states during training.

   1. Active state (on-state)
   2. Inactive state (off-state)
   3. Inhibited state (prevented from participation)

9. What are the two basic units of an ART1 network?

   The architecture of an ART1 net consists of:

   1. Computational units:
      The computational unit consists of F_1 layer, F_2 layer and the reset mechanism.

2. Supplementary units:

   It consists of gains, G_1 and G_2.

10. What is the importance of supplemental units in ART1 network?

    The ART1 network without supplemental unit faces two problems:

    1. The F_1 and F_2 units are required to respond differently at different stages of the process and a biological neuron does not have a method for deciding what to do and when.
    2. The operation of a reset mechanism is quite complex .i.e. the F_2 unit must be inhibited under certain conditions but returned to availability on subsequent trials.

    Both these problems can be solved using two supplemental units, G_1 and G_2.

11. What is the significance of ART2 network?

    ART2 network is designed to perform continuous-valued input vectors, the same type of tasks as ART1 does for binary valued input vectors. The differences between ART1 and ART2 reflect the modifications needed to accommodate patterns with continuous-valued components.

12. Why F_1 field is complex in ART2 unlike ART1?

    The F_1 field in ART2 includes a combination of normalization and noise suppression in addition to comparison of bottom-up and top-down signals needed for reset mechanism. Hence it is complex.

13. What are the two types of inputs used for ART2 network?

    1. Noisy binary signals and
    2. Truly continuous signals.

14. What is the activation function used in ART2 network?

$$f(x) = \begin{cases} x, & \text{if } x \geq \theta \\ 0, & \text{if } x < \theta \end{cases}$$

15. What is the use of noise suppression in ART2 network?

    The activation function treats any signal that is less than θ as noise and suppresses it. Noise suppression helps the net to achieve stable cluster formation.

16. How do we achieve slow learning in ART2 network?

    In slow learning, only one iteration of the weight update equations occurs on each learning trial. A large number of presentations of each pattern is required, but relatively little computation is done on each trial. For convenience, these repeated presentations are treated as epochs. However, there is no requirement that the patterns be presented in the same order.

17. How do we achieve fast learning in ART2 network?

    In fast learning mode, the weight updates continue until the weights reach equilibrium on each trial. Only a few epochs are required but a large number of iterations must be performed on each learning trial. In fast learning, the placement of the patterns on clusters stabilizes, but the weights will change for each pattern presented.

18. Differentiate between fast learning and slow learning.

Fast learning	Slow learning
In fast learning, the iterations of weight change followed by updates of F_1 layer proceed until equilibrium is reached.	In slow learning, only one iteration of the weight update step is required but a large number of learning trials is required for the net to stabilize.
The placements pattern in each cluster stabilizes.	Here, there is no requirement that patterns be presented in an exact order.

19. What are the assumptions employed in ART2 training?

 1. Reset cannot occur during resonance.
 2. A new winning unit cannot be chosen during resonance.

20. Give the expression for noise suppression?

The noise suppression parameter is given by $\theta = \left(1 - \sqrt{n}\right)$ where n is the number of input units. The sample value may be larger than desired in some applications. Components of normalized input vector less than this value are also set to zero.

REVIEW QUESTIONS

1. What type of learning does the ART use, and what kind of problems is it best fit for?
2. How many layers does an ART network have?
3. Explain the working principle of ART network.
4. What are the advantages of ART network?
5. Give an application for ART network.
6. What is the limitation of ART1 network and how it is overcome in the ART2 network?
7. Describe the characteristics of ART network.
8. Explain the major phases of ART classification process.
9. Differentiate between ART1 and ART2 networks.
10. Write the weight update equivalent for ART1 and ART2 networks.
11. How the weights of ART1 network are initialized?
12. Explain the working principle of reset mechanism of ART network.
13. Explain what is meant by plasticity.
14. Explain the significance of vigilance parameter.
15. Explain what is meant by stability - plasticity dilemma as referred to ART network.

CHAPTER

7

Special Networks

7.1 INTRODUCTION

As the revival of neural computing advances well into its second decade, the properties of learning and adaptation which this technique brings into computing in general has been well appreciated. There has been a growing interest in techniques that do not suffer from thc disadvantages of the dominant error backpropagation techniques. Radial basis functions is one such new technique. On the whole, the learning properties of neural networks are becoming more appreciated in pattern recognition tasks and are now used effectively in computing. Networks for specific functions, are being designed. This chapter gives a complete round up of few such networks, their functionalities and their purpose.

7.2 PROBABILISTIC NETWORKS [B40]

One of the special kinds of networks is the probabilistic network. These probabilistic networks are an improvement of the Hopfield networks. For certain kinds of network problems, the Hopfield network has a tendency to settle at local minima. Some of the local minima represent points in the 'energy landscape' where the stored patterns can be found. When an input vector is applied to the network, and it is close to one of these minima, it will move towards those minima because of the nature of the changes in the neurons, which always lowers the energy in the network. So, if a pattern is close to one of the stored patterns, it should produce that stored pattern at the output, once it has settled in the local minima.

There may also be local minima which are not related to stored patterns. The effect of this is that, the network can be given a particular input pattern and after a number of iterations, it will produce a stable output pattern. Later, the network could be given the same input pattern and because the system started in a different 'state', the output that is finally produced could be different, possibly even a complete new pattern.

The way to overcome this problem is to store the patterns at global minima and improve the method for finding minima. One way is to use 'Probabilistic Networks' where occasional jump to higher energy states are allowed rather than always moving towards lower energy. One such network is the Boltzmann Machine.

7.2.1 Boltzmann Machine

Assume that the energy flowing into the system is thermal noise and the system is in thermal equilibrium state. An effective method of finding the global minimum is to mimic a process called simulated annealing. Annealing is the process used for hardening metal, where it is first heated to a high temperature, so that the molecules have a lot of energy and therefore a lot of random motion. As the metal cools, the molecules settle into fixed positions with the tendency to look for minimum energy states.

In systems which are made of particles that can be in either of the two states, the probability of the particle being in state S_a or state S_b follows the Boltzmann distribution:

$$\frac{P_a}{P_b} = e^{-\frac{(E_a - E_b)}{T}} \tag{7.1}$$

and since $P_a + P_b = 1$, it follows that:

$$P_a = \frac{1}{1 + e^{-\frac{(Ea - Eb)}{T}}} \tag{7.2}$$

where T is the temperature and E is the energy in each state.

A network has been proposed called the Boltzmann machine in which the neurons produce '0' or '1' as outputs depending on the value of the weighted sum as before. The difference is that the outputs have a probability associated with them, so that the same weighted sum might produce a '1' output at certain times and a '0' output at others.

Fig. 7.1 shows a typical Boltzmann machine. The connections are bidirectional and the weights are symmetric. The energy associated with the two states of the neuron is assumed to be proportional to the weighted sum of the inputs.

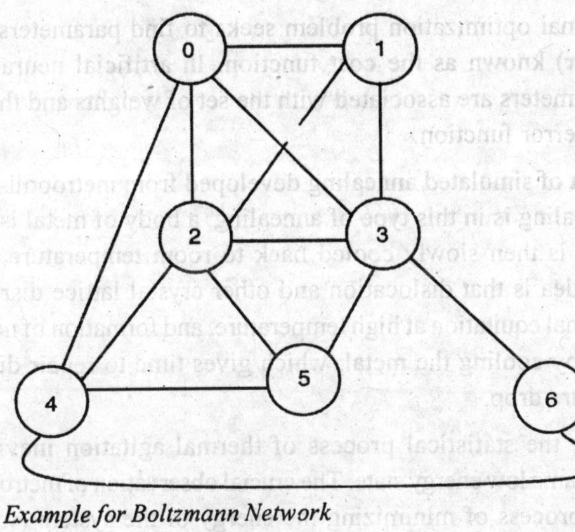

Figure 7.1 *Example for Boltzmann Network*

Thus, the energy can be represented as follows.

When $$y = 1,\ E_1 = -\sum_{i=0}^{n} w_1 x_i = -\text{net} \tag{7.3}$$

and when $y = 0$, $E_0 = 0$.

Substituting into the equation for the probability of the output being 1, P_1:

$$P_1 = \frac{1}{1 + e^{\frac{E_1 - E_0}{T}}} = \frac{1}{1 + e^{\frac{-\sum w_1 x_1}{T}}} = \frac{1}{1 + e^{\frac{-net}{T}}} \tag{7.4}$$

Training the Boltzmann machine Boltzmann Machine is trained by combination of simulated annealing and weight adjustment. Some of the neurons are chosen as inputs and some as outputs. Training has two different phases.

Phase 1 The input pattern and the corresponding output pattern are imposed on the input and output neurons. This is described as clamping the neurons, so that their activity is fixed irrespective of their own internal net values. The temperature is set to some arbitrary high value and the network is allowed to settle into thermal equilibrium. It is then gradually cooled by lowering the temperature by a small amount and then leaving the network to settle in thermal equilibrium. When the temperature reaches a low value, the network should be in a stable state, which should in principle be the global energy minimum for that set of weights.

Phase 2 The clamp on the output is removed and the process of simulated annealing is repeated.

7.2.2 Simulated Annealing

A close of probabilistic weight-change laws appears in neural models as simulated annealing, where it is primarily for combinational optimization problems with many variables.

A combinational optimization problem seeks to find parameters that minimize some function $F(x)$ known as the cost function. In artificial neural networks the configuration parameters are associated with the set of weights and the cost function is associated with error function.

The main idea of simulated annealing developed from metropolis algorithm and metallurgical annealing is in this type of annealing, a body of metal is heated to near melting point and is then slowly cooled back to room temperature (in contrast to quenching). The idea is that dislocation and other crystal lattice disruptions can be eliminated by thermal equitation at high temperature, and formation of new dislocations can be prevented by cooling the metal, which gives time to repair dislocations that occur as temperature drop.

By annealing, the statistical process of thermal agitation inevitably leads to approximately the same low energy state. The crucial observation of metropolis algorithm is that the global process of minimizing the energy of the system (which occurs in physical interactions) because of statistical energy transfer in mechanical molecular interactions can be attributed to the simple localized process of energy modification. The approximate solution obtained by using stimulated annealing is often within a few percent of the optimum.

Cauchy machine The Cauchy machine is a modification of Boltzmann machine and is also referred to as fast simulated annealing. It is based on the principle of adding more noise to the net input to increase the likelihood of escaping from a neighbourhood of a local minimum.

The unbound variance of the Cauchy distribution sometimes allows for larger changes in the confirmation of a system than allowed by the bounded variance of the Gaussian distribution. Noise based on Cauchy distribution is called "coloured noise" in contrast to the "white noise" of Gaussian distribution. The addition of Cauchy noise is equivalent to using an acceptance probability that makes it more likely for the net to accept a bad move.

The Cauchy machine can be included in the Gaussian form work of setting

$$\Delta t = T = 1$$

where Δt is time step to obtain,

$$\Delta u_i = u_i + \text{net}_i$$

where u_i is the input to unit u,

$$u_i(\text{new}) = \text{net}_i = \sum_{j=1}^{N} w_{ij} u_j + \theta_i + \varepsilon$$

where net_i is the input to unit u_i and ε is random noise.

Assuming that the noise obeys Cauchy distribution with mean zero and standard deviation $\sigma = T\sqrt{\frac{8}{\pi}}$ where T is the temperature.

Integrating the Cauchy noise distribution, the Cauchy acceptance function is derived as

$$\sum_{0}^{\alpha} \frac{1}{\pi} \frac{Tdx}{T^2 + (x - u_i)^2} = \frac{1}{2} + \frac{1}{\pi} \arctan \frac{u_i}{T} = A(I,T)$$

Note: $u_i = \Delta c(i)$

One of the potential advantages of the Cauchy machine is the possibility of using a faster cooling schedule. The Cauchy cooling schedule is

$$T = T_0/K$$

where K is the number of iterations that have been performed.

7.3 COGNITRON

In 1975, Fukushima put forward the following hypothesis of learning:

The synaptic connection from cell x to cell y is reinforced if and only if the following two conditions are true.

1. Presynaptic cell X fires.
2. None of the postsynaptic cells situated near the cell Y fires stronger than Y.

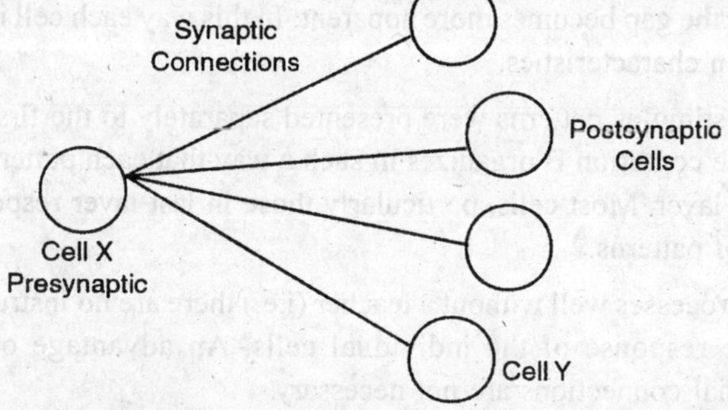

Figure 7.2 *Connection between X and Y*

Fukushima developed a model which he called cognitron as a successor to the perceptron which was able to take cognizance of symbols from any alphabet after training.

The cognitron is a self-organizing multilayer neural network. Its cells receive input from defined areas of the previous layer and also from units within its own area. The neural elements for input and output can take the form of positive analog values which are proportional to the pulse density of firing biological neurons. The cells use a mechanism of shunting inhibition, that is, a cell is bound in terms of a maximum and minimum activity and is driven towards these extremities.

Connectable area This is the area from which a cell receives input.

Vicinity area This is the area formed by the inhibitory cluster.

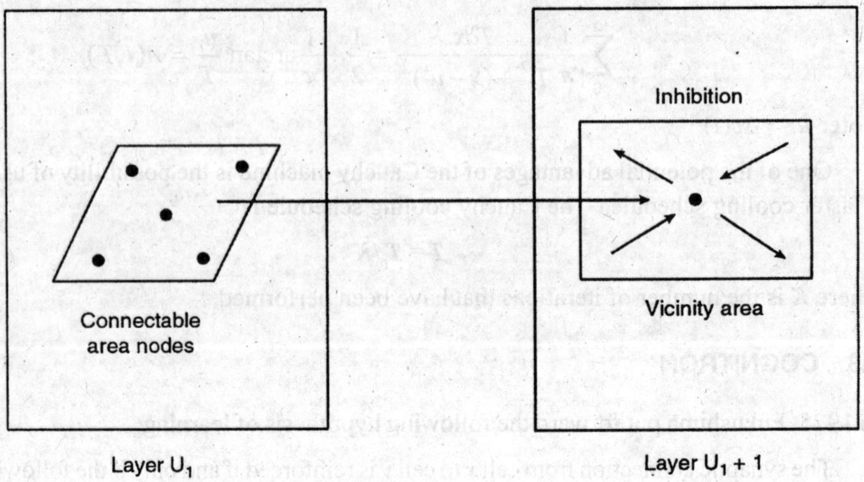

Figure 7.3 *Cognitron Model*

Because the connectable areas for cells in the same vicinity are defined to overlap, but are not exactly the same, a slight difference appearing between the cells will be reinforced so that the gap becomes more apparent. In this way each cell is encouraged to develop its own characteristics.

Training Five stimulus patterns were presented separately to the first layer. After the 20th cycle, the cognition B organizes in such a way that each pattern generates a response in each layer. Most cells, particularly those in last layer respond only to a selective group of patterns.

The model processes well without a teacher (i.e.) there are no instructions given, to determine the response of the individual cells. An advantage of this is that sophisticated initial connections are not necessary.

Applications For cognitron, the relationship between input and output uses the same expression as that used to approximate the nonlinear input to output relations of the sensory receptors (e.g.) cones in the retina of human eye. This is used in neurophysiology and psychology. As this bears such a close resemblance to the natural characteristics of a biological neuron, it is well suited for various kinds of visual and auditory information processing systems.

The cognitron model is a multilayer structure, so there is more capacity for information processing than previous models. This is not intended to be a complete system; additional units being needed at the input for initially getting the sensory input and at the output to act as a decision maker, which judges the results. Improvements could be made if the layers were modified. A suitable example could be backcoupling between cells of distant layers or cross coupling between cells of same layer. In either case, the algorithm would be varied.

However, a drawback of the cognitron was that it could not deal with the problems of orientation or distortion. So a new improved version called the neocognitron was developed.

7.4 NEOCOGNITRON

You would have noticed that almost all human beings are able to recognize people whom they know when they see them from a long distance. They do it even if it is raining or if it is foggy. You would have also observed that they are able to identify letters and numbers in different fonts and sizes even if they are distorted or displaced. This aspect of recognition which is possible by the human eye is amazing. During the early days of the neural networks, when perception was used to recognize patterns, the system failed if the same pattern was either distorted or displaced. It also failed if any pattern that was superficially similar to the trained input was presented. Thus, the research to develop a network to mimic the human eye began. But it was only in 1982 that Fukushima and Miyake were able to develop a model that could successfully accomplish this task. They called the network NEOCOGNITRON, a successor to the COGNITRON (1975) which was also developed by Fukushima.

7.4.1 Precursor: Cognitron

The cognitron is a self-organizing multilayer neural network whose basic form is very much like the general model we know. The only difference is that there are cascades of layers. Each layer receives input from the previous layer and also from units in its own area.

Learning hypothesis Fukushima, who putforth the cognitron also formulated the following hypothesis of learning in 1975:

The synaptic connection from cell X to cell Y is reinforced if and only if two conditions are true:

i. Cell X (presynaptic cell) fires and
ii. None of the postsynaptic cells situated near cell Y fires stronger (or brisker) than Y.

The situation is shown in Fig. 7.2 wherein the presynaptic cell (X) is shown along with the postsynaptic cells including Y, all connected by synaptic connections or weights.

Thus the training of the cognitron is based on a competitive learning mechanism.

Though the cognitron could recognize patterns once trained, it failed if the pattern was oriented or dissolved and this paved the way for the NEOCOGNITRON which was developed in 1982.

7.4.2 Improvement: Neocognitron

The defects of the cognitron were overcome in the form of Neocognitron developed by Fukushima and Miyake in 1982. A neocognitron is a multilayer feedforward neural network model for visual pattern recognition. The neocognitron is trained using a competitive learning procedure. A neocognitron model is shown in Fig. 7.4.

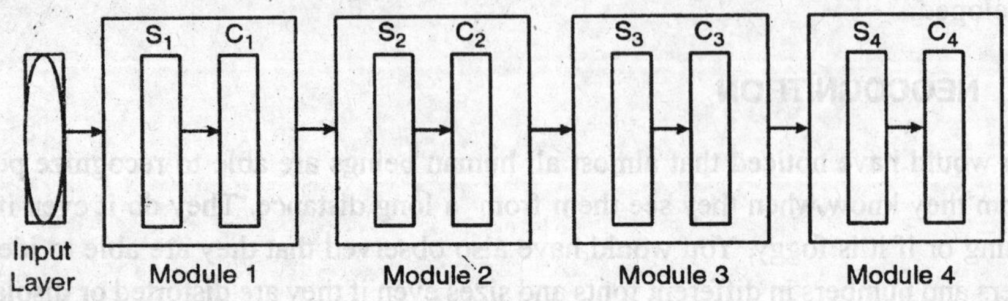

Figure 7.4 *Neocognitron*

The new model uses the same algorithm as the cognitron but this model can recognize patterns that are now position-shifted or shape-distorted. The neocognitron uses two types of cells:

S-cell These cells are trained to respond to only certain features in the previous layer.

C-cell This cell displaces the results of the *S*-cell in space-sort of "spreads" the features recognized by the *S*-cell.

Topology The network uses a hierarchy of many modules. Each module consists of two layers—a layer of *S*-cells and a layer of *C*-cells. *S*-cells receive the input from the previous layer, while *C*-cells receive the input from the *S*-layer.

Only the inputs to the *S*-layer can be modified during training. The *S*-layer is designed to detect specific features and the complexity of the features increases as we go higher up the hierarchy. The feature to be recognized by a node in S_1 layer could be a vertical bar or a horizontal bar but the feature to be recognized by a node in S_5 layer could be much more complex.

Each node in the *C*-layer corresponds to one relative position independent feature. This node receives the inputs from a subset of *S*-layer nodes for that feature. For instance, if one node in *C*-layer detects a vertical line and if 5 nodes in the preceding *S*-layer detect a vertical line, these 5 nodes will give the input to the specific node in *C*-layer in order to spatially distribute them.

Modules that are closer to the input layer (lower in hierarchy) are trained before the modules that are higher in the hierarchy i.e., module 1 will be trained before module 2 and so on.

The "receptive field" of each *C*-node must be fixed by the user before training. This is because the inputs to the *C*-layer cannot be modified. The lower level modules have smaller receptive fields while the higher level modules represent complex position independent features that depend on the detection of simpler features in the hidden layer. Fig. 7.5 illustrates the spreading effect used in neocognitron.

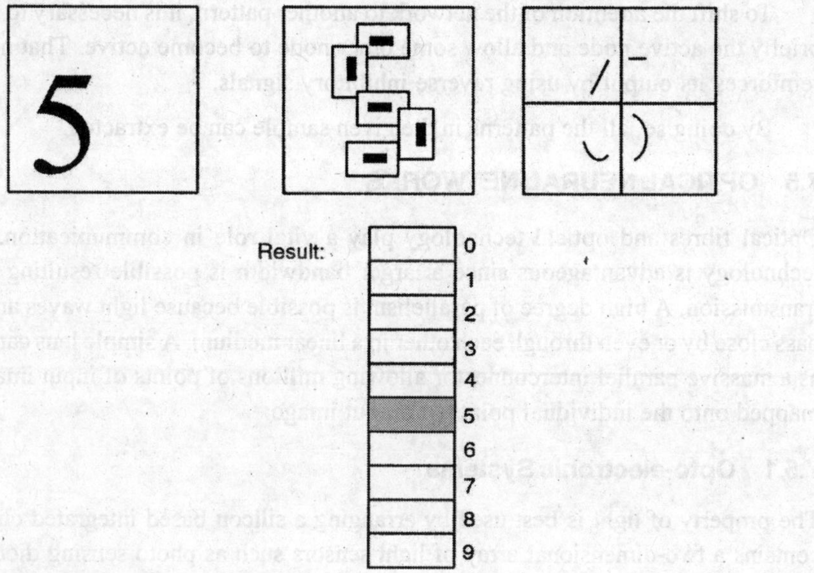

Figure 7.5 *The Spreading Effect*

Selective attention The model discussed so far is a feedforward network. In 1986, Fukushima came out with a closed net form of neocognitron that can recognize a particular pattern from a group of patterns. This model will focus on a given pattern, segment it from others and then recognize it. After that, attention is then switched on to the next pattern and the process is repeated until all the patterns are recognized. Such a model is found to recognize an imperfect pattern and recall the complete pattern with the defects and noise removed. This model is shown in Fig. 7.6.

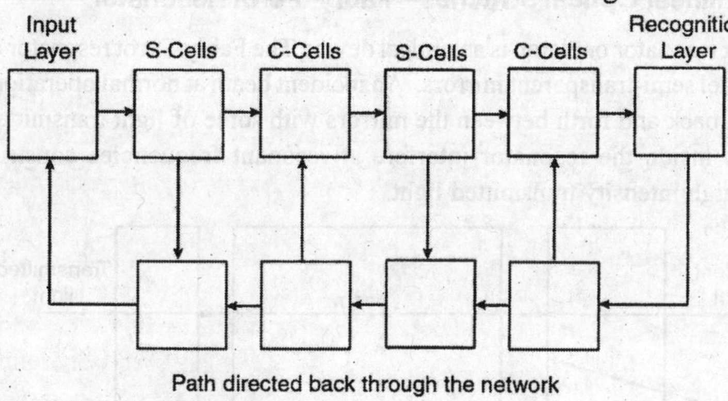

Figure 7.6 *Selective Attention*

Unlike the simpler neocognitron, the selective attention network has an "active input" layer. The reverse connections can turn off some of the units in this layer by inhibitory signals. Thus the reverse signals have the effect of suppressing those portions of the input image that did not contribute to the activation of the currently active node in the previous layer.

To shift the attention of the network to another pattern, it is necessary to suppress briefly the active node and allow some other node to become active. That node then reinforces its output by using reverse inhibitory signals.

By doing so, all the patterns in the given sample can be extracted.

7.5 OPTICAL NEURAL NETWORKS

Optical fibres and optical technology play a vital role in communication. Optical technology is advantageous since a larger bandwidth is possible resulting in faster transmission. A high degree of parallelism is possible because light waves are able to pass close by or even through each other in a linear medium. A simple lens can be used as a massive parallel interconnector allowing millions of points of input image to be mapped onto the individual points of output image.

7.5.1 Opto-electronic Systems

The property of light is best used by arranging a silicon based integrated circuit that contains a two-dimensional array of light sensors such as photo sensing diodes. This provides an interface between an image and the electronic circuits required to process the image. The output could also be a two-dimensional array of light emitting diodes such that electrical connections are necessary for image processing function of the chip.

Spatial light modulator is a two dimensional array of pixels that modulate electronic data, thus providing a means of entering parallel data into an optical computer. Optical devices must also be able to process the signals without the need to convert them into electronic signals.

7.5.2 Nonlinear Optical Switches—Fabry–Perot Resonator

Fabry–Perot resonator or elaton is an optical device.The Fabry-Perot resonator consists of two parallel semi-transparent mirrors. An incident beam at normal operation would be reflected back and forth between the mirrors with some of light transmitted. The light waves inside the resonator interfere at resonant frequencies constructively producing high intensity transmitted light.

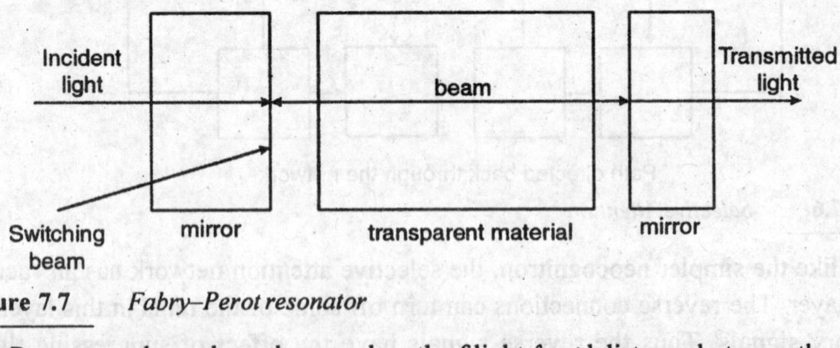

Figure 7.7 *Fabry–Perot resonator*

Resonance depends on the wavelength of light λ and distance between the mirrors d. In case of constructive interference, the path difference for various waves must be equal to whole number of wavelengths, thus,

$$2d = k\lambda$$

where k is an integer.

The resonator can be made into an optical switch by introducing non-linear material between the mirrors. The material has the property called photorefractive effect, where refractive index changes with the intensity of the light. This type of device will be produced by using wafer of non-linear crystal with sides covered with reflective layer. The device is called an etalon.

The refractive index of medium is defined as the ratio of speed of light in free space c_o to the speed of light in that medium c_m.

$$n = c_0/c_m$$

The relationship between frequency f and wavelength of light λ is

$$c = f\lambda$$

Combining both the equations gives

$$f = kc_0/2dn$$

so, as n increases, the resonant frequency decreases.

If frequency of incident beam is chosen to lie just below the resonance frequency, the output will be of low intensity level. Then if a small additional light signal is applied, the intensity increases and so refractive index increases and the resonant frequency comes down. Thus, an optical switch is produced, the output being either a small or large beam depending on the switching input.

Fig. 7.8 shows the switching characteristics of a resonator. As intensity of switching beam increases the intensity of output remains low until the threshold is reached, at which point the intensity switches to some higher value. If the switching beam's intensity is decreased now the intensity of the output stays high and then changes to a low value. This characteristic is known as hysteresis and can be useful in the construction of a bistable device.

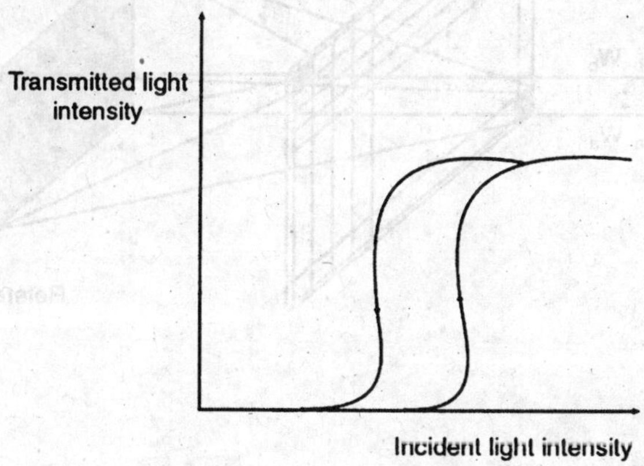

Figure 7.8 *Switching Characteristics*

7.6 HOLOGRAPHIC NEURAL NETWORKS

A hologram can direct a light beam in a direction determined by the information stored as an interference pattern on a tiny area of film. The familiar notion of a holographic picture which is seen in three dimensions is based on the property of being able to reconstruct intensity of light ray as well as the direction in which it is transmitted.

In principle, the proposed scheme is the basis for reaction of neural nets. In this arrangement, input to the neuron is obtained by means of an optical light modulator. The weight of each input is determined by the intensity with which each element of the SLM is illuminated. This intensity is controlled by a hologram which on being illuminated by a reference beam produces an accurate pattern of light intensities in the plane of SLM.

The light shining through each element is given by

$$W_a . X_a$$

where W_a is the amount of illumination coming from the hologram and X_a is the transmission value of SLM element.

The full lens arrangement for focusing the total light coming through SLM is not shown, but it is all directed towards detector output.

It is also quite possible to use a higher degree of parallelism. The hologram could be just one area of a larger M^*M sheet of such holograms. This means that SLM input neuron would be processed individually. The second neuron for high level of interest in holographic methods comes from the possibility that the entire processing procedure in a neural net could be done typically.

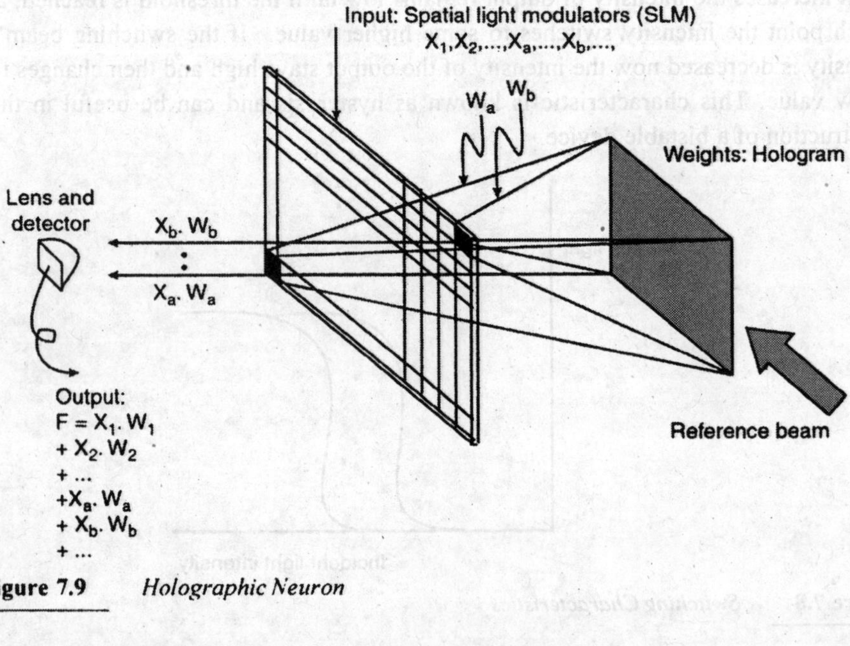

Figure 7.9 *Holographic Neuron*

Example 7.1 For a single cell with two inputs for a neocognitron model, find the Parameters a_1, a_2 and b after one iteration.

Solution

The input parameters are:

$$a_1 = 0; a_2 = 0; b = 0; c_1 = c_2 = 0.5; r = 1; q = 0.5$$

The input pattern is:

$$x_1 = 0; x_2 = 1$$

For the input pattern, $x_1 = 0$, $x_2 = 1$; the response is:

$$v = \sqrt{c_1 x_1^{\ 2} + c_2 x_2^{\ 2}}$$

$$u = r\phi\left(\frac{1 + a_1 x_1 + a_2 x_2}{1 + \frac{rby}{r+1}} - 1\right) = 0$$

$$\Delta a_1 = qc_1 x_1 = 0$$

$$\Delta a_2 = qc_2 x_2 = 0.25$$

$$\Delta b = qv = 0.35$$

So, $a_1 = 0$, $a_2 = 0.25$ and $b = 0.35$. If these values are substituted, the new value of u is 0.114.

SHORT QUESTIONS AND ANSWERS

1. What is a cognitron?

   A cognitron is a self-organizing multilayer neural network. Its cells receive input data from defined areas of the previous layer and also from the units within its own area. The neural elements for input and output can take positive analog values.

2. What is a connectable area?

   The area from which the input cell receives the input is called connectable area.

3. Justify that cognitron uses unsupervised training.

   The cognitron training model progresses well without a teacher. i.e. there are no instructions to determine the response of the individual cells. Hence, it uses unsupervised training. An advantage is that sophisticated internal connections are not necessary.

4. What are the disadvantages of cognitron?

   The drawback of cognitron is that it cannot deal with the problems of orientation and distortion.

5. What are the applications of cognitron?

   Cognitron is used in neuro-physiology and psychology. It is also used in visual and auditory information processing systems.

6. What are neocognitrons?

   The neocognitron is a model for visual pattern recognition and is concerned with biological plausibility. The network emulates the retinal images and processes them using two-dimensional layer of neurons.

7. What are selective attention networks?

   The selective attention network has an "active input" layer. The reverse connections can turn off some of the units in this layer by inhibitory signals. Thus, the reverse signals have the effect of suppressing those portions of the input image that did not contribute to the activation of the currently active node in the previous layer.

REVIEW QUESTIONS

1. Define the term 'OUT' related to Cognitron neuron.
2. What is meant by progressive redundant elemental feature coding?
3. What is the advantage of Boltzmann machine?
4. Differentiate Boltzmann machine from Cauchy machine.
5. How is Hopfield network converted to Boltzmann machine?
6. Why is simulated annealing used in many paradigms?
7. What is meant by fast simulated annealing?
8. Why are Boltzmann and Cauchy machines called probabilistic networks?
9. Discuss an algorithm for Boltzmann machine.
10. How do probabilistic networks solve the problem of local minima?
11. Define neocognition.

CHAPTER

8

Control Networks

8.1 INTRODUCTION

A complex network system may contain a neural network which controls or influences its processes. This network is termed as control neural network. It can be built out of a domain model based on domain knowledge. More than one network can be involved in the domain structure. Barto, Sutton and Anderson developed the first neurocontrol scheme. Their system involved two networks, both of which were simple table look-ups. Action and critic networks were clearly distinguished in their neurocontrol theory. Their approach has nourished a substantial line of research on neurocontrol. Lapedes and Farber developed another scheme which consisted of a master network and a slave network; the former set the weights for the latter.

Control decides the next action. This decision is based on the current situation and the goals to be pursued. Such information is described in the database or the working memory. The database is non-monotonic, since an action when executed may change it.

When there is more than one goal to be accomplished, the controller must determine the dependencies among goals and order them properly. In planning systems, there are different ways to order goals. An old approach is to use a linear stack, which processes goals by the 'last in first out' order. A blackboard-based model deals with goals in an asynchronously parallel manner. There are various heuristic approaches for ordering goals. The goal with the highest priority score is visited first. In the data-driven control, action is based on the current situation; in the goal-directed control, the action is based on the currently processed goal; and in the mixed approach, the action is based on both the current situation and the currently processed goal.

The mixed control strategy is more efficient than the other two since it offers bidirectional search for the solution.

8.2 NEUROCONTROLLER [B26]

No one in the field of control systems can be unaware of the growth of artificial neural networks. This is clearly indicative of the desire to use artificial neural network algorithms in control systems. Neural networks have the potential to provide a framework for modelling and control of nonlinear systems.

8.2.1 Schemes for Neurocontrol

Models of dynamic systems and their inverses have immediate utility and control. In the control literature, a number of well-established and deeply analyzed structures (schemes) for the control of nonlinear systems exist. Such models are made available in the form of neural networks which have been trained. The following control schemes, from the mainstream control theory viewpoint are of much importance.

Supervised control There are many control situations where a human provides the feedback control action for a particular task and where it has been proven difficult to design an automatic controller using standard control technique. In some situations, it is desirable to design an automatic controller which mimics the action of the human. Neural networks provide a possibility for this.

Direct inverse control This scheme utilizes an inverse system model. The inverse model is simply cascaded with the controlled system and the composed system results in an identity mapping between the desired response and the controlled system output. Thus the network acts directly as a controller in such configuration. Direct inverse control is common in robotics application. This approach relies heavily on the fidelity of the inverse model used as the controller. Absence of feedback leads to lack of robustness. This problem can be overcome to some extent by using online learning.

Model reference control Here the desired performance of the closed-loop system is specified through a stable reference model M which is defined by its input-output pair $\{r(t), y^r(t)\}$. The control system attempts to match the plant output $y^p(t)$ with that of the reference model output i.e.

$$\lim_{t\to\infty}\left\|y^r(t)-y^p(t)\right\|\le\varepsilon, \text{ for some specified constant } \varepsilon\ge 0.$$

Predictive control In the realm of optimal and predictive control methods, the 'receding horizon technique' has been introduced as a natural, computationally feasible feedback law. In this approach, the neural network model predicts the future plant response over the specified horizon. The predictions supplied by the networks are passed to a numerical optimization routine which attempts to minimize a specified performance criterion in the calculation of a suitable control signal.

Optimal decision control In this application, the state space is partitioned into regions corresponding to various control situations. The realization of a control surface is accomplished through a training procedure. Since the time-optimal surface in general is nonlinear, it is necessary to use architecture capable of approximating a nonlinear surface. One of the possibilities is to quantize the state space into elementary hyper-cubes in which the control action is assumed constant. This process can be carried out with linear vector quantization architecture. It is then necessary to have another network as a classifier. If continuous signals are required, a standard back-propagation architecture can be used.

Adaptive linear control A Hopfield network may be utilized as a dynamic controller for a linear system. In this case, elements of various structure theories are utilized to construct the controller. Hence, it is robust. It is possible to include adaptation through standard methods. The Hopfield network can also be used as a part of the adaptation mechanism. In this case, the network is included in the adaptation path and is used to minimize square-error rates of all the states simultaneously. Here, the output of the network represents the parameters of a linear model for the plant.

Adaptive control using a generic index (Reinforcement learning control) This kind of network makes use of low quality feedback signal. While the performance measure for a supervised system is defined in terms of a set of targets by means of a known error, reinforcement learning addresses the problem using any measure whose value can be supplied to the learning algorithm. Instead of trying to determine the target controller outputs from the target plant responses, one tries to determine target controller outputs that would lead to an increase in the measure of plant performance.

8.3 BRIEF OVERVIEW OF CONTROL SYSTEM CONCEPTS

8.3.1 Static and Dynamic Systems [B13]

The concepts of transfer characteristics, transfer functions and feedforward and feedback control are discussed below, as these are related to neurocontrollers. Solutions to a control problem depend directly on the precision with which the characteristics of the process are known. For example, in a single channel control problem, if the plant input is a scalar variable, the process if known can be described by a relationship between the plant actuating signal and the plant response. In general, this relationship is expressed as P, where P is the process transfer function. It has the form $P(s)$ where, s is the complex variable.

Plants are basically of two types. The static or the nondynamic plant is the one where the transfer function $P(s)$ is independent of s and reduces to simple functional relationship between the actuating signal and the response. For such plants, the transfer function becomes the transfer characteristics. In case of dynamic plants, they cannot be characterized by constants, not even by complex time-invariant functions because their responses, being solutions of differential or integro-differential equations, are functions of time. The transfer function for such plants is defined as the ratio between the integral transforms of the output and the input signal. The Laplace transform is the most commonly used transform to express the input and output signals of linear plants. The significance of the transfer characteristics in system and control theory is based on the fact that the response of a static system to an arbitrary excitation can be computed as a product of its transfer characteristics and of the excitation. Similarly, the transform of the response of a dynamical system can be expressed as a product of the transfer function and transform of the excitation.

8.3.2 Open-loop Configuration

For a plant that is completely known, any desired relationship between input and response can be realized by a simple open-loop control configuration as shown in Fig. 8.1. The feedforward controller consists of two parts connected in cascade. The second one cancels the process transfer function because its own transfer function has been chosen as the inverse of the known process transfer function. In addition, the front part of the controller introduces the desired overall transfer function of the controller and the plant, equal to *D*. Thus the controller's transfer function should be equal to *D*/*P*. This approach is known as inverse control since the most essential part of the controller provides the inverse of the plant's transfer function.

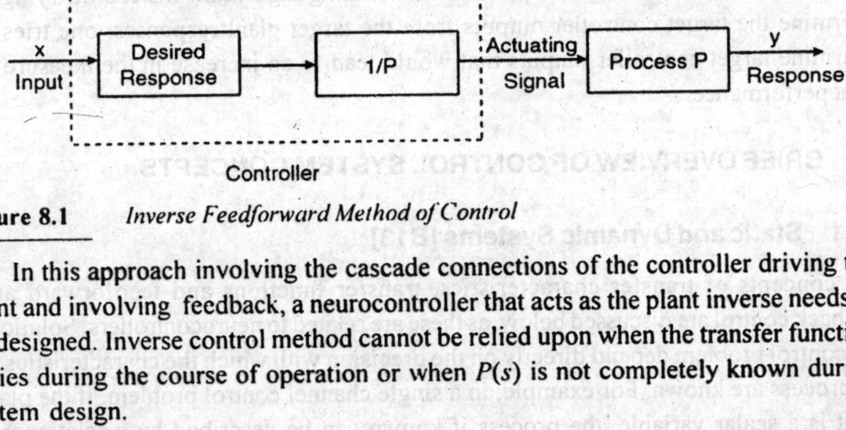

Figure 8.1 *Inverse Feedforward Method of Control*

In this approach involving the cascade connections of the controller driving the plant and involving feedback, a neurocontroller that acts as the plant inverse needs to be designed. Inverse control method cannot be relied upon when the transfer function varies during the course of operation or when $P(s)$ is not completely known during system design.

8.3.3 Feedback Control

It is a thumb rule to turn to feedback control systems to circumvent any or both of the above mentioned limitations. One of the most common feedback arrangements is shown in Fig. 8.2.

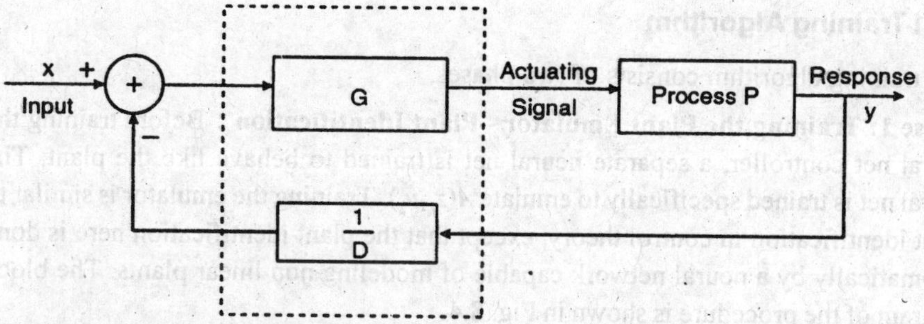

Figure 8.2 *Feedback Control*

For high and fixed loop gains, the output is independent of the plant transfer function, $P(s)$. Therefore, the use of feedback provides a useful means of overcoming both the parameter variation of the plant and ignorance of the transfer characteristics. These observations hold true for non-dynamic plants too.

In the proceeding sections, we shall see the various phases involved in designing a neurocontroller scheme, and plant identification schemes using neural networks.

8.4 CONTROL PROBLEM — IDENTIFICATION AND TRAINING

The standard representation of a finite-dimensional, discrete-time plant is shown in Fig. 8.3. The vector u_k represents the inputs to the plant at time k and the vector z_k represents the state of the plant at time k. The function, $A(z_k,u_k)$ maps the current input state onto the next state.

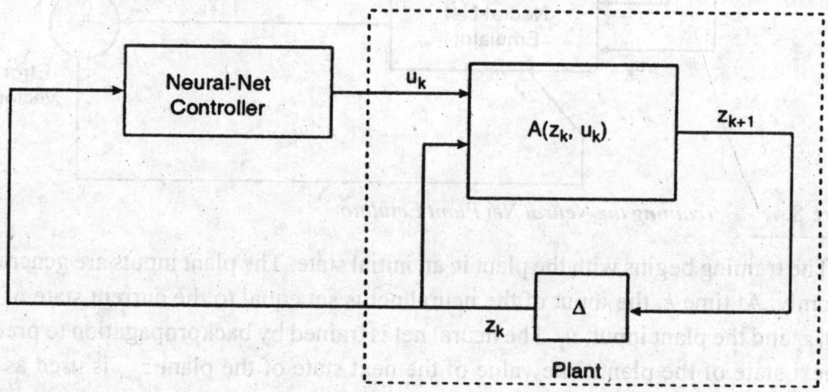

Figure 8.3 *Plant and Controller*

A common problem in control is to provide the correct input vector to drive a nonlinear plant from an initial state to a subsequent desired state z_d. Any of the previously mentioned schemes can be used to train the controller depending on application and trade-offs.

8.4.1 Training Algorithm

The training algorithm consists of two phases.

Phase 1: Training the Plant Emulator - Plant Identification Before training the neural net controller, a separate neural net is trained to behave like the plant. The neural net is trained specifically to emulate $A(z_k, u_k)$. Training the emulator is similar to plant identification in control theory, except that the plant identification here is done automatically by a neural network capable of modeling non linear plants. The block diagram of the procedure is shown in Fig. 8.4.

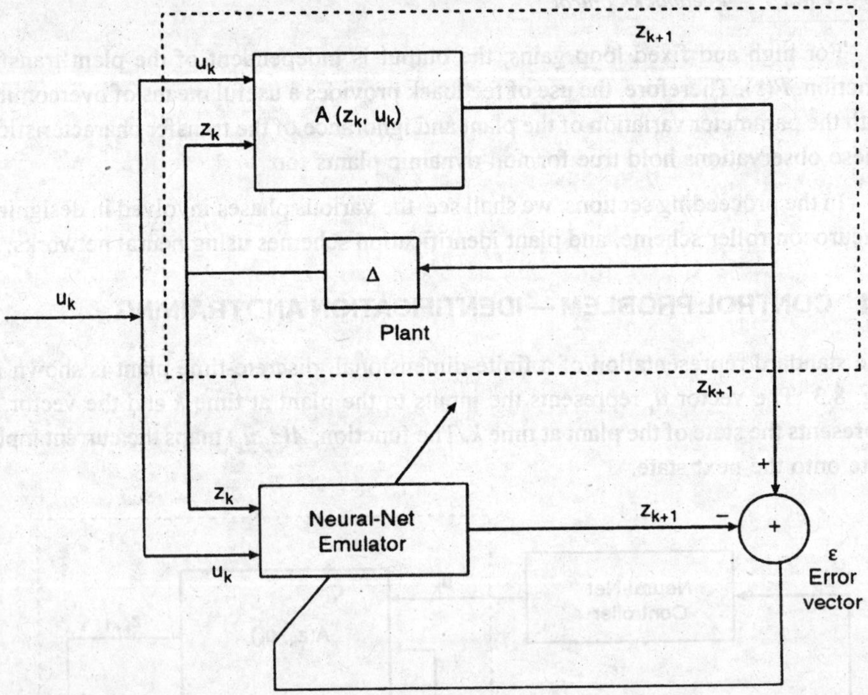

Figure 8.4 *Training the Neural Net Plant Emulator*

The training begins with the plant in an initial state. The plant inputs are generated randomly. At time k, the input of the neural net is set equal to the current state of the plant, z_k and the plant input, u_k. The neural net is trained by backpropagation to predict the next state of the plant. The value of the next state of the plant z_{k+1} is used as the desired response during training.

Phase 2: Training the Neural Network Controller Now that the emulator closely matches the plant dynamics, we use it for the purpose of training the controller. The controller learns to drive the plant emulator from an initial state z_o to the desired state z_d in k time steps. Learning takes place during many trials and runs, each starting from an initial state and terminating at a final state z_k. The objective of the learning process is to find a set of controller weights that minimises the error function J, where J is averaged over the set of initial state z_o.

$$J = E\left(\left\|z_d - z_k\right\|^2\right)$$

Training process for the controller is illustrated below:

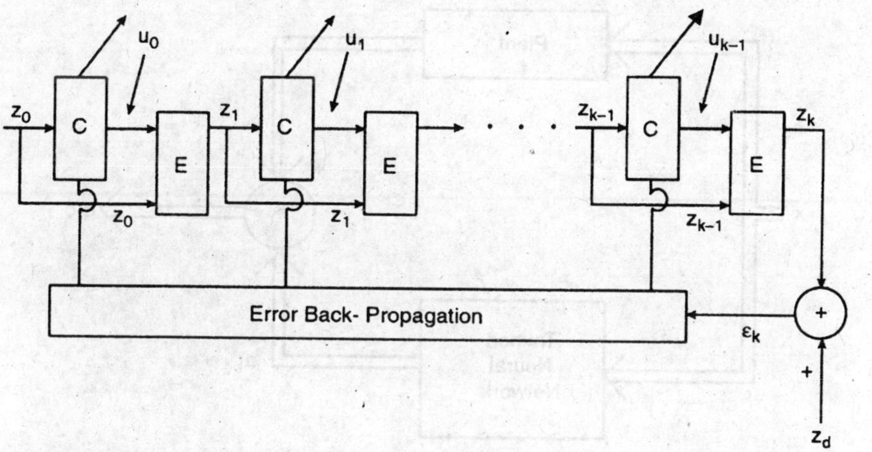

Figure 8.5 *Training the Controller with backpropogation (C = controller, E = emulator)*

8.5 SYSTEM IDENTIFICATION AND CONTROL [B9]

System identification is concerned with the construction of a model which describes an empirical relationship between system input and system output. System identification is often necessary for a control problem. The control problem deals with the setting of the input so that the output follows a desired curve. A mathematical model which relates the input and the output can help us to solve this problem because it allows us to calculate the desired input for a desired output. Suppose the model equation is:

$$Y(t) = F(X(t))$$

If the function F is invertible, then the desired input can be calculated from the desired output by

$$X(t) = F^{-1}(Y(t))$$

Thus, the control problem is solved by inverting the system dynamics.

8.5.1 Process Identification

In general, identification of the process should result in usable terms such as co-efficients of a plant differential equation or co-efficients of its transfer function. Neural networks used for identification purpose in the field typically have multilayer feedforward architectures and are trained using the error backpropagation technique.

The basic configuration for forward plant identification is shown in Fig. 8.6. A nonlinear neural network receives the same input x as the plant, and the plant output provides the desired response d during training. The purpose of identification is to find the neural network with response o that matches the response y of the plant for a given set of inputs x. During identification, the norm of the error vector $\| d\text{-}o \|$ is minimised through a number of weight adjustments.

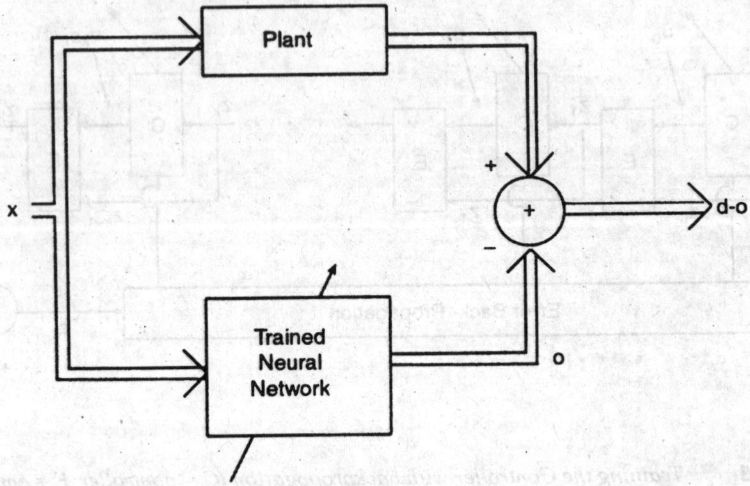

Figure 8.6 *Forward Plant Identification*

The inverse plant identification uses the plant output y as the neural net input as shown in Fig. 8.7. The error vector for the trained network is computed as $x\text{-}o$, where x is the plant input. The norm of the error vector to be minimized through learning is therefore $\|x - o\|$. The neural network trained in this way will implement the mapping of the plant inverse. Once the network is trained, it can be directly used for inverse feedforward control.

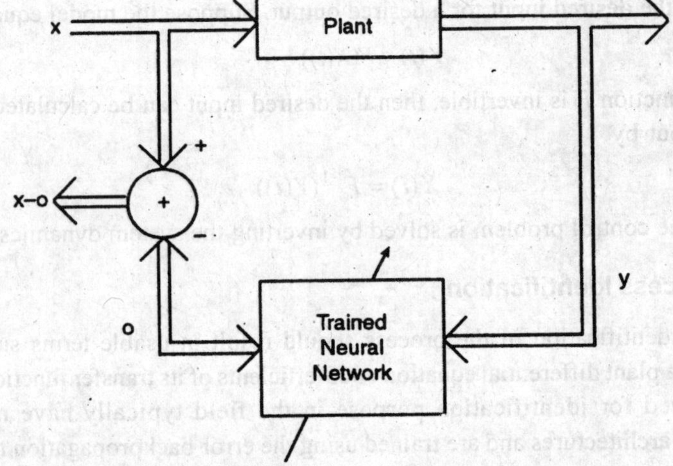

Figure 8.7 *Plant Inverse Identification*

The schemes used for modelling the two processes are described in the next section.

8.5.2 Forward Modelling

The procedure of training a neural network to represent the forward dynamics of a system will be referred to as forward modelling. A structure for achieving this is shown schematically in Fig. 8.8.

The neural network model is placed in parallel with the system and the error between the system and the network outputs are used as the network training signals. An issue in the context of control, is the dynamic nature of the systems under study. A possibility is to introduce dynamics into the network itself. This can be done either by using recurrent networks or by introducing dynamic behaviour into the network,

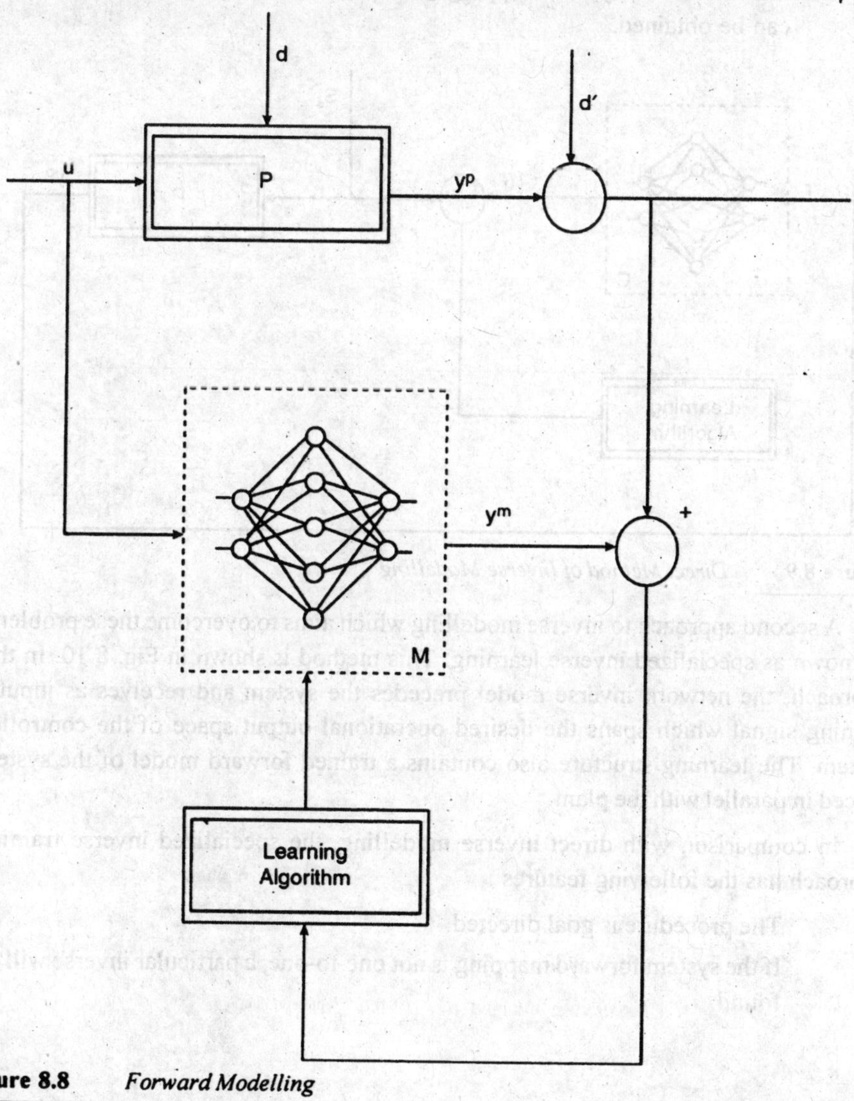

Figure 8.8 *Forward Modelling*

8.5.3 Inverse Modelling

Inverse models of dynamic systems play a crucial role in a range of control structures. However, obtaining inverse models raises several important issues which will be discussed. Conceptually, the simplest approach is the direct inverse modelling as shown schematically in Fig. 8.9. Here, a synthetic training signal is introduced. The system output is then used as an input to the network. The network output is compared with the training signal and the error is used to train the network. This structure will clearly tend to force the network to represent the inverse of the plant. However, there are drawbacks to this approach:

- the training procedure is not goal directed.
- if the nonlinear system mapping is not one-to-one, then an incorrect inverse can be obtained.

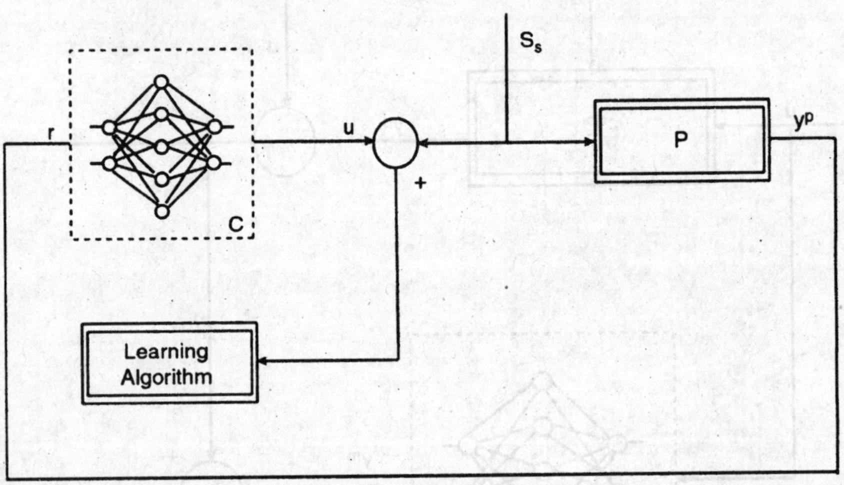

Figure 8.9 *Direct Method of Inverse Modelling*

A second approach to inverse modelling which aims to overcome these problems is known as specialized inverse learning. This method is shown in Fig. 8.10. In this approach, the network inverse model precedes the system and receives as input a training signal which spans the desired operational output space of the controlled system. The learning structure also contains a trained forward model of the system placed in parallel with the plant.

In comparison with direct inverse modelling, the specialized inverse training approach has the following features :

- The procedure is goal directed.
- If the system forward mapping is not one-to-one, a particular inverse will be found.

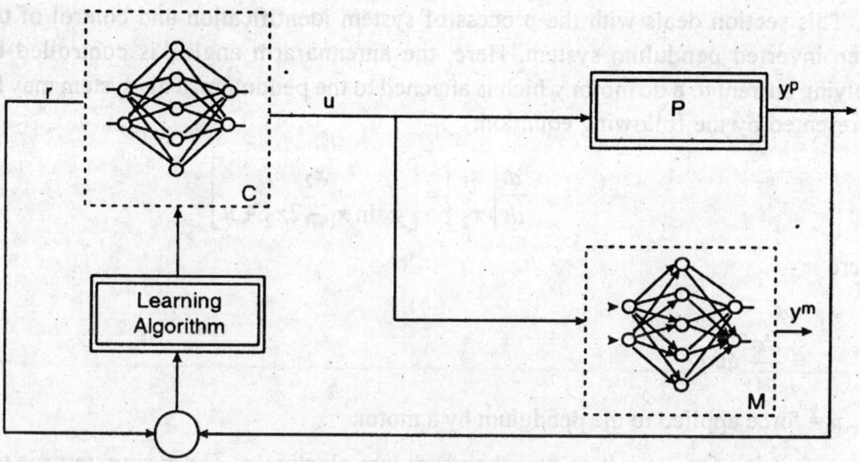

Figure 8.10 *Specialized Method of Inverse Modelling*

8.6 ADAPTIVE CONTROL OF DYNAMIC SYSTEMS

The adaptive control method enables a neural network to learn to control a plant in an autonomous way without a specific learning stage. The plant is treated as an additional and unmodifiable layer of the network and only simple qualitative knowledge of the plant is necessary. In order to avoid oscillations across the walls of ravines and to eliminate slow and long training caused by small gradients in plateaus, adaptive algorithms have been used to accelarate training. Independent adaptive step size parameters for each weight has been found more powerful than optimizing the global learning rate.

Certainly, an adaptive controller using direct control by backpropagation can be very sensitive to the dynamic properties of the plant. The various parameters that can be adaptively changed includes the learning rate, momentum factor, slope parameters and various other constants. The time to achieve convergence decreases significantly through local adaptation of these parameters.

8.7 CASE STUDY: INVERTED PENDULUM SYSTEM [B6, B42]

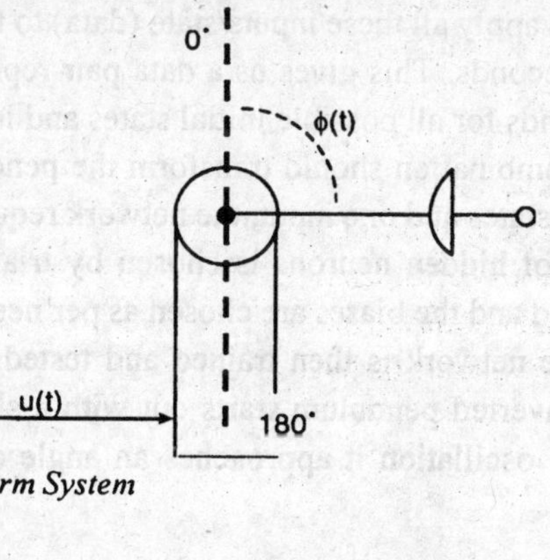

Figure 8.11 *Antenna Arm System*

This section deals with the process of system identification and control of the given inverted pendulum system. Here, the antenna arm angle ϕ is controlled by applying current to a dc motor which is attached to the pendulum. This system may be represented by the following equation:

$$\frac{d}{dt}\begin{bmatrix} x_1 \\ x_2 \end{bmatrix} = \begin{bmatrix} x_2 \\ g \sin x_1 - 2x_2 + u \end{bmatrix}$$

where

$x_1 = \phi$

$x_2 = \dfrac{d\phi'}{dt}$ and

u = force applied to the pendulum by a motor.

A positive force tends to turn the pendulum clockwise. The $g \sin x_1$ term is the force of gravity on the pendulum and the $-2x_2$ term is viscous friction against the velocity.

The aim is to apply a sequence of inputs, that is, forces of fixed magnitudes so that the pendulum is balanced. The problem is then defined by generating different pendulum angles, velocities and forces. By taking all possible combinations of these values, and by assuming a set of steady state conditions, we get a set of data represented by its angle and velocity. Input is the current provided to the dc motor.

Like the real system, the neural network model to be trained has three inputs.

1. Antenna position (ϕ).
2. Velocity (v).
3. Input current (u).

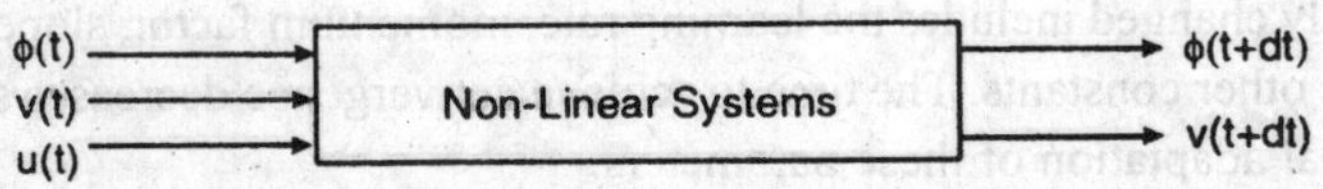

Figure 8.12 *System Representation*

The next step is to apply all these inputs/state (data) to the system and derive the next state after 0.05 seconds. This gives us a data pair representing the state of the system after 0.05 seconds for all possible initial states and inputs. The network when given an input/state combination should transform the pendulum state into the next state. As there are two states and one input, the network requires three inputs and two outputs. The number of hidden neurons is chosen by trial and error method. The weights are randomized and the biases are chosen as per need to model the nonlinear pendulum system. The network is then trained and tested to see if it provides the desired results. The inverted pendulum starts out with a slightly positive angle but falls quickly. After an oscillation it approaches an angle of 180° pointing straight down.

Controller design A second order sigmoid / linear network is trained to act as a controller for the antenna. Such controllers can be trained to produce systems with any desired behaviour.

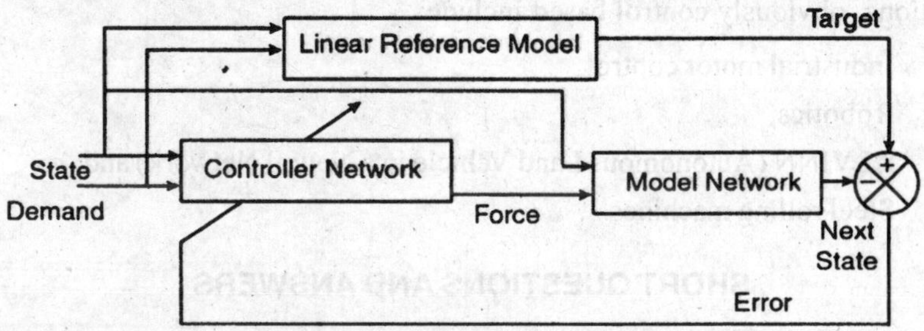

Figure 8.13 *Neurocontroller for Case Study*

The entire neurocontroller is shown in Fig. 8.13. The demand position r, the system initial position ϕ, and initial velocity v are presented to the controller. The controller will generate current u such that the antenna positions a time-step later without overshoot and remains there. In particular, the controlled neural network acts as a linear reference model described by the equation

$$\frac{dx_1}{dt} = x_2$$
$$\frac{dx_2}{dt} = -9x_1 - 6x_2 + 9r$$

After each time-step, the controller calculates the appropriate current (u), and the system reacts to the current and the gravity to arrive at a new state.

The controlled neural network has three inputs and one output. Once the controller network is initialized with random weight matrices and bias vectors, it is ready to be trained. The creation of input-output vector training pair is as in design of reference model.

The difference between the linear reference model's target response and the actual response of the neural controlled system are calculated as errors and are back propagated through the controller. However, weights of the system are not changed, only the neurocontroller is trained. Once the neurocontroller is designed, the reference model is discarded.

8.8 SUMMARY

Neural networks have many applications in control systems. In general, a neural network may be trained to respond to variations of the input such that the output is maintained as closely as possible to the desired one. As in traditional control, we may also consider an open loop and a closed loop control system.

Adaptive control using computers has progressed dramatically since the 1970's. Significant research in intelligent control continues and many applications have found their way in the market place using fuzzy logic and neural networks. The various applications, obviously control based include:

i. Industrial motor control,
ii. Robotics,
iii. ALVINN (Autonomous Land Vehicle in a Neural Network) and
iv. Steel rolling machines.

SHORT QUESTIONS AND ANSWERS

1. **Draw the block diagram of a neurocontroller?**

   The block diagram of a neurocontroller is shown below:

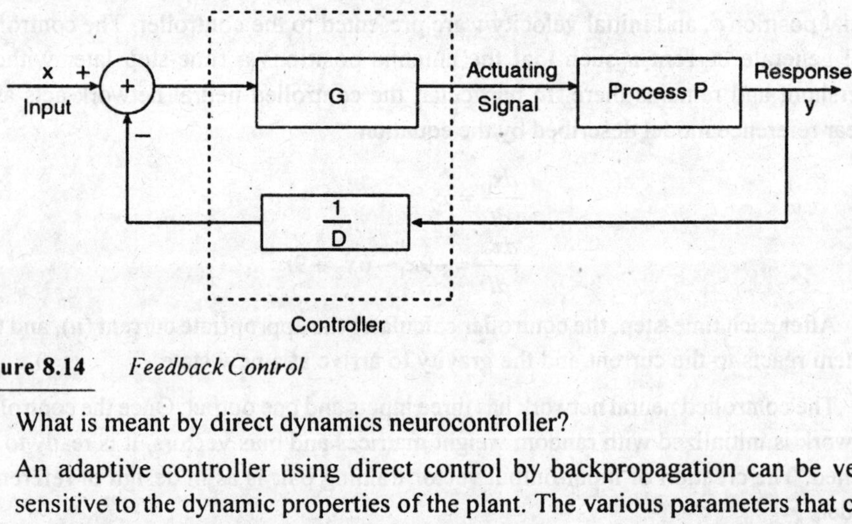

Figure 8.14 *Feedback Control*

2. **What is meant by direct dynamics neurocontroller?**

   An adaptive controller using direct control by backpropagation can be very sensitive to the dynamic properties of the plant. The various parameters that can be adaptively changed, include the learning rate, momentum factor, slope parameters and various other constants. The time to achieve the convergence decreases significantly through local adaptation of these parameters.

3. **What is meant by neural model of a process?**

   Process identification is concerned with the construction of a model which describes an empirical relationship between the system input and the system output. A mathematical model which relates the input and the output can help us to solve this problem because it allows us to calculate the desired input given a desired output. Suppose the model equation is:

$$Y(t) = F(X(t))$$

   If the function F is invertible, then the desired input can be calculated from the desired output by

$$X(t) = F^{-1}(Y(t))$$

Thus, the control problem is solved by inverting the system dynamics.

4. Bring out any two advantages of neurocontroller.
   1. The complexities of the calculations that need to be carried out and the non-linearities of the plant can be solved using the controllers.
   2. Irrespective of the domain, in automatic control systems measurements need to be translated into actions by a device called the controller.
5. What are the various control schemes for a neurocontroller?

   The following are the control scheme.
   a. Supervised control
   b. Direct inverse control
   c. Model reference control
   d. Predictive control
   e. Optimal decision control
   f. Adaptive linear control
   g. Adaptive control using a generic index (reinforcement learning control)

REVIEW QUESTIONS

1. Define neurocontrollers.
2. Differentiate static and dynamic systems.
3. Why is adaptive control using a generic index called reinforcement learning control?
4. Define "Receding Horizon Technique".
5. Explain briefly the neurocontrol schemes.
6. Write short notes on controller with inverse dynamics.
7. Define modelling of a plant.
8. Why is Hopfield network used in adaptive linear control?
9. Name the various features of control systems used in the modelling of a neurocontroller.
10. Mention the significance of transfer characteristics to both static and dynamic systems.
11. What are the demerits of open loop control? How is it rectified in feedback control?
12. Explain the various features of phase 1 and phase 2 training of neurocontroller.
13. Explain the advantages of neurocontroller to control systems.
14. Distinguish between forward modelling and inverse modelling.
15. Define system identification. Mention its significance in design of a neurocontroller.

Problems

1. Write a computer program to implement the Hebb net, for a single layer network with two input neurons, one bias and one output neuron.

   There are 16 different logical functions (with two inputs and one output) of which 14 are linearly separable. Show that the Hebb rule can find the weights for that have bipolar representation is used and a bias is included.

2. Assume the initial weight vector:

$$w^1 = \begin{bmatrix} 1 \\ -1 \\ 0 \\ 0.5 \end{bmatrix}$$

   The set of three input vectors are $x_1 = [1\ -2\ 1.0\ 0]^T$, $x_2 = [1\ -0.5\ -2\ -1.5]^T$, $x_3 = [0\ 1\ -1\ 1.5]^T$. For various learning constants, assuming bipolar neurons, find the final weights using Hebb net.

3. Use the Hebb rule to find the weights required to perform the following classifications. Vectors [1,1,1,1] and [–1,1,–1,–1] are members of the class (largest value 1); vectors [1,1,1,–1] and [1,–1,–1,1] are not members of the class (having target value -1).

   Test the same set of samples using the final weights.

4. Apply Hebb rule to the training patterns that define:
   (i) OR function
   (ii) AND-NOT function
   (iii) AND function
   (iv) X-OR function
   (v) NOR function

5. Write a computer program to classify various English letters framed by a 5×5 matrix grid using Adaline Learning algorithm.

6. Implement an ADALINE network to describe the function $y = x_1\bar{x}_2$. The learning rate is 0.1 and initial weights are –0.12, 0.4 & 0.65. The bias value is 1.

7. Using ADALINE model (without bias) find the weight after first epoch to perform the following classification. Vectors [–1 1 1 –1] and [–1 –1 1 –1] are members of first class and the vectors [1 1–1 1] and [–1 1 1 –1] are the members of second class. Assume $\alpha = 0.45$ and initial weights are zero.

8. With initial weights as 0.1, implement the AND function using ADALINE network. Assume learning rate as 0.2.
9. Write a computer program to simulate a Madaline to perform the XOR function.
10. Write a computer program to classify letters from different fonts using perceptron learning. Use as many output as number of letters. Compare the ability of perceptron to train ADALINE in this application.
11. Using perceptron learning rule, find the weights required to perform the following classifications. Vectors (1 1 1 1) and (–1 1 –1 –1) are the members of the first class. Vectors (1 1 1 –1) and (1 –1 –1 1) are members of the second class. Use two output neurons. Assume learning rate as 0.9 and initial weights of 0.25. Using the training vectors, test the response of the net.
12. Consider a two-layer perceptron with two input units, three hidden units and one output unit. Assume a hard limiting function as activation function and thresholds of all units as zero. There are two classes of patterns as

    (7,5), (6,3), (2,4) ∈ class A

    (6,0), (–1,–2), (3,–3) ∈ class B

    a. Will this network classify these patterns?

    b. Discuss the linear separability of these patterns.
13. Implement the following using perceptron:

    (i) AND function $y = x_1 x_2$

    (ii) OR function $y = x_1 + x_2$

    (iii) AND-NOT function $y = x_1 \bar{x}_2$
14. Simulate the auto-associative network through a C program. Also find how many patterns can be stored for a given configuration. Try to find out how much noise the net can handle.
15. Using the Hebb rule store the vectors (1, 1, 1, 1) and (1,1,–1,–1) in an auto-associative neural net. Find the weight matrix. Test the net using the vectors (1,1,1,1), (1,1,–1,–1) and (1,1,1,0). [Do not set diagonal terms to zero.]
16. Repeat the above problem with the diagonal terms in the weight matrix set to zero. Discuss the differences.
17. For the sample and target vectors given below, find the weight matrix to store the samples in a hetero-associative net.

	s_1	s_2	s_3	s_4		t_1	T_2
s	(0	0	0	1)	t	(0	1)
s	(0	0	1	1)	t	(0	1)
s	(1	0	0	0)	t	(1	0)
s	(1	1	0	0)	t	(1	0)

18. Given the sample and target vectors:

	s_1	s_2	s_3	s_4		t_1	t_2
s	(–1	–1	–1	1)	t	(–1	1)
s	(–1	–1	1	1)	t	(–1	1)
s	(1	–1	–1	–1)	t	(1	–1)
s	(1	1	–1	–1)	t	(–1	1)

Check whether the sample can be associated with the target using a hetero-associative network.

19. Find the weight matrix to store the following pattern using auto-associative network:

(i) [1 1 1 –1] (ii) [–1 1 1 –1]

(iii) [–1 1 1 1] (iv) [–1 –1 –1 1]

20. Using the weight matrix obtained in the previous problem, find the output y for input sample X = [1 –1 1 1].

21. Consider the TC pattern as shown below:

×	×	×	×	×	×
•	×	•	×	•	•
•	×	•	×	×	×

Use BAM to solve for auto-associativity of the pattern.

22. Write a computer program to implement the back propagation network.

23. Find the new weights for the backpropagation network shown below to train the following input / output pattern [0, 0, 1] – 1. The neurons are activated by binary sigmoidal activation function. Assume learning rate as 0.3.

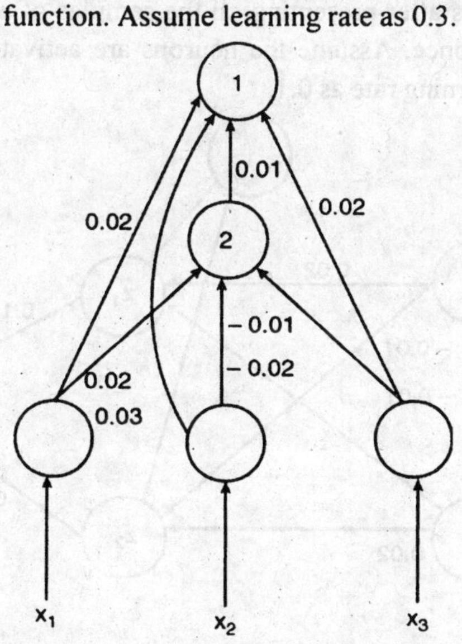

24. Repeat the above problem with a momentum factor of 0.7, learning rate of 0.4 and use bipolar activation function.
25. Find the new weights for the network shown below, when presented with the input pattern [−1 1] to associate a target pattern −1. Use bipolar activation function. Assume learning rate as 0.1. All the bias weights are 0.25.

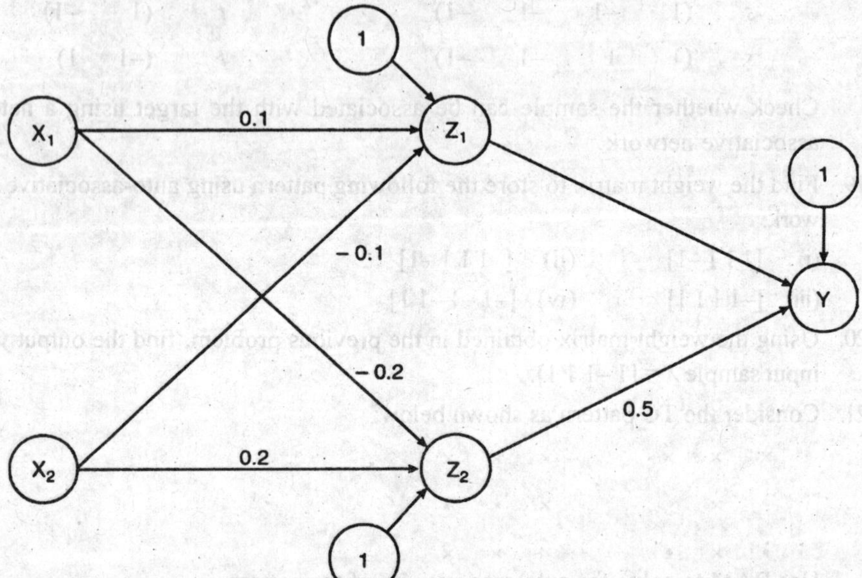

26. Repeat the above problem using binary activation function and a learning rate of 0.25.
27. A backpropagation network has initial weights as shown in Figure below. Determine the weights after presenting all the samples of an XOR problem (bipolar input / output) once. Assume the neurons are activated by sigmoid activation function and learning rate as 0.1.

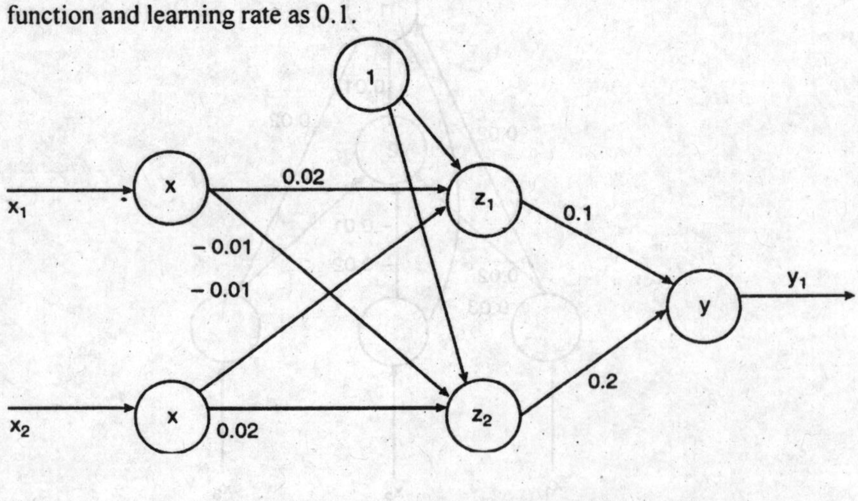

28. Repeat the above problem for binary input / output, with learning rate as 0.45 and momentum factor = 0.7.
29. For the network shown below, use backpropagation training algorithm to determine the weights after a single pass of all samples of an X-NOR gate for both binary and bipolar input / output. Assume learning rate and momentum factor as 0.2 and 0.9 respectively.

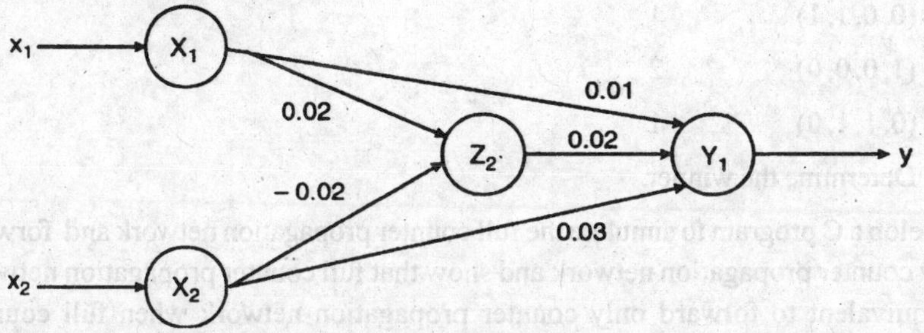

30. Repeat the above problem with a learning rate of 0.9 and a momentum factor of 0.2.
31. Simulate a hetero-associative net using a C Program. Test the hetero-associative net for various input-output pairs.
32. Use the hybrid (binary/bipolar) form of Hebb rule learning to find the weight matrix for the associative memory network based on the following binary input/output vector pairs.

    $S(1) = (1\,0\,0\,0)$ $\quad t(1) = (0\,0)$

    $S(2) = (1\,0\,0\,1)$ $\quad t(2) = (1\,0)$

    $S(3) = (0\,1\,1\,0)$ $\quad t(3) - (0\,1)$

    $S(4) = (0\,1\,0\,1)$ $\quad t(4) = (0\,1)$

33. Consider a BAM to store three pairs of vectors as follows:

Input	**Output**
$X_1 = (1,-1,-1)$	$Y_1 = (1,-1)$
$X_2 = (-1, 1,-1)$	$Y_2 = (-1.1)$
$X_3 = (-1,-1,1)$	$Y_3 = (1,-1)$

    Examine the network for test vectors $X = (-1,-1,-1)$.

34. Use a BAM to store three pairs of vectors as follows:

Original Vector	**Associated Vector**
[1,–1,1]	[–1,1,1,–1]
[–1,1,1]	[1,–1,1,1]
[1,1,1]	[–1,1,1,–1]

    a. Specify network structure and connection weights
    b. Examine whether the BAM can accurately retrieve the associated vector if each of the original vectors are given.

35. In a Learning Vector Quantization network the following input vectors represent two classes 1 and 2

Vector	Class
(1, 1, 0, 0)	2
(0, 0, 0, 1)	1
(0, 0, 1, 1)	1
(1, 0, 0, 0)	2
(0, 1, 1, 0)	1

Determine the winner.

36. Develop a C program to simulate the full counter propagation network and forward only counter propagation network and show that full counter propagation network is equivalent to forward only counter propagation network when full counter propagation network is concatenated for training input and target pattern.

37. Implement a full counter propagation network to store the letters *T* and *C*. Investigate the number of patterns that can be stored and recalled correctly. Solve the above problem using forward only counter propagation.

38. Write a computer program to implement a discrete Hopfield net to store the letters *T* and *C*. Investigate the number of patterns that can be stored and recalled correctly as well as the ability of the net to correspond correctly to noisy input.

39. Consider the action of a maxnet with four neurons and inhibitory weights. $\epsilon = 0.4$. The net is given the initial activations $a_1(0) = 0.5$, $a_2(0) = 0.3$, $a_3(0) = 0.7$ and $a_4(0) = 0.9$. Find the winner.

40. Given the weight values of ε as 0.2 and the excitations as $a_1(0) = 0.2$; $a_2(0) = 0.4$; $a_3(0) = 0.6$ and $a_4(0) = 0.8$, find the neuron with a non-zero value using maxnet architecture.

41. A Mexican hat network has a radius of positive reinforcement links as 1, connecting links as 2, positive reinforcement weights and negative reinforcement weights as 0.6 and – 0.4 respectively. The net is excited by an external signal $x_{max} = 2$. The excitation signal X is [0.0 0.5 0.8 1.0 0.8 0.5 0.0]. What is the new activation signal?

42. Classify the given samples into two clusters using Kohonen self-organizing map (1 1 0 0), (0 0 0 1), (1 0 0 0), (0 0 1 1). Assume the learning rate as 0.2.

43. Repeat the above problem for the samples:
(0 1 0 1), (1 0 0 0), (0 1 0 0), (1 1 0 0)

44. Write a C program to simulate a Mexican hat network.

45. A Mexican hat network is using the activation function,

$$f(x) = \begin{cases} 0, & \text{if } x < 0 \\ x, & \text{if } 0 \le x \ge 4 \\ 4, & \text{if } x > 4. \end{cases}$$

The radius of reinforcement region is 2 and the positive reinforcement is 1.

The excitation signal x is (0.0, 0.6, 0.9, 1.1, 0.9, 0.6, 0.0). The positive and negative reinforcement weights C_1 and C_2 are 0.6 and 0.4 respectively. Determine the activation after 2nd iteration.

46. Develop a C program to stimulate a Hamming net.

47. Given the exemplar vectors $e(1) = (-1, 1, 1, -1)$ and $e(2) = (1, -1, -1, -1)$, use a Hamming net to find an exemplar that is closest to each of the bipolar input patterns, $(1, -1, -1, 1)$, $(-1, -1, -1, 1)$, $(1, -1, 1, -1)$ and $(-1, 1, 1, -1)$.

48. Develop a simulation for a Kohonen's self organizing map using a computer program.

49. Find the winning neuron and the maximum update weight when the learning rate $\alpha = 0.5$ and the network is subjected to the following input. $X = [0.2, 0.2, 0.1, 0.1]$.

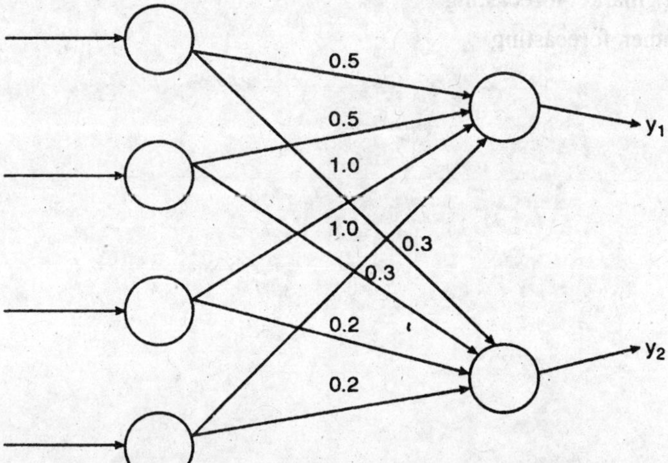

50. Simulate the ART network (both ART1 & ART2) algorithms through a 'C' program.

51. Consider an ART1 neural network with four F_1 units and three F_2 units. After some training, the weights are as follows:

Bottom up weights			Top down weights			
0.67	0.0	0.2	1	0	0	0
0	0	0.2	0	0	0	1
0	0	0.2	1	1	1	1
0	0.67	0.2				

Determine the new weight matrices when the vector (0,0,1,1) is presented if

a. the vigilance parameter is 0.3

b. the vigilance parameter is 0.7

52. Design a network for travelling salesman problem using:
    i. Hopfield network
    ii. Boltzmann machine
53. Design a Hopfield network for a digital to analog converter.
54. Explain and design a neurocontroller for DC motor speed control.
55. Design a neurocontroller for distillation column.
56. Design a neurocontroller for thermal process.
57. Design suitable networks for the following applications:
    i. Search and detection of land mines
    ii. To analyze the quality of wine
58. Suggest suitable neural networks for the following forecasting problems.
    i. DC machine load forecasting
    ii. Stock market forecasting
    iii. Weather forecasting

Bibliography

[B1] Alison Carling, *Introducing Neural Networks,* Galgotia Publication Pvt. Ltd., New Delhi, 1995.

[B2] Bernard Widrow and Michael A. Lehr, "30 years of Adaptive Neural Networks: Perceptron, Madaline, and Back-propagation," *Proceedings of the IEEE*, vol.78, no.9, pp.1415–1442, September 1990.

[B3] Carl G. Looney, *Pattern Recognition using Neural Networks,* Oxford University Press, Oxford, 1997.

[B4] Chun-Hsien Chen and Vasant Honavar, "A Neural-Network Architecture for Syntax Analysis," *IEEE Trans. on Neural Networks,* vol.10, no.1, pp. 94–114, January 1999.

[B5] Cihan H. Dagli, Editor, *Artificial Neural Networks for Intelligent Manufacturing,* Chapman and Hall, London, 1994.

[B6] Derrick H.Nguyen and Bernard Widrow, "Neural Networks for Self-Learning Control Systems," *IEEE Mag. on Control Systems,* pp.18–23, April 1990.

[B7] Dimitris A Karras and Stavros J.Perantonis, "An Efficient Constrained Training Algorithm for Feedforward Networks," *IEEE Trans. on Neural Networks,* vol.6, no.6, pp.1420–1433, November 1995.

[B8] Don R.Hush and Bill G.Horne, "Progress in Supervised Neural Networks: What's new since Lippmann?" *IEEE Signal Processing Mag.*, pp.8–39, January 1993.

[B9] Esther Levin, Raanan Gewirtzman and Gideon F.Inbar, "Neural Network Architecture for Adaptive System Modeling and Control," *Neural Networks,* vol.4, pp.185–191, 1991.

[B10] Fernando J.Pineda, "Generalization of Back-Propagation to Recurrent Neural Networks," *Phys. Rev. Lett.*, vol.59, no.19, pp.2229–2232, November 1987.

[B11] M.M.Gupta and D.H.Rao, "Dynamic Neural Units with Applications to the Control of Unknown Non Linear Systems," *Journal of Intelligent and Fuzzy Systems,* vol.1, no.1, pp.73–92, 1993.

[B12] Hecht–Nielsen. R, "Counterpropagation Networks," *Journal of Applied Optics* pp. 4979–4984.

[B13] K.J. Hunt, B. Sbarbaro, R. Zbikowski, P.J. Gawthrop, "*Neural Networks for Control Systems – A Survey,*". Pergamon Press Ltd., Oxford, England, pp. 1083–1112, 1992.

[B14] Igor Aleksander and Helen Morton, *An Introduction to Neural Computing*, International Thomson Computer Press, London, 1995.

[B15] Jacek M.Zurada, *Introduction to Artificial Neural Networks,* Jaico Publishing House, Mumbai, 1997.

[B16] Jacques de Villiers and Etienne Barnard, "Back-Propagation Neural Nets with One and Two Hidden Layers," *IEEE Trans. on Neural Networks,* vol.4, no.1, pp.136–140, January 1992.

[B17] James A. Freeman, *Simulating Neural Networks,* Addison Wesley Publishing Company, New York, 1994.

[B18] L. Jin, P.N. Nikiforuk, M.M. Gupta, "Direct Adaptive Output Tracking Control using Multilayer Neural Network," *IEEE Proceedings–D*, vol.140, no.6, pp. 393–398, Nov. 1993.

[B19] John.P.Cater, "Successfully using Peak Learning Rates of 10 (and greater) in Back Propagation Networks with the Heuristic Learning Algorithm," *IEEE First International Conference on Neural Networks*, pp.645–651, 1987.

[B20] Judith E. Dayhoff, *Neural Network Architecture – An Introduction,* Van Nostrand Reinhold, New York, 1990.

[B21] M.R. Kaimal, S. Dasgupta and M. Harishankar, Editors, *Neuro Fuzzy Control Systems,* Narosa Publishing House, New Delhi, 1997.

[B22] Kevin L.Moore, "Artificial Neural Networks weighing the Different ways to Systematize Thinking," *IEEE Potentials*, pp.23–28, February 1992.

[B23] Kishan Mehrotra, Chilukuri.K.Mohan and Sanjay Ranka, *Elements of ANN*, Penram International Pub., Mumbai, 1997.

[B24] Kosko. B, "Competitive Bidirectional Associative Memories," *IEEE First National Conference on Neural Networks*, San Diego, CA, pp. 759–766, 1987.

[B25] Kosko. B, "Bidirectional Associative memories," *IEEE Transactions on Sys. Man. And Cybernetics,* 18: pp 49–60, 1998.

[B26] Kumpati S.Narendra and Snehasis Mukhopadhyay, "Intelligent Control Using Neural Networks," *IEEE Mag. On Control systems,* vol.12, no.2, pp.11–18, April 1992.

[B27] Laurene Fausett, *Fundamentals of Neural Networks*, Prentice Hall, New Jersey, 1999.

[B28] Li Min Fu, *Neural Networks in Computer Intelligence*, McGraw-Hill Inc., Singapore, 1994.

[B29] Markus Hoehfeld and Scott E.Fahlman, "Learning with Limited Numerical Precision using the Cascade-Correlation Algorithm," *IEEE Trans. on Neural Networks*, vol.3, no.4, pp.602–611, 1992.

[B30] Nico Weymaere and Jean-Pierre Martens, "A Fast and Robust Learning Algorithm for Feedforward Neural Networks," *Neural Networks,* vol.4, pp.361–369, 1991.

[B31] Nicolaos B.Karayiannis and Anastasios N.Venetsanopoulos, "Fast Learning Algorithms for Neural Networks," *IEEE Trans. on Circuits and Systems-*II: *Analog and Digital Signal Processing*, vol.39, no.7, pp.453–474, July 1992.

[B32] Paul J.Werbos, "Back-Propagation Through Time: What it does and How to do it," *Proceedings of the IEEE*, vol.78, no.10, pp.1550–1560, October 1990.

[B33] Phil Picton, *Introduction to Neural Networks*, Macmillan Publishing Company.

[B34] Philip D. Wasserman, *Neural Computing Theory and Practice,* Van Nostrand Reinhold, New York, 1989.

[B35] Rajesh Parekh, Jihoon Yang, and Vasant Honavar, "Constructive Neural-Network Learning Algorithms for Pattern Classification," *IEEE Trans. on Neural Networks,* vol.11, no.2, pp.436–451, March 2000.

[B36] Reza Nekovei and Ying Sun, "Back-Propagation Network and its Configuration for Blood Vessel Detection in Angiograms," *IEEE Trans. on Neural Networks,* vol.6, no.1, pp.64–72, January 1995.

[B37] Richard P.Lippmann, "An Introduction to Computing with Neural Nets," *IEEE ASSP Mag.*, pp.4–22, April 1987.

[B38] Robert A.Jacobs, "Increased Rates of Convergence through Learning Rate Adaptation," *Neural Networks*, vol.1, pp.295–307, 1988.

[B39] Robert Hecht Nielsen, *Neuro Computing*, Addison Wesley Publishing Company, New York,1990.

[B40] Specht.D.F, "Probabilistic Neural Networks," *Neural Networks*, 3(1): pp. 109–118, 1990.

[B41] Stamatois V. Kartalopolous, *Understanding Neural Networks and Fuzzy Logic*, Prentice Hall of India Private Ltd, New Delhi, 2000.

[B42] Takayuki Yamada and Tetsuro Yabuta, "Neural Network controller using Auto tuning method for Nonlinear Functions," *IEEE Trans. on Neural Networks,* vol.3, no.4, pp.595–601, July 1992.

[B43] A.Van Ooyen and B.Nienhuis, "Improving the Convergence of the Backpropagation Algorithm," *Neural Networks,* vol.5, pp.465–471, 1992.

Index

A

B

C

D

E

F

G

H

I